D1055353

Twayne's United States Authors Series

EDITOR OF THIS VOLUME

Warren French

Indiana University

James Jones

TUSAS 366

James Jones

JAMES JONES

By JAMES R. GILES
Northern Illinois University

TWAYNE PUBLISHERS
A DIVISION OF G. K. HALL & CO., BOSTON

813.54
G

Library of Congress Cataloging in Publication Data

Giles, James Richard, 1937–
James Jones.

(Twayne's United States authors series; TUSAS 366)
Bibliography: pp. 215–21
Includes index.
1. Jones, James, 1921–1977—Criticism and interpretation.
PS3560.049Z68   813'.54   80–23295
ISBN 0–8057–7293–6

116925

Dedicated to
Three Beautiful People:
Wanda, Morgan, and Kaylie

Contents

About the Author

James R. Giles, a graduate of Texas Christian University and the University of Texas, is a member of the Department of English at Northern Illinois University. His main scholarly interests are American literary realism and naturalism and black American literature. He has published critical essays on Frank Norris, Jack London, Richard Wright, Zora Neale Hurston, John Rechy, James Baldwin, Willard Motley, anl Joyce Carol Oates in such journals as *Western American Literature, Phylon, Negro* (now *Black*) *American Literature Forum, Studies in Black Literature, Minority Voices, Chicago Review, College English, Forum, Southern Humanities Review, Arizona Quarterly,* and the *Dalhousie Review.* He is also the author of the Twayne United States Authors series volume *Claude McKay.* In 1973 and 1977, Giles presented papers at the Joyce Carol Oates seminars at the Modern Language Association conventions.

His interest in James Jones dates back to his initial reading of *From Here to Eternity* from the paperback rack of the Bowie, Texas, drugstore in the 1950s, and it has grown with his critical focus on post–World War II realistic and naturalistic writers. He believes that Jones is seriously underrated by the academic critic, especially in view of the novelist's ambitious and innovative army trilogy.

A native of Texas, Giles has published essays about his experience of Texas in the *Texas Observer,* an Austin-based journal of national reputation edited in the early 1960s by Jones's friend Willie Morris. He has published fiction in *Western Review, Story Quarterly, Quartet, Descant, Seems,* and other journals, and two of his stories have been anthologized in the Dell paperback collections *Innovative Fiction* and *No Signs from Heaven.*

He plans further work on contemporary American realistic writers such as Jones, Oates, Norman Mailer, William Styron, and Irwin Shaw. He also hopes to publish more short stories.

Preface

Since undertaking this study, I have become increasingly aware of the disparity between the academy's view of James Jones and the perceptions of the reading public and of other important writers. Beginning with *From Here to Eternity* in 1951, Jones's work always sold, sometimes spectacularly. Immediately after his death, William Styron and Irwin Shaw (who knew him) and Joan Didion (who did not) published tributes to his achievement. Within a year, Willie Morris finished his book-length reminiscence of Jones. During that time, traditional scholars printed nothing.

For almost thirty years, Jones was the friend, and frequently the benefactor, of American writers at home and abroad. Despite his clear importance in the writing community, the academy still largely ignores him. PMLA bibliographies from 1951 through 1976 list only ten articles about his work in scholarly journals and essay collections, three of which are in publications printed outside the United States. It often seems that, when academicians remember Jones, it is as the spokesman for an anachronistic male supremacy or as a writer of flawed naturalistic prose. There are exceptions: Edmond L. Volpe and Peter G. Jones have written sensitive and intelligent criticism of Jones's work.

Still, nonacademic critics have paid much more attention to James Jones. His novels were regularly reviewed in such publications as the *New York Times Book Review*, the *Saturday Review, Harper's*, the *New York Review of Books*, and the *Atlantic Monthly*. *From Here to Eternity*, his first novel, won the National Book Award. The popular success of this work also transformed him into an instant celebrity; personality profiles subsequently appeared in *Life, Newsweek*, and other mass circulation magazines. Edward R. Murrow interviewed him and Gloria Jones for a 1958 segment of "Person to Person" on the day when his second novel, *Some Came Running*, was released.

Despite this attention outside academia, there is still too little calm, objective criticism of Jones's work. There exists, for instance, amazingly little appreciation, or even understanding, of the power and ambition of his army trilogy—*From Here to Eternity* (1951), *The Thin Red Line* (1962), and *Whistle* (1978). This three-volume work is our most important fictional treatment of U.S. involvement in World War II. It is, moreover, an experimental trilogy. Three recurring character types unite the work, though they have different names and, to a degree, different backgrounds in each novel.

There is an ironic aspect to this experimentation since a central factor in the academic community's neglect of Jones is the prevailing opinion that his work is passé in a postmodernist literary period of narrative innovation. My aim in this study is to assess, thoroughly and objectively, James Jones's achievement in the specific context of what he attempted to do. I will examine some frequent criticisms of his work, especially the charges that he had a "bad" style, that he could write about nothing except war, and that he could not create believable female characters. Such an objective study is difficult, for Jones's work often elicits a strong emotional response from the reader. I will state now that the best of his writing, especially *From Here to Eternity*, produces such a response in me. Nevertheless, I intend to avoid the trap of uncritical admiration. Three of Jones's novels are, in fact, artistically flawed and unfocused.

One of my criteria for evaluating Jones's work will be his success in presenting two dominant themes—the evolution of a soldier and the sexual immaturity of the American male. After a first chapter devoted to biographical concerns and an introduction of these two themes, I will take up his works in chronological order, with one exception. Even though the short story collection, *The Ice-Cream Headache and Other Stories,* was not published until 1968, I will examine it in conjunction with the 1959 novella, *The Pistol,* because the two books demonstrate Jones's largely ignored expertise in the forms of short fiction.

I must mention a further point which is difficult to include in a scholarly study. In August of 1978 (about fourteen months after Jones's death), his wife, Gloria, invited me to visit Saga-ponack, Long Island, hoping that such a visit would enable me to gain a fuller appreciation of her husband's life and work. I spent three nights sleeping in Jones's study (the attic of the farmhouse the Joneses bought in 1975 and renovated) and three days in conversation with his family and his friends. I believe that I did gain an increased appreciation of James Jones, the man. The much-publicized gun and knife collections were in the study; they were smaller and more selective than one might expect. My own clearest memories of that light, clean room are of several abstract paintings, numerous books on aesthetic theory, and—side by side—his Bronze Star citation and a framed painting done by one of his children at about age six.

His friends still exhibit an intense loyalty to Jim Jones. Some of the people to whom I talked were established writers (Irwin Shaw, John Knowles, Willie Morris); some were young writers just beginning their careers (Winston Groom); some were painters and journalists and show business people; and some were people unconnected with the arts. All of them emphasized that James Jones was a man people liked to talk to, in large part because of his generosity and his wide-ranging interests and concerns—the Civil War; military strategy; theories of literature, art, and music; political and sociological change; Long Island potato farming; children and education. After that visit, I know more of James Jones, from meeting these people and seeing his places. But primarily, I know him through his work. And I am certain of one thing. The image of James Jones as a midwestern primitive, created by *Time* and other mass circulation magazines, was unfounded. Lacking a formal education, he was nevertheless a thoughtful and intelligent man who cared about life and art in all their manifestations. He was a writer's writer, one of the most human of persons.

JAMES R. GILES

Northern Illinois University

Acknowledgments

I wish to express my gratitude to several people for help in preparing this book. Northern Illinois University provided financial and other assistance, and special thanks must go to Professors James M. Mellard and William Williams for negotiating this support. Karen Duncan typed the first draft of the manuscript; I appreciate her decoding skills. In addition, Professors Rosalie Hewitt and Robert H. Wilson frequently and generously supplied me with primary and secondary Jones materials. Finally, all the English department staff—Pat Francis, Jo Jones, Karen Devault, Mary Starritt, and Jane Klink—were helpful and conscientious throughout the work on this book.

On Long Island, several of James Jones's friends and family members were particularly supportive and helpful. Ellen Adler suggested ways to improve the original manuscript, and all of her suggestions have been useful and pleasing. In an interview, Irwin Shaw helped immeasurably in understanding James Jones as a man and a writer. Lady Enid Hardwicke was as kind, perceptive, and generous as she is beautiful. Winston Groom talked with special warmth about Jones and the special problems of writing war novels. Willie Morris was helpful in so many ways that there is no sensible way to try to enumerate them; one very great kindness, however, was allowing me to read and quote from his book *James Jones: A Friendship* when it was still in galley proofs. During the three days I spent on Long Island, Willie was simply there, generous with time, ideas, self. Kaylie Jones showed a rare kind of courage in talking about her father and taking me to places on the Island that evoked him because they had been special to him. She also took me to James Jones's grave. Most of all, there was Gloria Jones, who invited me to visit her and stay in Jones's study. I discovered all the descriptions of her beauty, courage, integrity, and generosity to be true.

At G. K. Hall the production editors have given me a great deal of help. Finally, I want to thank three excellent editors who have made this book much better than it otherwise might have been: Warren French, Bill Riley, and Wanda Hancock Giles. That Wanda Giles helped in many other ways goes without saying.

Chronology

1921   James Jones, son of Ramon Jones and Ada Blessing Jones, born in Robinson, Illinois, November 6.

1939   Joins United States Air Force and is sent to Hawaii, where he transfers to Infantry.

1941   At Schofield Barracks, Hawaii, when Japanese bomb Pearl Harbor, December 7.

1942   Takes English courses at University of Hawaii after reading Thomas Wolfe and deciding to be a writer; Jones's father, Ramon, commits suicide.

1943   Wounded in battle of Guadalcanal (awarded Bronze Star and Purple Heart). Sent to U.S. army hospital in Memphis, Tennessee; meets Lowney Handy of Robinson, Illinois; in December, transferred to Camp Campbell, Kentucky, as a "Limited Duty Soldier."

1944   Discharged from United States Army, July 6. Moves in with Harry E. and Lowney Handy, who offer to help him in his ambition to become a writer, in hometown of Robinson.

1945   Maxwell Perkins of Scribner's rejects first novel, *They Shall Inherit the Laughter*, but asks to see other work; writing courses at New York University.

1948   Short story, "The Temper of Steel," published in the *Atlantic Monthly*.

1951   *From Here to Eternity*. Wins National Book Award for 1952. Jones sells film rights to Columbia Pictures for $82,500 and uses profits from novel to help the Handys organize a writers' colony and build a home in Marshall, Illinois.

1953   Film version of *From Here to Eternity*.

1957   Marries Gloria Patricia Mosolino in Haiti.

1958   *Some Came Running*; Jones moves to Paris. Film version of *Some Came Running* (MGM).

1959 *The Pistol.*

1960 Daughter, Kaylie Ann, born.

1961 Son, Jamie Anthony, born.

1962 *The Thin Red Line.* Works on script of Twentieth Century-Fox film *The Longest Day.*

1964 Film version of *The Thin Red Line* (Allied Artists).

1967 *Go to the Widow-Maker.*

1968 *The Ice-Cream Headache and Other Stories.*

1971 *The Merry Month of May.*

1973 Reportorial trip to Vietnam; *A Touch of Danger.*

1974 *Viet Journal*; returns from Paris to live in U.S. Teaches creative writing at Miami International University. Buys farmhouse in Sagaponack, Long Island, New York.

1975 *WWII.*

1977 Dies in Southampton, New York, May 9.

1978 *Whistle,* completed by Willie Morris from Jones's notes and tapes, published posthumously.

CHAPTER 1

A Mythical American

AFTER the publication of his first novel, *From Here to Eternity*, in 1951, James Jones's career became one of the most public in the history of American letters. In terms of both critical and popular reception, *From Here to Eternity* was a spectacular success; and its author was immediately elevated to celebrity status. This status was scarcely diminished by his failure to publish another critically successful novel during the last fifteen years of his life. His later novels continued to have at least some popular success; and, whether residing in Marshall, Illinois, or in Paris, James Jones, the man and the writer, remained in the public eye. He became an integral member of a group of writers and friends which included William Styron, Irwin Shaw, and Romain Gary.

However, Jones was thirty years old when *From Here to Eternity* was published, and the first three decades of his life had been far removed from celebrity or even material success. A sometime friend, Norman Mailer, in *Advertisements for Myself*, graphically appraises the initial impact of Jones on the American literary scene:

I felt then and can still say now that *From Here to Eternity* has been the best American novel since the war, and . . . it has also the force of few novels one could name. What was unique about Jones was that he had come out of nowhere, self-taught, a clunk in his lacks, but the only one of us who had the beer-guts of a broken-glass brawl.[1]

Having virtually no advanced formal education and possessing a literary style and public persona which seemed crude but powerful to some and vulgar to others, Jones, in 1951, did seem an American original who "came out of nowhere." After the

story of his unique literary apprenticeship was detailed by the
mass media, he was viewed as a personification of "the American
dream"—the obscure young man achieving, through grim determination and some improbable luck, sudden wealth and fame.
Thus, Jones's life can be divided into two distinct phases—the
first thirty years of obscurity and no little suffering, and the last
twenty-six years of celebrity.

The "nowhere" out of which he came—Robinson, a small south-
eastern Illinois town, and the huge, impersonal organization of
the United States Army—was crucial in forming the ideas which
dominate his books. James Jones was born November 6, 1921,
in Robinson; his parents were Ramon Jones, a dentist, and Ada
Blessing Jones. In an autobiographical statement prepared for
Twentieth Century Authors, Jones writes that his family had been
socially prominent in area farming for "several generations" and
that, when oil was discovered on their farm, his "grandfather
became a lawyer and moved to town." Ramon Jones became a
dentist, rather than the lawyer he wished to be. Jones's comments about his mother are brief and cutting: "She ... was considered a great beauty locally. She would have preferred to
remain a great beauty." His parents' marriage was an unhappy
one, and as a result Jones believes his "father took to drink
and ... [his] mother to religion."[2] Willie Morris's memoir, *James
Jones: A Friendship*, contains more information about the novelist's feelings toward his parents than has previously been acces-
sible:

His mother, Ada, came from Iowa and went to the University of
Chicago. She was a Christian Scientist and suffered from congestive
heart failure. He found her domineering, cruel, and deceitful; he
called her a "dwarf" and said she had "the mind of a mole." His
father, Ramon, was a dentist and the town drunk. There was affection between the father and son.[3]

Certainly he felt his home life as a child was not emotionally
reassuring: "I ... grew up in an atmosphere of hot emotions and
boiling recriminations covered with a thin but resilient skin of
gentility."[4]

When Jones was a junior in Robinson High School, his grandfather died and the family fortune disappeared as a result of the Samuel Insull stock scandal. Since James's father, Ramon, had always been a failure as a dentist, the decline in family prestige and security was immediate and total. After graduation from high school at the age of eighteen, James Jones took his father's advice and enlisted in the United States Air Force in 1939.

Sent to Hawaii, he soon transferred out of the air force into the infantry. Such a move was virtually unheard of, since most men dreamed of being in the air force. In a letter to scholar Lee A. Burress, Jr., Jones wrote that he made the decision to transfer after meeting a group of infantrymen on guard duty. He added that the experience was incorporated into *From Here to Eternity* in the scene in which Prewitt and his friends compose "The Re-Enlistment Blues"—it "is the only place that I myself appear . . . in the book: as the young Air Corps private, Slade."[5]

It is important that it was the old pre–World War II army with its rigid officer-enlisted men caste system which Jones joined. The descendant of a once prosperous family gone bankrupt, troubled by his parents' bitter marriage, the eighteen-year-old boy was hardly cut out to prosper in such a harshly regimented existence. He did not. He once summarized his army record of two promotions and subsequent reductions to the lowest enlisted grade: " 'Apted Cpl 13 May 42 Red to Pvt 3 Dec 43, Apt Sgt 1 Mar 44 Red to Pvt 20 May 44.' "[6] In an essay reprinted as an epilogue to *Viet Journal,* he remembers marching up the Kole Kole Pass in the Waianae Mountain Range ". . . with a full field pack and an escorting noncom, over some stupid argument with my company commander."[7] Jones was never sentenced to the brutal Schofield Barracks stockade which he helped to make infamous in *From Here to Eternity*; but he seems to have allied himself with the type of rebellious enlisted man personified by two of his fictional creations, Robert E. Lee Prewitt and Angelo Maggio.

In Hawaii, at the Schofield Barracks Post Library, he had a positive experience which was to be critical in his life. He read Thomas Wolfe's *Look Homeward, Angel* and ". . . realized [he] . . . had been a writer all [his] . . . life without knowing it or having written."[8] Later, after his initial success, Jones made his debt to Wolfe so public that it became somewhat fashionable to see *Look Homeward, Angel* as the only book that might ever have influenced him. In a 1959 interview, Jones argued that he had surpassed Wolfe "in viewpoint and style and even in selectivity; certainly ... in structuring novels." Still, he admitted: "Wolfe actually did influence me a great deal toward becoming a writer. ... I think he was a great writer."[9] Jones succinctly summarized the reasons for his emotional response to Wolfe in an interview with Willie Morris a few months before his death:

Reading about that crazy boy and his crazy family and his drunken father and his miserly mother is so like myself and my own family that I discovered I'd been a writer all along without really having realized it.[10]

On December 7, 1941, Jones was at Schofield Barracks, Hawaii, when the Japanese bombed Pearl Harbor, and thus he saw the birth of an impersonal and frightening new world:

I remember thinking with a sense of the profoundest awe that none of our lives would ever be the same ... and I wondered how many of us would survive to see the end results. I had just turned twenty, the month before.[11]

In the spring of 1942, Ramon Jones, whom James had loved despite the father's personal and professional failure, committed suicide after applying and being rejected for a commission in the army:

Later I would speculate often whether that turndown by the Army had not been such a slap in the face that it would awaken him to what he was, what he had become, and he could not stand to face it. ... He deserved a better fate.[12]

Approximately one year after Pearl Harbor, his division, the 25th "Tropic Lightning" Infantry Division, was sent to Guadalcanal. In *WWII*, published in 1975, Jones describes the "primitive" nature of the fighting on Guadalcanal in unforgettable detail. It was bloody jungle warfare, and it was something that left Jones with a vision of "the animal nature of man" that he was never to forget. He was to undergo two especially brutal

ordeals. In the worst kind of hand-to-hand combat, he killed
a Japanese soldier with a knife. It is revealing that, with one
glaring exception, Jones chose not to discuss this incident in all
his autobiographical accounts of the war. Nevertheless, it is
obviously the source of the short story "The Temper of Steel"
and the almost unbearable account of Bead's killing of the Japanese soldier in *The Thin Red Line*.

Jones himself suffered a head wound from a mortar fragment.
Ironically, the wound did not get him evacuated; but when he
later reinjured his right ankle which had been weak "since long
before Pearl Harbor," he was shipped, after surgery, first to New
Zealand and then to the United States. In *WWII*, Jones recounts
this experience and says that his "old first sergeant" had to talk
him into accepting evacuation: "I understood that numbers
were what counted in this war, vast numbers, of men and machines.... And I had no more romantic notions about combat.
... Finally, I went."[13] As with the experience of killing the
Japanese with the knife, Jones made fictional use of his evacuation; in *The Thin Red Line*, Fife reinjures an ankle, is offered
evacuation, and only accepts after being tricked by First Sergeant
"Mad" Welsh.

Back in the United States, Jones was sent first to the Army
General Hospital in Memphis, Tennessee, where he spent the
last seven months of 1943. He was awarded the Bronze Star and
a Purple Heart for his service on Guadalcanal, but he accepted
the code of the other wounded men in the Memphis hospital
and did not wear the decorations. Not surprisingly, Jones was
an intensely embittered young man at this point. Willie Morris
writes that it was during Jones's convalescence in Memphis
that he derived the vision, dominant in *Some Came Running* and
Whistle, of a profoundly changed America cut loose from its
old ethical certainties:

It was a different America altogether from the one so many of them
had left before the war. There was an unexpected affluence everywhere. Everyone had a cynical, knowing grin. Everyone seemed to
be getting rich.[14]

Upon his release from the Memphis hospital, he was transferred to a Quartermaster Gas Supply Company at Camp Campbell, Kentucky. In *Viet Journal* he describes this experience as being in an "outfit with a bunch of other cripples."[15] On July 6, 1944, he was discharged from the army.

It is difficult to reconstruct the exact sequence of certain events between late 1943 and his military discharge. In *Viet Journal* Jones mentions in an offhand manner "spending some time in a couple of Army jails."[16] Willie Morris, in a June 1978 *Atlantic Monthly* reminiscence of Jones, describes the future novelist's being imprisoned for refusing to return to combat because of his horror over killing the Japanese soldier:

... he was all alone in the jungle one day when a half-starved Japanese soldier came out at him from the undergrowth, and after a struggle he had to kill him with a knife, and then found the family photographs in the dead man's wallet; for a time he refused to fight again, and they put him in the stockade and busted him to private.[17]

However, a 1951 *Life* magazine article by A. B. C. Whipple, the biographical aspects of which Jones never refuted in print, depicts him as being on the verge of shellshock at Camp Campbell and going "over the hill" after being denied a furlough. According to the *Life* account, he returned to Robinson, Illinois, where his mother had died of diabetes; moved in with his aunt, Sadie Jones; and "got drunk and stayed drunk." The aunt then introduced him to Mr. and Mrs. Harry E. Handy, who set out to "rehabilitate" Jones and, after making him return to camp, got him a medical discharge "through a combination of Jim's head wound and Lowney's constant badgering of everyone in the Army. . . ."[18]

The conflicting evidence makes it difficult to be certain exactly when and why Jones was in military prison and the exact circumstances of his discharge. On the most significant point, Morris's recent reminiscence and the 1951 *Life* story may not really be in conflict. Clearly, Jones was deeply shaken by killing the Japanese soldier, and such an experience could have intensified his need for a furlough. However, the dates Jones gives in *WWII* for his recuperation in the hospital in Memphis and subsequent transfer to Camp Campbell do not clearly coincide with Whipple's 1951 account.

Two certainties emerge, however. In 1944 Jones was discharged from the army, greatly shaken by the horrors he had
experienced and by the tragic dissolution of his family. Sometime
in late 1943 or early 1944 (Whipple's *Life* account says November
1943) Jones met Mrs. Lowney Handy, and one of the most
unusual, and ultimately most publicized, literary apprenticeships
in the history of American letters was underway.

A 1953 *Newsweek* essay describes Lowney Handy as "... a
more dynamic version of Sinclair Lewis's Carol Kennicott in
'Main Street' " and as having been engaged in a lifelong "tragi-
comic combat with Midwestern provincialism" because of her
devotion to "art and culture."[19] Whipple's *Life* story depicts her
as growing up the daughter of a small-town Illinois sheriff,
"fascinated" with salvaging the people imprisoned in her father's
jail. After marriage, she devoted herself to Robinson's various
unfortunates and received much social condemnation. When
the war began, "she transferred her motherly affections to the
servicemen"; and the Handy home became a stopping-place for
returning GIs.[20] Thus "adopting" Jones was an inevitable act
for her—he was a young man with nowhere to go and no ambitions except the desire to be a writer. Simultaneously, he
touched her needs to protect outcasts and encourage art. Moreover, she had just written, and had had rejected, a novel.

Jones moved in with the Handys and began to write under
Lowney's tutelage. Her role extended, almost inevitably. Willie
Morris describes Jones's relationship with Mrs. Handy in this
way:

She was an attractive woman, and although she was almost eighteen
years older than he—she was thirty-nine, he was twenty-two—they
began an affair that lasted well into the 1950s, more or less with
the knowledge of the husband.[21]

Initially, they built a study for him on the back of the house;
but Jones became restless and Harry Handy went into debt to
buy him a trailer and a jeep. He toured the country in the trailer,
always writing. Ultimately, he finished a novel about embittered
war veterans entitled *They Shall Inherit the Laughter*, which he
took to New York and presented to Thomas Wolfe's editor,

Maxwell Perkins, at Scribner's. Perkins rejected the novel; and according to Whipple, Jones almost quit writing then; but Mrs. Handy interceded and coerced her protégé to enroll in a couple of writing courses at New York University.

Jones then got the idea for a novel about the prewar army and sent Perkins a sketch about the two characters who were to become Robert E. Lee Prewitt and Milton Anthony Warden. With some reluctance, Jones agreed to set aside *They Shall Inherit the Laughter* and concentrate on the prewar army novel. Perkins was especially impressed by Jones's ideas for the characterization of Prewitt:

Perkins believed that Jones had chosen to portray a "perennial character," and said: "It seemed to us from what you said, that you saw something truly important, and that you were right in your interpretation of the nature of that type of man, and that he had never been portrayed in a way to make him understandable."[22]

It is appropriate that Perkins, the almost legendary editor of Thomas Wolfe, Ernest Hemingway, Scott Fitzgerald, and other "lost generation" writers, should have discovered and nurtured *From Here to Eternity*, one of the celebrated World War II novels, through its early stages. The few published letters of Perkins to Jones indicate that the editor guided the struggling young writer with great tact and delicacy. Knowing of Jones's admiration for Wolfe, Perkins subtly advised him about precisely what to emulate in *Look Homeward, Angel*. He wrote to Jones about literary theory in a deceptively offhand but convincing manner: "One can write about nothing unless it is, in some sense, out of one's life—that is, out of oneself." When Jones added the incident of Prewitt's having accidentally blinded a friend while boxing, Perkins praised the "distinct improvement" in the character's "motivation."[23] Perkins died when the novel was only half completed (June 17, 1947), and Burroughs Mitchell and John Hall Wheelock assumed its editorship.

Lowney Handy remained a powerful factor in *Eternity*'s composition. Whipple writes that she objected to the title because it came from the Yale Whiffenpoof song until John Hall Wheelock convinced her that the Yale song actually originated with Kipling and, in its original form, referred to young British noblemen "sent into the army and packed off to far places and forgotten."[24]

In 1951 *From Here to Eternity* was published by Scribner's with advance publicity proclaiming it as important as the first novels of Thomas Wolfe and Scott Fitzgerald. In his "Acknowledgment," Jones expresses gratitude to Maxwell E. Perkins, John Hall Wheelock, Burroughs Mitchell, and "Mr. & Mrs. Harry E. Handy of Robinson, Illinois, without whose initial impetus I would never have started out to be a writer at all, and whose material and spiritual expenses over a period of seven years provided me with necessary nourishment."

Scribner's had reasons to be uncertain about the critical and popular reception of *From Here to Eternity*. It was over eight hundred pages long. Publishing such a sprawling first novel by an unknown writer was a gamble. More importantly, in its dialogue and treatment of sexual relationships, the novel's level of frankness was revolutionary in 1951. Jones's depiction of the brutality of military "justice" was equally unrestrained; the novel's stockade scenes horrify the reader. Some critics—as could have been expected—reacted negatively to such a "new" frankness in such a long novel. In addition, the unevenness of Jones's style became an ongoing subject of debate.

Bernard DeVoto linked Jones's novel with Norman Mailer's *The Naked and the Dead* as "dull" novels of arrested intellectual and psychological development; *Eternity*'s "obscenities" were "childish," he asserted.[25] In the *Nation* Ernest Jones attacked "this preposterously overpraised novel"; he argued that "the prose alone should make it impossible to take very seriously" and that its largely positive reception cheapened all contemporary American fiction.[26] John Lardner, in the *New Yorker,* took a middle ground:

It is a slovenly, furious book. If it is also the most realistic and forceful novel I've read about life in the Army . . . it's because the English language is capable of absorbing, and condoning a good deal of abuse from a man who has something to say and wants very desperately to say it.

Lardner conceded that, even when the novel failed in parts, it was "honest."[27]

As the defensive nature of DeVoto's, Ernest Jones's, and Lardner's criticism indicates, most reviewers were strongly positive in their assessments. David Dempsey, in the *New York Times Book Review*, wrote that "... in James Jones an original and utterly honest talent has restored American realism to a preeminent place in world literature."[28] The *New York Herald Tribune Book Review* also praised the novel. In the *Atlantic Monthly*, C. J. Rolo asserted that

the book as a whole, however, is a spectacular achievement; it has tremendous vitality and driving power and graphic authenticity. Prewitt and Warden are magnificent creations, ...

while still expressing the fear that Jones was "... another of those emotionally retarded he-men to whom toughness is the supreme Good...."[29] The most perceptive initial review of *Eternity* was Ned Calmer's in the *Saturday Review of Literature*. Calmer called the novel "for the non-squeamish adult ... the best picture of Army life ever written by an American, a book of beauty and power despite its unevenness...." Calmer perceived that the characterization of Prewitt gave the novel a "deeper" level of significance "as social protest" and that Prewitt was searching for "that rarest moment when one human could find and touch the soul of another."[30] Calmer thus touched on two of the novel's major supporting themes: proletarian protest and the need for, and difficulty of, human communication.

On the whole, *From Here to Eternity* was a critical success, even though highly controversial. There was never any doubt about its popular appeal. The Book-of-the-Month Club made the novel an alternate, rather than a main selection, because of its frankness. Still, the original hardback editions sold almost a half-million copies; and in November 1953 *Newsweek* reported that the paperback reprint had gone through five printings of "1,700,000 copies ... in the past six weeks." There were avenues of reward other than direct sales: Jones received $82,500 for movie rights and $101,000 as advance reprint royalties. All this made Jones, according to *Newsweek*, "the most successful novelist in American literary history."[31] Still, he worried about whether he was considered a good writer; and when *Eternity* won the 1952 National Book Award, he was pleased: "In my own particular case, because the novel with which I won it was such a commercial success ... I think it gave me a certain literary status and prestige which might not otherwise have been accorded me."[32]

His new wealth enabled Jones to build a new house, described by *Newsweek* as a "mansion," in Marshall, Illinois (twenty-eight miles from Robinson).[33] However, he put all of his initial profits from *Eternity* into a writers' colony in Marshall, directed by Lowney Handy. The colony received as much publicity as Jones's initial apprenticeship with Mrs. Handy. Reassured by Jones's spectacular success that she knew genius when she saw it, Lowney Handy ran the colony with iron discipline and enforced acceptance of her unique philosophy of developing writers. Her theory combined physical labor, mandatory periods of silence, rigid diet, great sexual restraint, and "copying" great masterpieces in a regimented existence which must have reminded Jones of the army.

The "copying" was perhaps the most controversial of all Mrs. Handy's theories—she believed that, by copying on typewriters all of a great novel, the men would necessarily absorb genius which would later be reflected in their own work. A 1958 debunking article by David Ray describes his experience as a member of the colony. Ray says that he first met Jones in Arizona (Jones was still traveling extensively in his trailer) and was referred immediately to Mrs. Handy. Accepted into the colony, he soon became aware that "Jones was a 'priest' writer and the boys were all 'apprentices.'" Lowney Handy decided which books one could read. "We were not to read Proust, Wallace Stevens, Kafka, and other 'phony' writers: we were encouraged to read Wolfe, Jones, Hemingway, Tess Slesinger, Faulkner and Raymond Chandler." In 1957, three novels by colony members were published: Edwin Daly's *Some Must Watch*, Gerald Tesch's *Never the Same Again*, and Tom T. Chamales's *Never So Few*.[34]

Factors which were to force Jones's abandonment of the colony had been growing for some time. Since the appearance of his first novel, he had been a celebrity, and the 1953 film version of

From Here to Eternity enhanced his position. Jones submitted a script (which was revised by Daniel Taradash) and acted as an advisor on the film, becoming friends with several members of the cast—Frank Sinatra, Montgomery Clift, Deborah Kerr. Besides having written the novel, perhaps Jones's most important contribution to the film was an indirect one. Prior to the picture's filming, he attended a party given by Vance Bourjaily in New York, where he first met Montgomery Clift. Jones decided immediately that Clift should play Robert E. Lee Prewitt and convinced producer Buddy Adler and director Fred Zinnemann that he was right. They got the role for Clift over the objections of Columbia Pictures studio head Harry Cohn.[35] Clift's performance was brilliant—he was the definitive Prewitt, perfectly capturing the character's mixture of sensitivity and toughness. Jones's continuing friendship with this brilliant, but personally tormented, actor is described in two recent biographies of Clift.[36] Given the common view of Jones as devoted to a "he-man" cult, it is significant that he was aware of the actor's sexual ambivalence and went out of his way to maintain the friendship as long as it was possible.

Columbia's motion-picture version of his novel justifiably angered Jones in some ways. It downplays the stockade brutality and has "Dynamite" Holmes relieved of his command in disgrace, rather than promoted. Still, it was one of the most successful and influential American films of the 1950s; named the "best picture" of 1953 by the Motion Picture Academy of Arts and Sciences and the New York Film Critics, it was filmed simply, in black and white, at a time when Hollywood was experimenting with 3-D and other gimmicks in an attempt to combat television. The powerful emotions of its characters and story proved a potent weapon against mere visual tricks; it has been credited with helping Hollywood see that it can produce nothing better than honest movies about believable characters. The success of the film also enhanced Jones's position as celebrity and friend of celebrities. Marshall, Illinois, was fast becoming too small a stage for him.

In addition, he became restless under Lowney Handy's stern discipline and began to want new experiences. In the mid-1950s he decided to learn skindiving and was soon an ardent diver.

Most importantly, writer Budd Schulberg introduced him to the beautiful Gloria Mosolino of Pottsville, Pennsylvania. Willie Morris writes:

She came to New York City after Syracuse University with the idea of going to law school, after having been an honor student and even a saxophone player in the Syracuse Orchestra, but she taught dancing for a while at Arthur Murray's, and wrote a novel which was never published, and did a little acting, and was Eva Marie Saint's and Marilyn Monroe's stand-in in some movies.

In 1957, James Jones and Gloria Mosolino were married at the Olafson Hotel in Port-au-Prince, Haiti, "by a black voodoo master who was also a judge." Morris says, "Their marriage would be the first and last for them, and was of another order; I have never seen one quite like it. . . . They loved each other passionately, and she was fiercely loyal to him. . . ."[37] Jones's associations with the Marshall Colony and Lowney Handy were over. For a few months, he and Gloria lived in New York City and then, in 1958, moved to Paris.

   In the 1959 *Paris Review* interview, Jones discusses the writers' colony and his move to Paris. The Marshall project had been one of his dreams for years: "I honestly believed that if you gave guys who wanted to write a place to do it where they could live and eat free, then they *would* write." He admits its failure, however: "I guess you just can't pick up any Joe off the street and turn him into a writer by setting him down to copying the great books. . . ." There is something peculiarly American, if not Midwestern, about such a statement: Jones had honestly believed that virtually anyone could become a writer through dedication and hard work. It was not in his background to view artistic talent as the possession of an elite. Had not his own experience proved the unlimited possibilities for literary success in America? Significantly, he never mentions the Handys in this discussion; his break with Lowney was apparently abrupt and bitter.

   Concerning the move to Paris, he says that he came to get material for a novel about the jazz guitarist, Django Reinhardt, mentioned in *From Here to Eternity*; the novel would investigate the question of "... whether Django's type of individuality can exist today in any form...." The exile from his homeland was, in no sense, a gesture of political defiance: "I'm an American, and always will be. I happen to love that big, awkward sprawling country very much—and its big, awkward, sprawling people."[38] The Reinhardt novel was never written because Jones came to feel that it was impossible to obtain sufficient information about the guitarist.[39]

The year 1958 was significant in Jones's life for another, less pleasant reason than the move to Paris. Like any author of a spectacularly successful first novel, Jones had worried about the reception of his second book. *Some Came Running*, over twelve hundred pages long, appeared to almost unanimous critical condemnation. An involved account of the lives of a large number of characters living in a small Illinois town, it was dismissed by the *New Yorker* as "twelve hundred and sixty pages of flawlessly sustained tedium."[40] David Dempsey, who had so admired *From Here to Eternity*, wrote in the *New York Times Book Review* that *Some Came Running* "becomes, at length, a relentless and often tedious *seductio ad absurdum*."[41] Some critics who had not liked the first novel took the opportunity to condemn both books. One review which especially hurt Jones was Edmund Fuller's in the *Saturday Review*. Fuller saw Jones as a glorifier of the "semi-literate" Yahoo:

This novel offers us the Yahoo as social arbiter, as do many others nowadays. Swift loathed his Yahoos as projections of the subhuman in man. Jones creates Yahoos with abiding tenderness toward them.[42]

Though insensitive criticism did inflict both pain and error, *Some Came Running* is undeniably a failure. It is a "tedious" book, even though Jones argued its superiority to *From Here to Eternity*, probably because it contains much which is central to his artistic creed. Norman Mailer places much of the blame for the novel's failure on Scribner's; someone, he argues, should have told Jones that the book was far too long and unfocused before it was published.[43] A recent *Esquire* article offers the possibility that, had he lived, Maxwell Perkins might have prevented Jones from being distracted from "his Army trilogy"

(Jones conceived the idea for the trilogy in 1947 while writing *Eternity*) by such "detours" as *Some Came Running*.[44] Still, the novel's failure did little to diminish Jones's position as a celebrity.

It was news when Jones moved to Paris in 1958, when the movie version of *Some Came Running* failed to repeat the success of *From Here to Eternity*. For the next sixteen years, he and Gloria lived on the Île St. Louis, the center of a distinguished group of American and European writers, artists, and actors. Jones came to love Paris during these years, and Willie Morris's memoir thoroughly discusses that time. While Jones felt estranged from "the French intellectual establishment," his home was a refuge for expatriate Americans, especially writers and artists, comparable to the 1920s salons of Gertrude Stein, Natalie Barney, and Sylvia Beach. A list of more or less regular visitors to the Jones house would include William Styron, Irwin Shaw, Mary McCarthy, James Baldwin, William Burroughs, Allen Ginsberg, Gregory Corso, James T. Farrell, Gore Vidal, Jerzy Kosinski, Arthur Miller, Thornton Wilder, Nelson Algren, Bernard Malamud, Tennessee Williams, Alice B. Toklas, Henry Miller, Alexander Calder, and Kurt Vonnegut. There were also show business people: Adolph Green, Betty Comden, François Truffaut, Lauren Bacall. Jones soon had the reputation of the man for people in trouble to see: "He and Romain Gary were known as the easiest touches in Paris."[45]

While he continued to write, it was suggested more than once that living abroad was a mistake for one of the most American of writers. Norman Mailer asserted in 1959 that the author of *From Here to Eternity* "sold out badly" to wealth and fame.[46] John W. Aldridge, who had admired *From Here to Eternity* and who published as much criticism about Jones as anyone else, dismissed the novelist in the early 1960s as having been creatively destroyed by the voluntary exile:

The result . . . appears to be that his experience of American life stopped with the period of the war and its immediate aftermath, and having so far been unable to put his European experience to creative use, he has been obliged since *From Here to Eternity* to keep returning obsessively to that period. . . .[47]

In fact, Jones was unable to write successful *long* fiction about anything other than the army for the rest of his career. In 1960, he published *The Pistol,* a brilliant and generally well-received novella set in Hawaii during and just after Pearl Harbor. Eleven years after *From Here to Eternity,* the second volume of his army trilogy, *The Thin Red Line,* appeared. The critical reception was primarily favorable. Maxwell Geismar argued that the combat novel effectively refuted Aldridge's evaluation of Jones as a " 'has-been' ":

Jones . . . has apparently remained impervious to all the temptations of popular and commercial success; he has kept his integrity, his own version of life. And he proves his talent and his integrity once again with "The Thin Red Line."[48]

Lewis Gannett agreed: "Set this down about James Jones: Among the once bright battalion of 'promising' World War II novelists he has continued to write and continued to grow."[49] The favorable reception of *The Thin Red Line* in 1962 marked the second, and last, peak of critical acceptance during Jones's lifetime.

He continued to prosper in other ways, however. In 1964, he received $35,000 for "nine hours of work" on the film script of Twentieth Century-Fox's epic about the Normandy invasion, *The Longest Day* (virtually everything he wrote for the film was eventually cut). The following year, he left Scribner's to sign a multi-book contract with Delacorte. Other "detours" arose before he turned to the third volume of his army trilogy. In 1967 he published a long, and unsuccessful, novel set in the world of skindiving, *Go to the Widow-Maker.* The following year saw the publication of his much underrated collection of short stories, *The Ice-Cream Headache and Other Stories.* In 1971, he published the last novel he was ever to complete, *The Merry Month of May.* Organized against the background of the 1968 Paris student rebellion, it is a weak and poorly focused novel. Nine years had passed since *The Thin Red Line,* with no novels except *Go to the Widow-Maker* and *The Merry Month of May* to show for the decade's work. Thus, John W. Aldridge felt vindicated in dismissing Jones much more brutally than he had before: Jones had "a thoroughly commonplace mind seemingly arrested forever at the level of his first adolescent ideas"; he belonged in the literary company of "writers like Robert Ruark, Leon Uris, and Harold Robbins"; and "his approach to fiction ... [was] antiquated and provincial ... because it ... [could] no longer be depended upon to yield a valid or original impression of reality."[50]

In a "Letter Home" column for *Esquire* in 1963, Jones responded to his two most persistent critics. Subtitled "Sons of Hemingway," the column describes Jones, Gloria, and friends attending a fiesta in Pamplona, Spain, and being haunted by the "ghost" of Hemingway. Jones discusses the appeal and the danger of Hemingway's "masculine" myth: "It meant, to me, that for quite a while yet, there still would be heroes, great generals, and war." Then, in a sarcastic postscript, he replied to Mailer (the Hemingway-Mailer association was not meant to be missed): "I hadn't really believed Norman was all that smart. I know I was helped immensely by his criticism of my writing, my courage, and my integrity. . . ." He asserts that Mailer's criticism had been more helpful than Aldridge's ever was and, thus, he had to wonder if Mailer "was not cut out to be perhaps the greatest critic of our generation and not a novelist at all." He ends the essay by expressing the hope that he can someday write a novel which will stimulate his former friend into competition: "After all, that's my main reason for writing them." The refutation of Mailer is effective in its cutting irony; however, the postscript also contains a hint as to why *Go to the Widow-Maker* and *The Merry Month of May* would fail as they did.

Jones writes that he likes Mailer's image of "the novel as the Great Bitch": "It's an apt description of the dark shadow so many American males fight and swing at, but can never hit in frantic efforts to save their masculinity through external objects." He continues with the remark that he prefers to think of the novel as Sleeping Beauty, whom he must sexually awaken.[51]

As the 1970s began, Jones had still not produced the third volume of his army trilogy. He had his first attack of congestive heart failure in 1970 and felt an increasingly intense need to complete the three-part work upon which he knew his literary reputation would ultimately rest. There were to be yet more "detours," however. In 1973, he published a private detective thriller, *A Touch of Danger*, and journeyed to Vietnam to report his views of the tragic U.S. involvement there. Essays about Vietnam appeared in the *New York Times Magazine*, *Harper's*, and *Oui*; and, in 1974, the book-length *Viet Journal* was published. Jones attempted to be scrupulously honest in reporting the Vietnam situation; still his discussion of Viet Cong atrocities involved him in a controversial letter to the editor of the *New York Times* (August 5, 1973, pp. 40–41).

In 1974 Jones, Gloria, and their children returned to the United States. Appropriate to the novelist's status as celebrity, the move was announced in the *New York Times*: " 'The United States is where it's all happening today, that's where the cultural revolution is really going on,' " Jones is quoted as explaining.[52] Initially, he accepted a position as writer-in-residence at Miami International University. Jones took his teaching quite seriously and enjoyed working with students. However, neither he nor Gloria really felt at home in Florida, and in late 1974 they bought, renovated, and eventually settled into a farmhouse in Sagaponack, Long Island, New York. Near some of his closest friends (Willie Morris, William Styron, and Irwin Shaw), Jones planned to work on the third volume of his trilogy.[53] Yet another project intervened. Art Weithas, the art director of *Yank* magazine, suggested that the novelist collaborate with him on a book about World War II "graphic art"; and Jones accepted. *WWII*, published in 1975, is an important book. Weithas's art reproductions are brilliant and Jones's commentary is a sharp, unforgettable analysis of his personal involvement in the war, the overall military strategies of both powers, and, most importantly, Jones's concept of "the evolution of a soldier."

Determining that nothing else would interfere with the completion of his trilogy, Jones now plunged into the writing of *Whistle*, the last volume. He had not quite finished the novel when he died on May 9, 1977. His death occasioned a flood of tributes from friends and admirers. Irwin Shaw, William Styron, and, later, Willie Morris, three of his closest friends for years, published eulogies, as did Joan Didion, who had never met him. The emotional intensity of all the reminiscences of James Jones made evident that, whatever his critical standing, Jones was greatly admired by other writers and personally loved by virtu-

ally everyone who had known him. As far back as 1959, Norman
Mailer had written: "There is not a man alive he cannot charm
if he chooses to. . . ."[54]

The May 15, 1977, memorial service for Jones underscored
the great affection he had inspired in his closest friends. Styron
read William Butler Yeats's "Sailing to Byzantium"; Willie Morris
read Prewitt's "Taps" scene; Irwin Shaw said, " 'Goodbye, Jim.
The adventure is over.' " A master bugler from the U.S. Army,
Master Sergeant Patrick Mastroleo, volunteered to play Taps,
as he had done for three U.S. presidents.[55] "The adventure" was
not quite over. Almost a year after Jones's death, *Whistle*, completed by Willie Morris from Jones's notes, was published. Thus
the trilogy, if not exactly "finished," stands as the signal achievement of his career.

There is something almost mythically American about the life
of James Jones. A product of the small-town Midwest, child of
an unhappy marriage, emotionally staggered by the horrors of
war, he became, through talent, determination, disciplined work,
and some luck, one of the successful writers of his time. The boy
who felt rejected by his mother, the infantryman wounded on
Guadalcanal, the embittered returning soldier died an international celebrity.

CHAPTER 2

The Evolution of a Soldier, Part 1: From Here to Eternity

IN *Viet Journal* Jones makes it clear that he viewed *From Here to Eternity* as the first volume in "a trilogy on World War II and soldiering" (p. 19). Thus on one level the novel is an introduction to the theme of the evolution of a soldier. (The reader remembers that *Eternity* is dedicated to "the United States Army.") Jones believed that the crucial evolutionary step came when individual combat soldiers submerged their own individuality into a necessary mass anonymity. In art as well as life, however, necessity is often painful and even tragic; and much of the emotional impact of this novel derives from Jones's application of his concept of unavoidable anonymity to Robert E. Lee Prewitt and Milton Anthony Warden.

I *The "Good Soldiers"*

Both Prewitt and Warden are "good soldiers." They are, in fact, the best soldiers in Schofield Barracks, Honolulu, Hawaii, in 1941. Each understands the demands that the army must make of him, including the ultimate demand, surrender of self. However, two important factors complicate this theme and give the novel a power that transcends Jones's considerable violation of stylistic and structural niceties. Both Prewitt and Warden are rich, unforgettable characters who represent rare types of individuality that cannot be destroyed without real damage to humanity. Each embodies strengths that force the reader to care a great deal about him. But these strengths are accompanied by humanizing weaknesses. It is important that most of the novel takes place before December 7, 1941, when the United States is not in military combat. Prewitt's and Warden's combat is essentially and paradoxically with the army they serve. In *Viet Journal*, Jones reminisces about his own military experience: "I had both loved and hated the Army" (p. 49).

Understanding this ambivalence is crucial to comprehending the mood of *From Here to Eternity*. Jones's army (as well as Prewitt's and Warden's) was what professional soldiers now call the old army, which had not been tested in combat for more than twenty years and which had lapsed into a rigid, self-perpetuating caste system. Any institution which continues to exist after its *raison d'etre* has been virtually forgotten will inevitably become corrupt. Secondary, tertiary, and outright inappropriate purposes assume dominance. In both *Viet Journal* and *WWII* Jones discusses the unnatural protection enjoyed by the officers of the old army which virtually rendered this army incapable of the sudden, decisive action necessary in December 1941. *WWII* especially stresses the idea that initial U.S. failures in that war had much to do with the difficulty of the officer class in becoming reaccustomed to responsible decision making after years of having every menial task performed for them. In *Eternity*, then, one cannot be surprised at the phenomenon of a "Dynamite" Holmes obsessed with winning a boxing trophy.

Like James Jones, Prewitt and Warden both love and hate the army. What they hate, presumably, is the corruption, forgotten purpose, and incompetence that accompany directionlessness. What they love is more complex. It is partly a concept of what the army should be, and soon will have to be. The two good soldiers know there is a war coming and that the army will have to be the main protector of the United States, its territories, its traditional values, and its ideals. Warden, especially, has already begun to move toward the requisite anonymity as the novel opens. The army has been for years a refuge for men like Robert E. Lee Prewitt, their pasts dominated by political and economic oppression and their fortunes outside the army bleak. Being a soldier allows such men a profession, which they could not easily find anywhere else.

Much of the power of *From Here to Eternity* comes from three perceptions which are reconciled with pain and difficulty: an

awareness that human individuality, personified by Warden and
Prewitt, must be sacrificed in the war that comes as the novel
ends; a sense of the irreplaceable value of both men's individuality; and the realization that for most of the novel the two
are threatened by the institution to which they have devoted
their lives. The existence of such primary complexity and contradiction allows Jones to introduce supporting themes that make
his book much more than a novel about the army. *From Here
to Eternity* is also concerned with the nature of artistic creation
and the difficulty of human communication. Jones also contrasts
idealism and realistic awareness as solutions to the complexity
of functioning within a corrupt organization, and he explores
the degree of compromise an honest person can make in such
a situation without loss of sanity. Prewitt represents artistic creation and idealism while the question of the possibility of compromise without insanity is associated with Warden, the realist.
The difficulty of communication is a problem for Prewitt and
Warden both with each other and with the women they love.
Finally, as a picture of the life of all the men in Schofield Barracks the novel has implications as proletarian fiction.

Richard P. Adams has written a perceptive study of the novel's
structure; it is based upon "the form of the letter X," he writes.
One line of the X corresponds to Prewitt's downward movement
to death and the other to Warden's upward movement to
"dominance of G Company under the nominal authority of Lt.
Ross." Adams sees also that the two men assume symbolic importance in each other's eyes. Prewitt's devotion to Warden
almost permits the private to save himself from destruction,
while Warden comes despite himself to view Prewitt as a symbol
of "the integrity of the Company." The two soldiers represent
personal and social approaches to the issue of moral integrity.[1]

Robert E. Lee Prewitt represents so much that is admirable
that Jones had to give him significant flaws so that he would be
a credible character. He emerges as a most believable character
because his weaknesses are very real and are intricately related to
his strengths. Often the character flaws are simply mirror images
of the qualities that make him admirable. One is aware immediately, for instance, that Prewitt personifies an idealism carried to
such an extreme that it must be modified or it will play a part in

his destruction. During "The Treatment," when Dynamite Holmes attempts to break his will and force him to box, Prewitt goes through an introspective period. He realizes that he has been shocked by the pervasive brutality of "The Treatment" because he himself would never have caused another human being such pain:

... having suffered as you have from an overdeveloped sense of justice all your life, not to mention being a hotly fervent espouser of the cause of all underdogs all your life (probably because you have always been one, I imagine).

But he had always believed in fighting for the underdog, against the top dog. (p. 275)[2]

This self-analysis shows the abstract nature of Prewitt's idealism. He acknowledges that, while underdogs and top dogs change places, his commitment is totally to underdogs. He is sympathetic to the Communists in Spain, but not in Russia. He is always sympathetic with blacks "because the Negroes were nowhere the top dog, at least as yet" (p. 276). The nonideological nature of Prewitt's philosophy of life in further illustrated by its primary inspiration. His conscious commitment to underdogs was inspired by seeing American Depression films: *Dead End*, *Winterset*, *The Grapes of Wrath*, and the gangster "on-the-bum and prison pictures" (p. 275) featuring John Garfield, James Cagney, and Henry Fonda. The approach in these films varied widely. John Ford filmed a serious study of oppressed people in *The Grapes of Wrath*, whereas most Garfield and Cagney films appeared to be entertainment with no overt political or social message. However, a message was always implicit in even the prison and gangster films of the 1930s. One sympathized with or, if like Prewitt, even identified with Garfield, Cagney, and Fonda precisely *because* they were outside the law. Civilization appeared to have failed; and one responded to characters who tried to take back, by whatever means necessary, the security lost in massive economic failure. Prewitt recognizes that his total commitment to the oppressed is "a very irrational and emotional philosophy," but asserts to himself that "this is a very irrational and emotional age." His beliefs are exactly right for "this disunited world"

(p. 276). Jones's choice of Hollywood as the source of Prewitt's ideology is an aesthetically sound decision. At this point, Prewitt has read very little; when he does discover books, he values writers who reinforce the views he already holds. It should be remembered too that Prewitt is only twenty-one and that his idealism is intense and youthful. Complex and important corollaries result from Prewitt's basic idealism. He is a young man devoted to moral purity: "It was like with a virgin, one wrong decision was enough to do it; after one you were not ever the same again" (p. 8). He understands and accepts the inevitable challenge to such an uncompromising stance:

You decided one thing right, with much effort, and then you thought you'd coast a while. But tomorrow you had to decide another thing. And as long as you decided the way you knew was right you had to go right on deciding. Every Day a Millenium, he thought. (p. 7)

In the context of his own definition of morality, Prewitt does remain remarkably "pure" despite much self-doubt. His primary ethic is fair and decent treatment for everyone and especially for society's underdogs who have experienced nothing but oppression. A logical result of total commitment to society's victims is determination to oppose any social institution acting in a corrupt or even capricious manner. Prewitt must especially challenge the army, the one institution which has given him a sense of identity and purpose, if it appears to behave arbitrarily or unfairly. For a Prewitt that which is most loved must be most above reproach. Since so much of his personal identity derives from the army, corruption in that institution threatens his individual integrity. Edmond L. Volpe writes that "Prewitt's history is an eloquent paean to a concept of individualism rapidly becoming anachronistic in an increasingly bureaucratic society."[3]

It is important to remember that Prewitt comes to Dynamite Holmes's G Company after requesting a transfer out of the Bugle Corps. He transfers because the Bugle Corps's commanding officer wrongly passes him over as First Bugler. The novel opens with one of Prewitt's friends from the Bugle Corps begging him to apologize to "the Old Man" and to accept the secondary position. Prewitt cannot settle for second because he is "the best bugler in the Regiment, bar none." (p. 4). To humiliate himself by accepting unfair judgment would be to cooperate with the kind of corruption which he has vowed always to oppose. In the context of Prewitt's idealism it is almost a secondary consideration that he is the victim in this instance. When an institution exhibits symptoms of corruption, anyone can become a victim at any time, and it is the responsibility of the moral virgin to oppose all such threats.

James Jones's intense awareness of the near impossibility of what Prewitt demands of himself makes this a powerful part of *Eternity*. To vow to remain pure within the confines of a corrupt institution is to will one's own destruction. The very qualities which make Prewitt most memorable and most admirable foreshadow his annihilation.

One of Warden's roles in the novel is to prophesy the self-destructive futility of Prewitt's ethical position. Warden's reaction to G Company's young transfer from the Bugle Corps is complex. On one level, however, he foresees that death inevitably awaits Prewitt and is outraged at the waste: ". . . he was a good soldier" (p. 806). In part, Warden's initial harassment of Prewitt originates in his perception of Prewitt's dedication to the army and vision of a higher purpose for that institution. Other than Sgt. Warden and Pvt. Prewitt, not many men in G Company share such dedication and vision; and the sergeant is tormented by the premonition that the former bugler will be dead before any foreign enemy ever attacks Hawaii. The thirty-four-year-old Warden tries to convince himself that his recent transfer's idealism is ordinary stubbornness, and he first sets out to break his youthful charge of what he thinks of as "bolshevik" intransigence. However, Warden soon responds positively, and almost in spite of himself, to the purity of the young man.

Warden also recognizes the impossibility of changing Prewitt. The "irrational and emotional" nature of the private's ethical position has such deep personal origins that it can only be eradicated by death. When he is released from the Stockade and kills the sadistic guard Fatso Judson, Prewitt reviews his life as a history of "scars":

There were the scars he got in the Stockade, still new and red. And there were all the scars he'd got in all the barracks, coming in drunk and falling over the footlockers. He had lots of scars. He had a real history. *Robert E. Lee Prewitt*, a history of the United States in one volume, from the year 1919 to the year 1941, uncompleted, compiled and edited by We The People. There were the scars he got on the county road gang in Georgia, and the scars he had got in Mississippi in the city lockup. There were the scars he had got from the police, and the scars he had got from the enemies of the police. (p. 676)

The son of a Harlan County, Kentucky, mining family, Prewitt grew up in grinding, hopeless poverty. His father beat him; his mother died of consumption when he was in the seventh grade; and all the adults around him were trapped in an environment which stripped away dignity and self-respect. There were two possibilities of escape. Prewitt's Uncle John Turner had been in the army as a young man and still liked to talk about the "adventure" of "The Profession." Second, the music of Appalachia suggested a beauty somewhere away from Prewitt's environment.

Prewitt's first dramatic confrontation with social repression comes when the Harlan County miners attempt a strike. The strikers are overwhelmed; Prewitt's father receives multiple stab wounds and a fractured skull, then is imprisoned; and Uncle John Turner goes down in a blazing gun battle with several deputies. It is at this time that the young man makes a deathbed promise to his dying mother that is to shape so much of his later life. She extracts from him a "sacred" pledge: " 'Promise me you wont never hurt nobody unless its absolute a must, unless you jist have to do it' " (p. 16). Prewitt is the product of fundamentalist religious faith, and his need to uphold that "sacred" pledge is deeply embedded in his consciousness.

Prewitt leaves Harlan County when he is seventeen and, after a period on the bum, enters "The Profession." The army is initially good for him, especially when he receives a "call" upon learning to play the bugle. However, he picks up another skill which is to hound him for the rest of his life. He becomes an excellent amateur boxer. It is the bugle that matters to Prewitt, however; and he reaches the high point of his life when he is chosen to play "Armistice Day Taps at Arlington, the Mecca of all Army buglers." After that, however, "the other people began to come into it" (p. 18). Prewitt has an affair with a "society girl" from whom he gets a venereal disease. While such a fate is not regarded in Prewitt's army as anything serious or unusual, it is a "bad mark" on his official record, and it indirectly costs him his rating in the Bugle Corps.

Jones's intent in having the son of Harlan County miners catch a venereal disease from a rich society girl is obvious, perhaps too much so. Nevertheless, this rich girl is the first in a series of upper-class characters who victimize the young man, whose primary desire is only to play his bugle; Dynamite Holmes is the culmination of the diseased chain begun by the society girl. The society-girl episode is critical in its effects on Prewitt, who felt he "was no longer the virgin. . . . Up to then he had been the young idealist. But he could not stay there. Not after the other people entered into it" (p. 18). This is a quixotic young man, and it is natural for him to fight the most bitterly and intransigently for his moral purity when he feels that it may already be gone. He seems almost to attempt virginity again.

The next person who comes into Prewitt's life and irrevocably complicates it is Dixie Wells. In contrast to the society girl, Dixie Wells is physically damaged by Prewitt, and in a tragic, permanent way. Prewitt has been pressured back into boxing; Wells is a friend and sparring partner. In a workout Prewitt "caught Dixie wide with this no more than ordinarily solid cross" (p. 21). Wells is blinded. Jones's hero must connect this tragic incident with the deathbed promise to his mother:

> It would probably, after Dixie Wells, have been the same whether or not he had been haunted by his promise to his mother. But the old, ingenuous, Baptist-like promise was the clincher. Because the uninitiated boy had taken it, not like a Baptist, but literally. (p. 22)

The "uninitiated boy" determines never to allow himself to box again, unknowingly setting up his victimization by Holmes. However, the physical ruination of Wells by Prewitt is perhaps the simplest level on which the incident affects him. This time Prewitt has hurt somebody when it was certainly not "absolute a must." While he no more meant to blind Wells than to become infected by the society girl, he cannot accept a self-vindication based on the assertion of Wells's or his own free will. For Prewitt, morality is not a matter of choice. He is a literalist, and it is undeniable that he hurt somebody. He has to find a way of avoiding any excuse:

My god! he wondered. Are you a misfit? What happened to you does not bother any of these others. Why should you be so different? But fighting had never been his calling, bugling was his calling. For what reason was he here, posing as a fighter? (p. 22)

The blinding of Wells does then involve a choice he made—allowing himself to become a boxer again. Such an assumption of guilt hardly clarifies things for Prewitt; rather, it makes his ethical position more complex and hopeless. Much like Hemingway's Nick Adams, who, in "The Killers," "can't stand to think about" the Swede being killed, Jones's character is tormented by the pain of reality. Prewitt is a "misfit" in the same way that Nick Adams is. Both young men are compassionate idealists trying to exist in a brutal, naturalistic universe. Prewitt finally cannot deny this side of himself any more than the guilt he assumes for Wells's blinding. "Other people" have confused Prewitt's ethical stance almost irrevocably—but only almost. Peter G. Jones stresses Prewitt's guilt more than any other critic: "Prewitt knows from the moment he breaks his mother's deathbed request that he is guilty and he devotes the rest of his life to insuring that his punishment will result."[4]

The society girl and Dixie Wells may have temporarily taken his moral purity from him, but Prewitt's inherent decency and concern for others tell him that it can perhaps be regained. But there is no room for any more mistakes. If he is to become a moral virgin again, Prewitt must be unequivocally pure from now on and so must those things he loves and derives his identity from— the "calling" of the bugle and the "Profession" of the army. Such a demand ironically will lead him to Dynamite Holmes's G Company, with its concern for nothing but boxing. There, a result of his determination to fulfill his deathbed promise to his mother will be the killing of Fatso Judson, the sadistic stockade sergeant. "Perhaps it was his temperament, but he seemed to have a very close working alliance with irony" (p. 20). Robert E. Lee Prewitt, quixotically attempting to be faithful on a literal level to an idealism he fears is already lost, can hardly avoid irony.

II Sgt. Warden

Sgt. Milton Anthony Warden, tortured by his awareness of the essential complexities in remaining loyal to an obviously corrupt institution, has worked out an apparent solution to this dilemma. He understands what the army should be and what it soon must become if any traditional American values are to survive in a world threatened by fascism. He is also painfully aware of how far the pre–Pearl Harbor army is from representing any kind of workable force against the Axis powers. Moreover, Warden creates a complex role for himself. He will be the best sergeant in Hawaii. Further, he intends to protect himself against the disillusionment of seeing his work undone by Dynamite Holmes and others through perfecting a manner of uncaring cynicism. Warden knows a test is coming which cannot be failed. He hopes that there are enough men like himself to keep alive some degree of integrity in the army until that time. Meanwhile, he seeks to protect his own psyche against present corruption by not caring and not feeling.

The danger in such suppression of emotion is madness. By attempting to become a one-dimensional man, Warden renounces communication with other people and with himself as a totality. He has taken an important first step in accepting the necessary anonymity of war, but at a much greater cost than he would admit. Throughout Schofield Barracks, there is a legend of Warden—the ultimate top sergeant, tough, hard, demanding, and unfeeling. It is a legend which Warden has worked hard to create and one he is proud of. But in private moments he is locked in bitter conflict with the truth underneath the legend.

The most memorable view of Warden comes early in the novel. Dynamite Holmes has just ordered him to issue an "open Pfc." to another undeserving boxer. After protesting Warden fills out the papers. However, when Holmes leaves, the sergeant takes a "regulation .45 pistol" out of his desk and plays a desperate game with it. He first points the unloaded pistol at an empty closet and calls out in defiance:

"Re-enlist, will you? I'm Wolf Larsen, see? and nobody re-enlists. Not without answering to old Shark. . . . No you don't!" (p. 106)

Wolf Larsen is Jack London's classic personification of insanity resulting from denial of the total self. Larsen's repudiation of every aspect of his personality except calculating brutality makes him something less than a man. Warden's game becomes even more desperate. He loads the pistol, points it at his own head, and "lightly" fingers the trigger. This act leads to a moment of introspection:

Just where is, he thought, the line that separates insanity? Any man who would pull this trigger now would be insane. Am I insane? because I put it loaded to my head? or because I touch the trigger? (p. 106)

Warden's spiritual and psychological descendant in Jones's Guadalcanal novel *The Thin Red Line* is Sgt. Edward "Mad" Welsh, who has come even closer to crossing the "line" into insanity. Welsh is simply Warden carried to a predictable end; cynicism and love of combat have almost removed all normal emotions from his personality. One result of this suppression of feeling is that Welsh is an excellent combat sergeant. He is the "good soldier" Warden will become after December 7, 1941. But now, before Pearl Harbor, Warden is painfully aware of the cost of a one-dimensional personality. He has given up too much of himself. The question Warden must continually face is how much of a man's basic self can be repudiated without loss of sanity. One source of the title of *The Thin Red Line* is an old Midwestern saying: "There's only a thin red line between the sane and the mad." In *From Here to Eternity* Warden knows how difficult it is to walk that line.

Examples of Warden's flirtation with madness occur throughout the novel. He loves to tease a subordinate with his knowledge of books and painting and then abruptly deny any such knowledge. Old Pete Karelsen, a veteran soldier, is the closest thing to a friend Warden has. Suddenly Warden says Karelsen embodies "the disease of the human race" transmitted by "intellectuals." A short page later Warden has completely forgotten that he began the argument. The first description of Warden in the novel is as "the meanest son of a bitch in Schofield Barracks" (p. 10); and he appears to thrive on such an image.

However, just as "other people" confuse things for Prewitt, they also enter Warden's life and complicate it. Warden's "other people" are essentially two—Karen Holmes and Prewitt. Warden initiates a plan to seduce Karen Holmes for two reasons. She has a reputation of being "easy," and she is commanding officer Dynamite Holmes's wife. The legend of Warden demands that he sleep with an attractive, promiscuous woman; and his hatred of officers compels him to seduce this one in order to make a political statement. When he first visits her house, risking imprisonment in Leavenworth, he demands that they go to Holmes's bed:

[Karen:]   "You take your cuckoldry seriously don't you, Milt?"
[Warden:] "Where Holmes is concerned I take everything seriously."
(p. 120)

Karen Holmes turns out to be a greatly more complex woman than Warden imagined. In their first encounter Warden explains to her his definition of "sin":

"I believe the only sin is a conscious waste of energy. I believe all conscious dishonesty, such as religion, politics and the real estate business, are a conscious waste of energy. I believe that at a remarkable cost in energy people agree to pretend to believe each other's lies so they can prove to themselves their own lies are the truth . . . ." (p. 118)

The principal wasters of energy, Warden knows, are the officer class. Covert counterattacks against this elite, such as seducing their wives, are necessary for him to maintain his balance on the thin line between sanity and insanity. However, such a strategy will work only as long as Warden can view Karen Holmes merely as an extension of her husband. Soon she forces him to recognize that she is a victim of, rather than a participant in, Dynamite's corruption.

In a hotel room, Warden cruelly assaults her with the accusation, spread primarily by G Company's mess sergeant, Maylon

Stark, that she is notoriously promiscuous. Karen first speaks of
the depths of her hatred for men and then gives Warden a new
definition of "waste of energy." Showing him a long scar on her
abdomen, she lectures on the medical and psychological meaning
of hysterectomy:

"A hysterectomy is a uterectomy. A uterectomy is an operation in
which they excise the uterus. But they call it hysterectomy. You know
what hysterectomy comes from, of course? From hysteria. Hysteria
and womb and women are synonymous in the medical profession,
you know. That's where they get their biggest source of income,
you see. . . .

"God knows what the medical profession would do if it didn't
have its hysterectomies and their hystro-derivities. Probably all go
broke and vote for socialized medicine after all, I guess. At the
hospital I was in they performed as many as nine hysterectomies in
a morning. . . .

"But," . . . "you're still not a woman any more. You still go to bed,
the men still get what they want, but the purpose of it all is gone.
The meaning of it is gone, too. You're not a woman and you're certainly not a man, you're not even a poor freak of a hermaphrodite.
You're not anything. You're a gutted shell. . . ." (pp. 331–32)

Warden tries to stop her, but Karen Holmes continues to explain
that her hysterectomy resulted from infection by her husband's
gonorrhea. She further states that she did sleep with Maylon
Stark after the surgical invasion in order to cleanse herself: " 'I
was dirty' " (p. 334). Warden now has to begin seeing her as a
beautiful, victimized woman whom he comes increasingly to love.
Because she is married to Holmes and because of the old army
caste system, their relationship is hopeless unless he too becomes
an officer. Now the legend of Warden is seriously compromised.
Not only does he feel the emotion he has struggled to deny, but
he is forced to contemplate becoming a member of the officer
class he despises. Throughout much of the remainder of the novel,
Warden struggles to accept this compromise. He even takes the
officers' candidacy examination and passes with ridiculous ease.

But despite his genuine love for Karen, Warden simply cannot
let go of the "legend" he has so elaborately constructed. He does
try, however, and undergoes great inner turmoil. In a nicely

condensed statement of his dilemma, Warden has a moment of introspection in which he comprehends that the moment he told Karen he loved her, "he was no longer a free agent, and as a result the old wild terrible strength that had been the power and pride of Milt Warden was gone" (p. 627). But still inescapable is the fact that "when he was with her, he only thought about how fine it was to be in love" (p. 627). The only clear solution to Warden's conflict is not to be "with her"; and Karen Holmes seems always to know that separation from Warden is inevitable.

Still, they truly love each other; and such a solution is not possible without a last attempt to deny the external and internal truths that haunt their relationship. They go to a little known hotel, which succeeds by "holding the world back out of evidence" (p. 702) and try for a romantic idyll. No hotel can keep the world out of their minds, however; and the combination of guilt and anticipation of defeat denies them any chance of escape. They start to make each other "pay" for all the external factors that complicate their relationship and force them into a secret rendezvous and for all their inner doubts and torments. In desperation Warden tells himself that love cannot exist because it must lead to marriage and then torments himself with a vision of marriage dominated by combat imagery. Nothing could more quickly destroy "the legend of Milt Warden" than marriage; and the sergeant upbraids himself for having succumbed to "the virus of the illusion of romantic love, . . . Warden's Bacillus" (p. 705). His self-castigation does not yet release Warden: "If a man could just hang onto one illusion he could still love. The main trouble with being an honest man was that it lost you all your illusions" (p. 705). The surrender of all illusions is, of course, the main principle underlying Warden's adopted persona; and the fact that he regrets such a surrender now indicates how deeply he does love Karen Holmes.

His love for her is great enough that he is unable to regain the legend of Milt Warden without help. Such help comes first from the Japanese. December 7, 1941, represents the first of three major steps in the release of Warden from his own self-doubt. It is no accident that Warden takes over in this crisis and restores a degree of order in the barracks. The Japanese attack is the moment of crisis which he has prophesied throughout the novel and it is the time in which the anonymity of the soldier will be necessary. Warden feels exhilaration as he organizes whatever resistance he can. His desperate bargain with self and sanity which his love for Karen Holmes has compromised is once more controlling. The world is now at war, and there is need only for soldiers (especially good soldiers) and not for lovers and husbands. Warden is almost free to become "Mad" Welsh.

Only almost, because Karen Holmes and Robert E. Lee Prewitt will still play important and symbolic roles in Warden's evolution into the anonymity of a soldier. Karen Holmes, who seemingly has always known that her love affair with Warden must end, attains a peace and understanding after December 7 which she transmits to the sergeant. Ironically, their last meeting takes place at the home of Maylon Stark's mistress. Stark is the man who, out of rage and frustration over a failed affair years before with Karen, has started the widespread rumors about her promiscuity. When Warden sees Karen, she is "at peace"; she tells him that she can accept their separation because " 'maybe we only love the things we cannot have. Maybe thats all love is. Maybe its supposed to be that way' " (p. 824). Whether that is correct or not, Karen says Warden has freed her from Holmes by making her know that she is "attractive" and "loved" (p. 825). The two then share a night of intense, but nonphysical, lovemaking. The avoidance of intercourse is a sign Karen demands, and to which Warden willingly assents, that their relationship has changed immeasurably since the day Milt Warden came to seduce Karen Holmes as a political statement. They say goodbye, and now Warden can resume his persona of the man who does not love or share more than his body with any woman.

Prior to this farewell scene between Warden and Karen Holmes, Prewitt has been killed; and the death of "the misfit" transfer is the third key factor in Warden's final liberation. While the Japanese brought war and the necessity of completing the "evolution" of a soldier, and Karen Holmes freed the sergeant from the confusion of love, Prewitt's death plays at least as important a role in releasing him from complexity. As mentioned, Warden's response to Prewitt, from the beginning, is complicated. The sergeant understands that the young transfer is, like himself, "a good soldier," but is frustrated by the private's idealism.

Knowing intuitively that such idealism can lead only to self-destruction in a corrupt institution such as the army, Warden attempts to convince himself that Prewitt is merely stubborn and initially participates in the harassment of the young bugler. However, Warden always knows that Prewitt is an infinitely stronger and better man than "Dynamite" Holmes and the others engaged in organizing "The Treatment." Moreover, the stubborn "bolshevik" comes to personify for Warden the emotion, passion, and artistic egotism which he is struggling to deny in himself. Ultimately, Warden even breaks some of the army's and, more significantly, his own rules in an attempt to protect Prewitt.

In fact, the top sergeant is so drawn to G Company's "misfit" that he allows himself to violate the most basic element in his code—before Prewitt arrives, Warden had successfully committed himself to emotional noninvolvement in the lives of the men serving under him. Early in the novel, Warden saves Prewitt from the stockade; however, he must see it as a game in which he defeats "Dynamite" Holmes, rather than as a favor to a "stupid fool of an antediluvian . . . trying to live up to a romantic, backward ideal of individual integrity" (p. 288). The "romantic misfit" knows instinctively that it is "the Top" who saved him and reacts in a manner that typifies the two men's relationship at this point in the novel: "I dont know what the hell business it is of his. . . . Why cant he keep his big nose out of things?" (p. 291)

Both men are so locked into their own self-imposed roles that neither can yet make a gesture of simple, direct affection or respect for the other. In fact, the novel's most beautifully written scene, relevant not only to the "evolution" of Warden but also to the novel's theme of failed communication, occurs when "the Top" and Prewitt get drunk together and *come close* to admitting their feelings for each other. After some wonderfully funny dialogue, they both pass out and are almost run over by a truck. The truckdriver is seemingly unable to arouse Warden, but Prewitt does recover long enough to see that his sergeant is taken care of and to state that Warden is the " '. . . Best fuggin soljer ina Compny.' . . . '*Ony* fuggin soljer ina Compny' " (p. 481). The private passes out again, and his sergeant immediately regains consciousness he had never really lost. Warden has dreamed up an excuse for Prewitt that will save him trouble with G Company and tells Weary Russell, the truckdriver, that the "bolshevik misfit" is " 'the best fuckin soljer in the Company.... The *ony* fuckin soljer in the Compny....' " When Russell protests, Warden proclaims: " 'We got to take caref him while we can, see?' ... 'This man may not be with us for long, and we got to take caref this man' " (p. 482). While each man still pulls back from a direct, open statement of respect for the other, mutual admiration is clearly present. Moreover, Warden is already "taking care" of Prewitt, which clearly constitutes a violation of his principle of emotional noninvolvement.

Only when the young private is awaiting the stockade can "the Top" drop his mask and let his personal affection and concern show. This gesture makes Prewitt "feel proud, because for some obscure reason he valued that respect more than he valued anybody else's respect..." (p. 520). For the reader, the reason is complex, but not "obscure." Prewitt admires Warden's devotion to being the total soldier, a devotion which he is ironically complicating by touching the sergeant's emotions; and he responds to Warden's recognition of his own devotion to "The Profession."

After Prewitt kills "Fatso" Judson and deserts, Warden completely drops his pretense of not caring about the young private and carries him present on the company roster; the sergeant reassures himself that the AWOL will return because "thirty-year-men did not desert" (p. 700). Such an action torments him, however; and he attempts to understand what is happening to him. He first admits that "Prewitt seemed to hold the key to something," that "Prewitt had become a symbol to him of something." Then he reaches an even more painful level of self-examination: he is taking Prewitt's desertion "... as if it really meant something to him personally." This thought must be resisted as much as possible: "Probly its because you feel guilty about becoming an officer, he told himself. Probly that's all it is" (p. 714). That's not all it is, but it is a clue. Prewitt represents to Warden the doomed idealist and is, then, the embodiment of his own troublesome "backward romanticism." This aspect of his personality made the Top vulnerable to Karen Holmes's love, which is why he is considering becoming an officer.

The last meeting between Warden and Prewitt contains one of the novel's most effective examples of indirect communication. "The Top" has explained to his troublesome private that, while the murder of Judson can be covered up, Prewitt will have to spend some time in the stockade for desertion when he returns to the Company. Prewitt flatly refuses to risk any more time in the stockade; and Warden explodes: "'. . . I don't know why the fuck I'm down here bothering to talk to you right now.'" The "bolshevik" answers simply: "'Because you're ashamed of being an officer'" (p. 735).

When Prewitt is killed by an American guard patrol as he attempts to return to his company after the bombing of Pearl Harbor, Warden must identify the body. He does more—he sees to it that the private's record will read "Killed in Line of Duty" and arranges for burial in the permanent army cemetery at Schofield. When one of the guards asks if Prewitt was a friend of his, "the Top" replies: "'No.' . . . 'Not a friend.'" The guard then adds, "'Well, I wanted you to know we were all awfully sorry.'" "'Everybody's always very sorry.' Warden said. 'Afterwards'" (p. 796). These brief remarks by "the Top" constitute Prewitt's epitaph, as well as the end of Warden's torment. Warden is paying final tribute not only to another "good soldier," but to the end of his own romantic individualism, which in the twentieth century of war is not a "friend." He, like everyone who will have to endure it, is "sorry" about the anonymity which now cannot be avoided; but it is too late for such regret to be meaningful.

Moreover, it must be remembered that Prewitt was killed not by a military enemy, but as a result of his idealism colliding against the corruption of the "old Army." "Dynamite" Holmes is the novel's most powerful representative of such corruption, but finally not its most unforgettable. A great deal of *From Here to Eternity*'s shock effect in 1951 came from the stockade scenes and the characterizations of S/Sgt "Fatso" Judson and Major Thompson. It is an example of Prewitt's "close working alliance with irony" that he eventually winds up in the stockade as an indirect, rather than a direct, result of "The Treatment" ordered by Holmes. In *Viet Journal*, Jones discusses reaching a "breaking point" in combat; he argues that an isolated incident, in itself not sufficient to destroy a man's control, can in an environment of unremitting outrage and horror have such an effect. If one remembers that Prewitt is always in a special kind of "combat" with his own army, this concept is applicable to him. It is finally a ridiculous fight with a man named Bloom, every bit as much a victim as Prewitt, which triggers the events that push the former bugler over the edge and into the stockade.

III   *The Symbol of the Stockade*

The stockade operates in the novel as a symbolic microcosm of all the "old army's" corruption. Jones's juxtaposition of hideous brutality with official, bureaucratic assault upon the dignity of the self causes these scenes to be reminiscent of the excesses of Nazi Germany, a parallel intended to be drawn indirectly, but strikingly. Prewitt is immediately made aware that there is no intention of reform in the Schofield Barracks Stockade—he is shown a clipping which informs each new prisoner that it was in the Schofield stockade that John Dillinger first served time. The clipping ends with these words: "IT WAS SO TOUGH THAT JOHN DILLINGER UPON BEING RELEASED FROM IT SWORE TO HAVE VENGEANCE UPON THE WHOLE UNITED STATES SOMEDAY, EVEN IF IT KILLED HIM." Beneath this, someone has printed: "WHICH IT DID" (p. 532). Shortly after seeing this clipping, the idealistic private is introduced to Major Thompson and the grub hoe handle torture. Major "Father" Thompson, "an officer ever since 1918" (p. 533), is the epitome of the caste system of the old army. While he interrogates the new prisoners, they are ritualistically beaten in the kidneys by guards armed with the omnipresent grub hoe handles. While undergoing this torture, Prewitt first notices "Fatso" Judson:

. . . S/Sgt Judson somewhat [resembled] Porky Pig in the Walt Disney cartoons. S/Sgt Judson was staring at him with the deadest eyes he had ever seen in a human being. They looked like two beads of caviar spaced far apart on a great white plate. (p. 535)

"Father" Thompson provides the "philosophical" justification of the stockade's brutality (" '. . . the quickest, efficientest, least expensive way to educate a man is to make it painful for him when he is wrong, the same as with any animal,'") (p. 534), while Judson serves as the enforcer.

It is significant that Prewitt undergoes great brutality and humiliation, and sees his friend Private Angelo Maggio suffer even worse without promising himself revenge. However, after being forced to watch Judson supervising the murder of a man named "Blues" Berry, whom he has never met prior to entering the stockade, he vows to kill "Fatso." That the former bugler even feels a degree of pride in being able to take the worst that "Fatso" can give is a clue to the degree of masochism that is always present in his psychological makeup. However, the murder of Berry is the worst violation of his mother's creed of never hurting anybody that Prewitt has ever seen, and the "literalist" can see no way to right this wrong except to kill Judson. He is told more than once that "Fatsos" are infinitely replaceable, as are "Father" Thompsons; still "Blues" Berry was an almost classic underdog destroyed by the institution upon which the young man from Harlan County has based his identity. Moral restitution must be made. The most chilling detail concerning "Fatso" Judson is his total inability to comprehend Prewitt's need for vengeance. As he dies of the knife wound inflicted by his former stockade victim, he expresses surprise:

"You've killed me. Why'd you want to kill me," he said and died. The expression of hurt surprise and wounded reproach and sheer inability to understand stayed on his face like a forgotten suitcase left at the station, and gradually hardened there. (p. 672)

Judson is a man born without a moral or ethical sense, and much of the grim point of Jones's novel is that he represents what corrupt institutions have done to twentieth-century man. Prewitt is himself cut badly in the knife fight with Fatso—the wound is in the back and side. He makes his way to the home of his mistress, Alma Schmidt, clutching his bleeding side all the way. The wound in Prewitt's side initiates an emphasis upon Christ imagery which climaxes in the former bugler's death. Such symbolism is relevant both to Prewitt's role in the novel as a devout fighter for the underdog, as well as to an unusual form of mysticism introduced in the stockade section of the novel and arising directly from Jones's proletarian emphasis. Still, the depiction of Prewitt as Christ figure seems forced and flaws the novel.

Cut off from "the Profession" at Alma's, the "romantic bolshevik" goes through a period of obsessive drinking and reading until December 7. It is one of the novel's sharpest ironies that Prewitt, one of the novel's two "good soldiers," is isolated from the army at this most crucial of times, sleeps through the actual attack, and assumes that it is the Germans bombing Pearl Harbor. However, he undergoes a complete reversal when he reads that all the prisoners have been released from the stockade and vows to return to his company. His farewell scene with Alma is one of the most powerful moments in the novel:

"What do you want to go back to the Army for?" she cried, getting her breath. "What did the Army ever do for you? besides beat you up, and treat you like scum, and throw you in jail like a criminal? What do you want to go back to that for?"

"What do I want to go back for?" Prewitt said wonderingly. "I'm a soldier." (pp. 779–80)

Indeed, he is "a soldier"; "the Profession" was the first thing in his life that gave him a sense of pride and identity.

Prewitt's return to G Company is virtually impossible. Because of the bombing, all of Hawaii is under tight security and army patrol cars are everywhere. It is not long before he is captured attempting to cross the Waialae Golf Course. After being taken into custody, Prewitt is able to escape momentarily because of "the old, narrow, clear, hard, crystal something which was the trademark of Harlan Kentucky" (p. 787). The class conflict, which is always a major underlying theme in the novel, is given a clear focus when the son of Harlan, Kentucky, miners dies on a golf course, the plaything of the rich. Running from the patrol, Prewitt attempts a zigzag maneuver across the course until he comes to the edge of a sandtrap, where he stops, turns and faces his pursuers, and is shot three times before sliding into the sandtrap. Jones focuses upon the former bugler's dying thoughts which emphasize the religious imagery which has been pervasive in the novel since the knifefight with Judson. Shortly before he stops, he hears one of his pursuers yell, "'This guy wasn't no soldier'"; and his turning to face death is, in part, a doomed attempt to refute such a total falsehood:

And these were the Army, too. It was not true that all men killed the things they loved. What was true was that all things killed the men who loved them. Which, after all, was as it should be. (p. 789)

Throughout his flight, the young private has been impressed with the competency with which the ground patrol is doing its job; and he decides finally to die facing, not running from, such "good soldiers."

Jones also utilizes Prewitt's dying thoughts to emphasize the proletarian-based mysticism introduced in the stockade section of the novel. In fact, the young idealist's final vision encapsulates Jones's vision:

But then, as if in a way he was seeing double, he realized that it wasnt really going to end after all, that it would never end. . . . How that there was always an endless chain of new decidings. (p. 791)

Thus, Prewitt's martyrdom is to the army as it is and as it should be, to the exploited proletariat, and to his own peculiarly puritanical idealism that demanded "Fatso's" life for the murder of "Blues" Berry. Despite the fact that he is clearly doomed from the start (as are all idealists in corrupt institutions), it is ironic that he would not have had to die when he did had he been able to resist killing Judson.

The primary external pressures which have been punishing him since he joined G Company have been removed. "Dynamite" Holmes has moved upstairs to a position of increased power in the army; and, as Warden ironically proclaims over Prewitt's body, the Japanese have effectively canceled the boxing season. However, the quixotic idealist could have come to no other decision. One exchange of dialogue concisely captures the vast difference between Prewitt's self-destructive idealism and Milt Warden's self-denying realism. In their last meeting, Warden attempts to talk his troublesome private out of killing "Fatso," logically pointing out that the Judsons of this world are plentiful and killing one means less than nothing. Prewitt responds: " '... Nobody's got the right to do that to another human being.' " " 'Maybe not, but they do it,' Warden grinned. 'All the time' " (p. 736).

In Warden's last meetings with Prewitt and Karen Holmes, the barriers which have made communication difficult are almost completely transcended. These are only two relationships in the novel which involve Jones's treatment of the difficulty of open communication. The main characters in *From Here to Eternity* adopt personae which hide their inner selves and thus complicate openness with others. Jones has been quoted as saying, "In life ... conversation is more often likely to be an attempt at deliberate evasion, deliberate confusion, rather than communication. . . ."[5] Prewitt's mistress, Alma Schmidt, is in her own way as extreme an example of the tendency to adopt a mask as Milt Warden. Alma has come to Hawaii to escape a small Oregon town where she has always been vulnerable and hurt because her family is not respectable. Her plan is to work as a prostitute long enough to become financially secure and then return to the mainland: "Because when you are proper, you are safe" (p. 260). Alma is, of course, aware of the inherent contradiction in her plan—to become "proper" by becoming a prostitute. She attempts to negate this contradiction by becoming hard and unfeeling and by becoming someone else. Her working name is Lorene; and, when she tells Prewitt about her decision, she uses military imagery. She is a "volunteer" who has "enlisted" (p. 258). Alma has her war; and, initially, there is no place in it for emotions, feelings, or involvement with a "twenty-year-man" from Harlan County, Kentucky.

While she does ultimately fall so in love with Prewitt that she is willing to sacrifice her dream of becoming "proper," she never tells him until it is too late. Significantly, she tells her roommate, Georgette, earlier. Throughout Jones's novel, characters can most comfortably express strongly positive feelings about others to a third party. By the time Alma tells Prewitt of her real love for him, he has hurt her in several vindictive ways. He has even slept with Georgette, whom he cares nothing for. Moreover, the Japanese have attacked, and Prewitt must attempt his return to G Company. The name *Alma* means "soul"; and Prewitt's inability to attain a true understanding with his mistress is symbolic of his failure to attain peace with his own soul. Moreover, Alma's adopting the name *Lorene* in order to become a prostitute is representative of her attempt to deny her own spirituality. In the novel's last chapter, Alma meets Karen Holmes on a ship taking civilians to the mainland and tells her about Robert E. Lee Prewitt, her dead "fiancé" from "an old Virginia family" who was killed at Hickam Field and posthumously awarded the Silver Star. Alma, while admitting the totality of her love, must still revise some crucial aspects of reality. Karen Holmes, who knows all about Prewitt and who has herself had a painful experience involving the masking of emotion and feeling, feels "all the grief that had been in her boiling over into a wild desire to laugh out loud" (p. 855).

IV *Jones's Artistry*

Since communication is the basis of art, Jones's treatment of the motif of denied feeling and sharing allows him to incorporate the related theme of artistic creation. Prewitt's bugling is the central metaphor of artistic creation in the novel, but there are others. In a universe necessarily devoted to the annihilation of individuality, Jones can only treat artistic creativity in a despairing and painful manner. Individuality, complete realization of the self—these are the essential elements in art; and they have no place in the evolution of a soldier.

In *Viet Journal* Jones writes about the overwhelming fear he experienced in World War II:

I could remember being terribly afraid under mortar barrages in World War II. Getting to shoot back at the enemy and hurt him had helped that fear a lot. Anyway, I was younger. Back then, I had been afraid of dying without having made my voice heard in the world, without having the fact of my existence at least known. I did not want to be lumped namelessly together with a lot of dead heroes who got remembered only collectively. A perhaps legitimate vanity. (p. 219)

In fact, this was the most "legitimate" of "vanities" because the need to make one's "voice heard in the world" is the central motivation behind all art. One of the most painful implications in *From Here to Eternity* is that art almost certainly must be destroyed by the requisite anonymity of warfare. In later novels, Jones is concerned with the possibility that the inhuman technology of the twentieth century may endanger this highest expression of the self even in peacetime.

Robert E. Lee Prewitt became an artist as soon as he received "the Calling" of the bugle. An archetypal underdog from Harlan County, he must, in part, symbolize the proletarian artist. In a magnificent scene early in the novel, Prewitt, surrounded by other musicians, plays Taps in the darkness of the quad. From this scene, one can deduce much about Jones's aesthetic theory during the writing of *From Here to Eternity*. Prewitt's masterful bugling rises "triumphantly high on an untouchable level of pride above the humiliations, the degradations":

This is the true song, the song of the ruck, not of battle heroes; the song of the Stockade prisoners itchily stinking sweating under coats of grey rock dust; the song of the mucky KPs, of the men without women who collect the bloody menstrual rags of the officers' wives, who come to scour the Officers' Club—after the parties are over. . . .
This is the song of the men who have no place, played by a man who has never had a place, and can therefore play it. Listen to it. . . . This song is Reality. Remember? Surely you remember? (pp. 218–19)

"This song" is also *From Here to Eternity*—a novel about the underdogs in a brutal caste system, soon to be faced with collective anonymity, desperately wanting their existence "at least known."

This scene is masterfully handled; while Prewitt's notes "hovered like halos over the heads of the sleeping men in the darkened barracks, turning all grossness to the beauty of sympathy and understanding" (p. 218), the almost constant brutality of the novel ceases as Jones creates a moment which both emphasizes and transcends the suffering which dominates his novel. Prewitt's bugling is a pause in the narration—but a pause of critical importance to all that Jones is saying. Two critics have devoted extensive discussion to Prewitt's role as proletarian artist. Richard P. Adams argues that the "simple" Prewitt is treated as "artist-philosopher" and that such characterization is an example of the "romantic doctrine of quasi-mystical primitivism of low-brow sentimental anti-intellectualism...."[6] Leslie Fiedler puts *Eternity* in a literary tradition which glorifies "the bum" "on the run."[7] Jones, in response to the Fiedler argument that Prewitt is the "heir" of an American romantic tradition which glamorizes the apparently inarticulate artistic wanderer, said: "What's interesting is that if Prewitt is *their* heir, Prewitt as the wanderer had no place left to go *except* into the army—where he became, artist or not, a ward of the government."[8]

There are other examples of Jones's concern with art in the novel. Warden removes from Prewitt's dead body a copy of "The Re-Enlistment Blues" and a list of books the dead bugler had planned to read. "The Re-Enlistment Blues" is a classic example of the manner in which proletarian art is created—it is jointly written by Prewitt and two of the novel's other "lonely" musicians.[9] The list of unread books is the result of Prewitt's discovery of literature while in the stockade and subsequent reading binge while AWOL at Alma's. Also, as mentioned, though he constantly attempts to suppress the fact, Warden, too, knows more than a little about painting and literature.

Still, music is the most emphasized art form in the novel; and the types of music (country and western, the blues) to which Jones refers illustrate his concern for the common man. At least in the 1950s, country-western music was primarily identifiable with the rural Southerner; and the blues, of course, has traditionally been the music of the oppressed black American. Thus the use of "the common man's music" serves as a supporting metaphor for Jones's proletarian concern. That the novel is intended as a work about an exploited class is evident on virtually every page. Jones cares most for the lonely private living in the paradise of Hawaii, but unable to experience the pleasures inherent in this environment. Relatively overt statements of proletarian consciousness occur throughout the novel. Warden's refusal to become an officer (such refusals constitute a recurrent theme in Jones's fiction) ultimately arises from concerns which transcend the army. Essentially he hates and distrusts the middle class:

"Who do you think it was put Hitler up? The workers? No, it was the same middleclass. Who do you think gave the Communists Russia? The peasants? No, the Commissars. That same goddam middleclass. In every country everywhere that same middleclass holds every rein. Call it Fascism or call it Individual Initiative or call it Communism, and you still dont change it any. . . ."

"And now I'm supposed to go on and become an Officer, the symbol of every goddam thing I've always stood up against, and not feel anything about it. . . ." (pp. 621–22)

This speech of Warden's makes clear that, while Jones is writing from a proletarian viewpoint, he does not embrace communism. In fact, he wishes to repudiate all totalitarian systems. One of the most chilling scenes in *From Here to Eternity* depicts Dynamite Holmes's recruitment by a power-mad brigadier general named Slater. Slater argues that, in the old army, Honor and Fear of Authority equally motivated men; however, he asserts, "the advent of materialism and the machine age" have made Honor obsolete and men can now be controlled only by the negative concept of Fear of Authority. He then goes to the logical conclusion of such a theory and extends it beyond the army: "The lot of modern man has become what I call 'perpetual apprehension.' It is his destiny for several centuries to come, until control can become stabilized." A few men who, like himself, are blessed with "logical" minds must master this method of control-through-fear, just as it has been mastered in Germany, Japan, and Russia (p. 342). Slater obviously embodies Jones's vision of the men who have brutally risen to power throughout the twentieth century world by using technology as a means of intimidating the masses. Jerry H. Bryant sees the Slater episode as a crucial thematic center of the novel. Comparing Slater to General Cummings in Norman Mailer's *The Naked and the Dead,* he argues that both novelists are warning against ". . . the fascists within our own system, bent on establishing . . . a non-living society." Prewitt's individualism poses a threat to Slater's plan for a totalitarian society and, thus, the bugler must be killed.[10]

In *From Here to Eternity*, Jones finds himself in a position confronted by more than one twentieth-century American writer —he responds deeply to the lower classes, is suspicious of any systematic attempt at organizing the masses, and longs nostalgically for a vanished American individualism. One of Jones's literary idols, John Steinbeck, dealt with essentially this same dilemma in *Of Mice and Men*, *The Grapes of Wrath*, and, most specifically, *In Dubious Battle*. Jones's "solution," not unlike Steinbeck's, is to turn to a highly personal kind of mysticism. The focal character in *Eternity*'s mystical vision is Jack Malloy.

Malloy has preceded Prewitt to the stockade, where he has been preaching a doctrine of Passive Resistance derived from Ghandi, the Wobblies, and his own highly individualistic life. Soon after meeting Prewitt, Malloy begins to educate the newcomer for the purpose of converting him to "a new religion." In his summary of Malloy's past, Jones begins to establish the mythic significance of his character: "There was a singular quality about Jack Malloy. . . . He had been almost everywhere and done almost everything in his 36 years" (p. 639). In fact, Prewitt and the reader hear Malloy spoken of in reverential tones even before the character is introduced. As a boy, Malloy learned to read from the Wobblies whom his father, a Montana county sheriff, imprisoned; and he has never ceased to read voraciously. The Wobblies gave him copies of Veblen's *Theory of the Leisure Class* and Joe Hill's *Little Red Songbook*, and the first book he ever bought for himself was Whitman's *Leaves of Grass*. Becoming an IWW activist just as the movement was breaking up, Malloy was a veteran of the Centralia, Washington, massacre, "where they castrated first, and then lynched, Wesley Everest and afterwards sentenced seven other Wobblies for 2nd degree murder for having fought back. . ." (p. 642). Later, Malloy was a follower of the California radical movement centered around "the memory of Jack London and the old group of Socialists in Frisco, George Sterling, Upton Sinclair, and the rest . . ." (p. 642). Sinclair's movement later came to disgust him because of its excessive puritanism. Malloy introduces Prewitt to names which constitute a capsule history of American radicalism: Whitman, Veblen, Joe Hill, London, and Sinclair. Then he outlines the manner in which the legacy of these people must be utilized,

and transcended, in order to create a "new religion" of the proletariat.

First, the prudery about sex which Malloy feels was a primary
factor in destroying the viability of Sinclair's movement must be
dropped. Malloy has always been promiscuous, but he insists
that he never slept with a woman he did not love at the time.
Part of his thesis is that, if puritanical guilt can be removed
from sexuality, love will be more possible. He further feels that
the utilization of propaganda has been a traditional mistake of
radical movements: " 'The masses are one thing, the amalgam of
individuals is another. And you cannot escape that paradox by
leveling them off to a fourth-grade-mind common to all...' "
(p. 643). It is time, Malloy announces, for the evolution of "a
new religion" from "the amalgam of individuals":

"Every religion starts at the bottom level, with the whores, publicans,
and sinners. Logically, it has to start there, with the dissatisfied.
You cant get the satisfied to accept new ideas.
    "And every religion brings martyrdom to its innovators. That part
is a test of natural selection. If the new faith is strong enough, it
conquers persecution and goes on to glory." (p. 645)

However, the central tenet of Malloy's new faith is belief in
a constantly changing, eternally evolving god. (" '... Mightnt the
new religion teach that instead of being permanently fixed God
is growth and evolution, a God which is never the same twice?' "
p. 646). Further, the Old Testament concept of a "God of Vengeance" and the New Testament emphasis on a "God of Forgiveness" must be replaced by an evolutionary "God of Acceptance,
the God of Love-That-Surpasseth-Forgiveness, the God who saw
and heard and spoke no Evil simply because there was none"
(p. 647). In Malloy's mind, both the Old and New Testament visions of God are hopelessly compromised by the idea of guilt.
Faith, even in a benign "God of Forgiveness," of necessity arises
out of human feelings of sin and unworthiness. Reincarnation, the
final article of Malloy's faith, is a natural corollary of his vision of
a changing God. There is a bit of Emerson in Malloy's concept of
God as "the amalgam of [eternally evolving] individuals." In prais-
ing Joe Hill, Malloy remarks: " '... He must have done something

great, back a long time ago before he was ever Joe Hill, to have earned a chance at a ticket like that one.'" A baffled Prewitt asked when, and Malloy replies: "'In one of his previous lives'" (p. 648).

It is really not illogical that Malloy, spokesman for the proletariat who simultaneously fears all attempts at organization of the masses, finally settles for a mystical faith in reincarnation as the basis of his "new Religion." Artistically, however, the Malloy characterization with its attendant philosophizing does damage to Jones's novel, because Malloy's theory of reincarnation is not intellectually profound, even though Jones devotes much space to it. Malloy's mysticism comes to dominate far too strongly and implausibly the characterization of Prewitt after his release from the stockade. One of the many problems with *Some Came Running* is that a variation of this "new religion" is introduced into that novel in an extremely obtrusive manner.

V *Jones and the Underdogs*

Jones is infinitely more powerful in depicting the sufferings of underdogs than in developing philosophical solutions for them. In fact, the primary contribution of Pvt. Angelo Maggio to *From Here to Eternity* is his identity as a classic, and unbreakable, proletarian underdog. Maggio, from Brooklyn, represents the urban lower classes, balancing Prewitt, who is from a rural Kentucky background. The physically small Italian-American also enters the stockade before Prewitt and introduces his friend from G Company to Jack Malloy.

Maggio's arrest outside the Royal Hawaiian Hotel provides the novel with one of its most memorable scenes of social protest. Maggio, a confirmed heterosexual, has just walked out of the apartment of a homosexual named Hal whom he occasionally visits when desperate for money. The humiliation of being reduced to visiting Hal on the chance of picking up money has reduced him to desperation, and he runs drunkenly into the night wearing only his trunks. Prewitt goes to save him from the Military Police and finds him outside the Royal Hawaiian. This hotel is known to soldiers as the place where movie stars and other famous, wealthy people stay. Of course, it is strictly off limits to them. Maggio is not quite conscious when his friend initially finds him, and this interlude allows Jones one of his most effective treatments of the failed communication theme. Prewitt fantasizes a movie star coming out and asking him to her room. When his friend awakens, he repeats almost the same fantasy; and Prewitt merely laughs at him.

Prewitt is attempting to get Maggio away when two M.P.s discover them; and, then and there, the little man from Brooklyn stages his rebellion:

> "Sure, I'm drunk. Sure I am. So what? Cant a man get drunk? Cant a man do anything? Cant a man even put his goddam hands in his goddam pockets on the goddam street? Why not get picked up? You might as well be in Leavenworth, anyway, instead of always on the outside looking in and never getting past the glass front, like a kid outside a candy store. Why not get picked up? I aint no coward, to be running from *them*. I aint yellow. I aint no coward. I aint no bum. I aint no scum." (p. 400)

After this speech, Maggio attacks the military policemen, and Prewitt is unable to rescue him.

A crucial factor in *From Here to Eternity*'s success is Jones's ability to create sympathy not only for the obvious victims of injustice like Maggio and Prewitt, but for less sympathetic characters as well. There is Bloom, a favorite of Dynamite Holmes because he is a good boxer and intensely disliked, partially for that reason. Bloom is reminiscent of Robert Cohn in Ernest Hemingway's *The Sun Also Rises*. Both characters are Jewish and have been isolated all their lives. Their isolation results in a desperation which makes them even more unpopular. In confusion and despair, both finally see their alienation as the result of anti-Semitism in others. It is Bloom who becomes involved in a ridiculous fight with Prewitt which sets off the chain of events ending in the ex-bugler's imprisonment. Moreover, Bloom has had homosexual experiences and is desperately insecure about his masculinity. As a result, he plays a major role in a vice investigation that sweeps the island. Unable to understand the contempt Prewitt and others feel for him except in terms of anti-Semitism and his own and other people's suspicion of his homosexual leanings, Bloom commits suicide by blowing off the top of his head with a rifle. Ironically, when Prewitt learns of Bloom's death in the stockade, he wishes that he could play Taps at his old enemy's funeral: "'Every dogface deserves to have at least one good Taps. At his funeral'" (p. 583).

The most striking example of Jones's ability to create sudden compassion for a previously unsympathetic character is his depiction of Preem, the original head of the mess room. Preem is totally incompetent and does nothing to encourage any positive feeling from the reader until he is replaced by Maylon Stark. Stark's promotion is the result of the machinations of Warden, who is interested primarily in his covert "war" with Holmes. The scene in which Stark replaces Preem is brief and strangely moving. As Preem says, he is thirty-eight, but looks fifty-eight, and has absolutely nowhere to go for the rest of his career. As Preem, a defeated and alienated man, walks out of the mess hall alone, the reader understands that blind favoritism, an inevitable result of the old army's corruption, isolates everyone.

James Jones's first novel is a long, complex attempt to unite several disparate themes. Literary influences on the novel are many, and Jones overtly states several of them in his description of Prewitt's obsessive reading while AWOL. Prewitt responds to Jack London for two reasons: London's own concern with the "lower classes" and his interest in reincarnation as expressed in novels like *The Star Rover* and *Before Adam*. London echoes are strong throughout the novel, and one would expect Jones to respond to a writer like London who stressed so often the theme of physical survival in an almost exclusively male world. Neither is one surprised to find Prewitt responding to Thomas Wolfe because, after all, it was Wolfe who first inspired James Jones to write.

The power of *From Here to Eternity*, however, is Jones's own highly personal achievement. The novel transcends more than a little loose organization and awkward writing, as well as the obtrusiveness of the Jack Malloy characterization, for a quite basic reason. Jones depicts in this novel the brutal and doomed struggles for dignity and simple survival of a group of unforgettable characters. At one point in the novel, Warden reflects on Prewitt and Maggio in the stockade and tries to dismiss them as "common ordinary verynormal fuckups" (p. 631). In terms of social class, all the novel's enlisted men, including Warden, could be so described. However, because they embody values which are so essential to the best in the human race, Prewitt, Warden, Maggio, and the women are anything but "ordinary." The fact that, in various ways, all these characters are doomed gives Jones's novel a beauty derived from pain which will always affect a substantial number of readers.

CHAPTER 3

Some Came Running : *The New Peons*

LIKE many authors of enormously successful first novels, Jones worked long and hard to make certain his second book would be a triumph; and like more than one such author, he failed. *Some Came Running*, which was written over a six-year period, is over twelve hundred pages long and is seriously flawed. In various interviews Jones insisted that his second novel was superior to *From Here to Eternity* because it was more honest and less romantic and adolescent. In fact, *Some Came Running* attempts to expand two of the major themes of Prewitt's and Warden's stories—examination of the lower classes and the sources of art. In addition, Jones investigates at great length two other themes that dominate much of his subsequent fiction. Like *Go to the Widow-Maker* (1967) and *The Merry Month of May* (1970), *Some Came Running* is a study of the sexual maladjustment of American society—especially of the American male. The concept that post–World War II American society is doomed and decaying, an undercurrent in virtually all Jones's fiction, receives extensive analysis in his second novel. There is a connection between these last two ideas—Jones views America's sexual immaturity as one major cause of its inevitable destruction.

In addition, Jones was attempting a narrative experiment in the novel. He renounces what he calls a "classic style" for "colloquial forms" which yield "the immediacy of experience."[1] He believed that standard literary usage produced writing that was foreign to life; thus, he discarded many accepted rules of punctuation and grammar. In particular, he tried to exorcise the apostrophe. Such rebellion against standard usage has caused some critics to call the book "subliterary."

69

I   *Sources of Jones's Failures*

For an understanding of why *Some Came Running* fails, it is necessary to investigate Jones's handling of each of his main themes. In *From Here to Eternity* Jones had, in the enlisted man of the old army, an obvious representative of an oppressed proletarian class. The second novel, set in peacetime, has no such convenient symbol of the proletariat; and Jones falls back upon a highly romantic veneration of the nonrespectable elements of a small Midwestern town. Jones's approach to these undesirables is more than a little reminiscent of the John Steinbeck of *Tortilla Flat* and *Cannery Row*. Steinbeck is evoked frequently in the novel; for instance, Dave Hirsh, Jones's main character who has once been a writer, owns a five-volume library—the Viking Portable editions of Fitzgerald, Hemingway, Faulkner, Wolfe, and Steinbeck, "the five major influences" (p. 12).[2] *Tortilla Flat* and *Cannery Row* are successful novels, however, because they are dominated by a comic mood which mitigates excessive romanticism. In contrast, the tone of Jones's glorification of undesirables is extremely serious, despite the romanticism inherent in such an approach being carried to implausible extremes. It is necessary to say, however, that the romanticism is blunted by the novel's recurrent emphasis that the undesirables are doomed.

There is a different reason behind the failure in this second novel of Jones's analysis of the nature of art. In *From Here to Eternity*, Jones brings the plot of his novel to a momentary halt while Prewitt plays Taps on the bugle. He then describes in a few eloquent paragraphs the pain and oppression out of which Prewitt's music comes. One understands and feels Jones's statement—the most significant art results from the suffering of the common man. In *Some Came Running*, the author and four of his main characters lecture the reader at great length on the sexual, proletarian, and other sources of artistic creativity. Some of this overt philosophizing is embarrassingly obvious, while some of it is so arcane that one must wonder how seriously to take it.

Jones fails in all three of the long novels in which he focuses on the sexual maladjustment of the American male. The essential difficulty with this aspect of *Some Came Running* is the same as

with *Go to the Widow-Maker* and *The Merry Month of May.*
Jones could write moving short fiction about essentially Oedipal
origins of male sexual abnormality. But in novels he tended to
try for shock effects, which seem contrived, to illustrate inadequacies produced by childhood trauma. While Jones believed
deeply that he was one of the few Americans to write honestly
about this defect in the national character, his insights on the
origins of sexual maladjustment were, finally, neither original nor
profound. Such writers as Scott Fitzgerald and Ernest Hemingway can be similarly criticized for a lack of fresh insight into
American sexual problems. Jones's naturalistic style and tendency
to overt lecturing, however, make his limited vision in this regard
more obvious.

Only in its depiction of America as a crumbling, decadent
society does *Some Came Running* come alive. This is especially
true when he presents America's moral and spiritual decline as
the result of a war which irrevocably established the legitimacy
of dehumanizing technology, mass destruction, and a rigid caste
system based on rampant consumerism. In fact, certain minor
figures in *Some Came Running* who are depicted as spiritual
casualties of the war come more memorably alive than the novel's
main characters.

How much Jones believed in *Some Came Running* is made
evident by his placing a quotation from *Don Quixote* at the
front of the novel: "'At last he was free of the damnable books
of Romance.'" He is clearly implying that *From Here to Eternity*
was a young, romantic book he had to write before going on to
other, more serious work. Like other writers before and after
him, Jones seems to have gradually developed something of a
resentment toward his first novel. He became aware that everything else he wrote would be judged in the context of *From
Here to Eternity*'s success. In its own way, however, *Some Came
Running* is as obsessed with a doomed romanticism as *Eternity*;
and it is infinitely less absorbing.

II *The Story*

Dave Hirsh, returning after a long absence to his hometown
of Parkman, Illinois, as the novel opens, allows Jones to interrelate

his motifs of the glorification of the lower classes and the nature of artistic creativity. Dave is a former writer, returning to Parkman after nineteen years away. Having originally left his hometown in disgrace, he comes back partly out of a defiant need for revenge. Dave's father, known to the town only as Old Man Herschmidt, deserted the family to run away with the wife of a local doctor; he returned alone five years later, but never resumed any contact with his family. Thus Dave's brother Frank, a senior in high school at the time of the father's desertion, was forced to take over management of the family affairs.

As a high-school senior himself, Dave was accused of having got a thirteen-year-old country girl pregnant. In fact, he and two other friends had been sleeping with her "night after night each with a good bit of friendliness among the four"; but the girl's father named Dave as his daughter's lover because Frank had by then gone into business in Parkman and started to become prosperous. Frank reacts bitterly to Dave's disgrace: "Like father like son!" he says and gives the younger brother five dollars and orders to leave town. After initially joining a carnival, Dave has held a series of barely respectable jobs until becoming a key figure in a group of writers on the West Coast. In World War II, Dave participated in the Battle of the Bulge, and he returns to Parkman as a thirty-six-year-old ex-GI.

His older brother is the main motivation behind Dave's return; but he is really not certain whether he desires a confrontation or a reconciliation with Frank. He initially lays down a challenge that the older brother can accept in whatever spirit he desires. Frank is equally uncertain about how to receive Dave. While the younger brother is a painful reminder of scandal in a family which has had too many, Frank lacks an heir for his successful business. He has a daughter, but his extremely poor relationship with his wife makes the possibility of a son remote. Briefly, Frank contemplates the possibility of Dave as a son-substitute; and, briefly, the younger brother is not averse to such an idea.

However, it is not long before Frank's hypocrisy and animosity to writing offend Dave; and the returning prodigal soon encounters a group of the town undesirables with whom he feels a kinship. The complexity of Dave's response to Frank is indicated in their final meeting. Dave "felt again the luxurious sense of security

he had always felt with his older brother, and had not felt anywhere else in the world since." In part, Dave desires to accept
his successful brother as a father figure; but the rebellious independence that is a crucial part of his psychological makeup
abhors such a desire: "You cant let your damned emotions run
away with you, by God. Quite suddenly he hated Frank" (p. 97).
Dave's attitude toward Frank remains complex for most of
the novel.

In contrast, his response to the town undesirables is immediately clear—he likes them and identifies with them:

> Every town had a group like that, living on the fringes, always
> within the law, always strictly within the law, not criminal, but at
> the same time not respectable. A little wild. It always did attract
> him. Probably mainly because the respectables always bored the hell
> out of you, with their lies about themselves they'd convinced them-
> selves of finally. Why shouldn't it attract you he thought miserably,
> youre one. (p. 23)

Especially when put in the context of *From Here to Eternity*,
this passage reveals much about the problems Jones has with
Some Came Running. Prewitt, Warden, and Maggio are intensely
sympathetic characters because of what they are; the veneration
of the not-quite-criminal class in Dave Hirsh's story seems to
depend largely on what they are not. Jones's assertions that they
are not boring and they don't lie are generalizations, and much
artistic control would be required to make them convincing. A
writer who values characters from an essentially negative context
inevitably opens himself to serious aesthetic difficulty.

Three characters, 'Bama Dillert, Ginnie Moorehouse, and Jane
Staley, emerge as the primary representatives of the novel's
undesirables; and two of them only add to Jones's artistic problems. Dave is not back in town long before he meets 'Bama
Dillert, a professional gambler who intensely desires the returning prodigal's friendship. With Dave and 'Bama, Jones attempts
to create an example of male affection comparable to that between Prewitt and Maggio. He does not succeed, however,
because it is finally difficult to care very much about 'Bama.
Maggio dramatically acts out his fierce independence; 'Bama

Dillert talks about his for page upon page. Jones is attempting something very difficult with 'Bama—he wants to make him the personification of much that is valuable and admirable, while still stressing his human weaknesses. This approach is precisely the strength of *From Here to Eternity*. The characterization of 'Bama, however, simply becomes incoherent. Not only is he unbelievable at times, but one often has difficulty in distinguishing which aspects of his character Jones intends as admirable.

'Bama is immediately set up as a foil for Frank; and Dave is faced with choosing between the two. The choice is forced when, after Dave has entered into a taxicab business with his older brother, 'Bama urges him to become a partner in his professional gambling operations. The younger brother decides for the undesirable and tells Frank why:

"Bad reputation or not, I trust him—and like him—more than I do the respectable people in this town. And that includes you.... If he was going to cheat you, at least he wouldn't do it in the name of God, or Business, or Social Responsibilities." (p. 613)

Again, Jones's formula is upheld—the "undesirables" are honest; the "respectables" are not.

'Bama is much more than just honest, and sorting out all the central elements of his character is almost impossible. Despite his solitary existence, 'Bama is married and has children; he sees his family only when in the mood and then only under appallingly sexist conditions. He explains early in the novel that a man has to be married because "men like sex but women dont," and "nice women" will only sleep with men because of societal pressure to have children (p. 155). It is difficult to take such a passage seriously; but when Dave eventually visits 'Bama's family, the scene is depicted idyllically.

In fact, 'Bama gives several lectures on male-female relationships that are simply embarrassing if they are read as serious authorial attempts to communicate. At one point he speaks on the art of seduction and says that, for a man to be successful, he simply has to not care. It is all a battle for control, anyway, he argues: " 'Women are smart; theyre shrewd; and they have absolutely no ethics, nor morals, nor integrity, and that's why men don't understand them.... The reason I can handle them is I don't have any ethics or morals or integrity, either, you see? I sort of meet them on their own ground, and they aint used to a man doin' that' " (pp. 539–40). In a novel which has as a central theme the immaturity of American sexual relationships, it is at least possible to view such speeches as evidence that 'Bama is also a victim of arrested male adolescence. However, one cannot be sure if this is what Jones intends because of the generally positive nature of the 'Bama characterization and because the gambler's family life is presented as something greatly desirable.

During an extended Florida gambling trip, one of the novel's least defensible digressions, 'Bama, a Southerner himself, also gives Dave Hirsh a long lecture on Civil War history and the psychology of Southerners. When Dave says many Northerners fear Southerners as irrational, violent people, 'Bama asserts that, contrary to popular belief, white people in the old Confederate states are still fighting the injustices of Reconstruction, as opposed to the Civil War itself. He then explains that, instead of being inherently vicious, white Southerners are "more primitive," less "sophisticated" than Northerners. This lack of sophistication makes them at times prone to spontaneous and brutal acts arising from emotion. Such emotional reactions often lead to spectacular and bloody fights; but if both combatants are still alive afterward, they are likely to unite in warm and sincere friendship (pp. 515–16).

During their odyssey South, Dave and 'Bama observe just such a brutal, senseless fight, followed immediately by an equally incomprehensible reunion. 'Bama's lecture, especially as it comes accompanied by an incident illustrating its validity, so inspires Dave that he formulates the idea for a long short story in praise of Southern primitivism. When published under the title "The Confederate," the story constitutes a major turning point in Dave's struggle to return to writing. There is seemingly little room for doubt that Jones intends the reader to accept 'Bama's speech on the nature of Southerners. Ironically, it is merely a

reversal of the romantic condescension that white writers have
frequently applied to blacks: they are psychologically more
healthy than whites because they are less "sophisticated."

Yet 'Bama's speech inspiring Dave to write a story illustrates
another way in which not only the gambler, but all the undesirables in the novel, are idealized. They are seen as the primary
inspiration for art; this view is a natural corollary of Jones's
vision of the proletariat. But in contrast to *From Here to Eternity*,
Jones's presentation of this theme is extremely awkward. In
large part, this failure is the result of the author's repeatedly
talking about the idea, rather than dramatizing it. In the course
of the novel, 'Bama becomes something approximating Dave
Hirsh's artistic conscience. When the gambler discusses the responsibilities and duties of people like Dave who are "creative"
and who have "talent," one is somewhat reminded of Hemingway's "The Snows of Kilimanjaro":

"But a person who has a talent has a responsibility to it, by God. . . .
Talent is the only single damned thing that separates human beings
from dogs or cats. And not very damned many people have talent.
Too damned few. . . . But when a person has talent, it dont just
belong to him. It belongs to everybody. And that gives him responsibilities to it." (p. 771)

Like Hemingway in his famous story about a dying writer, Jones,
through 'Bama, is establishing the power of creativity as a unique
gift which carries the unavoidable ethical obligation to produce
enduring work for "everybody."

In fact, the gambler does bring about a rebirth of Dave's
artistic conscience and talent: "A friendship . . . had begun, and
was to embrace, the most productive period of Dave Hirsh's
life." In theory, such a result makes a kind of sense—it is Jones's
way of actualizing his belief that aesthetic inspiration should be
sought in those on society's fringes. However, because of the
shallowness of so much of what 'Bama says, the artistic elaboration of this theory is often incoherent.

III   *Idealization and Failure in the Novel*

Jones dramatizes some of the ideal qualities 'Bama is meant

to represent. A marathon gambling session early in the novel illustrates the gambler's endurance, self-possession, and insistence on protecting himself with no external help. He is also meant to personify an old-fashioned pride in "craft" as well:

"You know, . . . gamblin's really a profession, a craft, just like anything else. A fellow gets into it he has to learn his trade, his craft. . . ." (p. 490)

In describing Dave and 'Bama's trip South, Jones gets into what initially seems an unnecessary disgression on the gambler's expertise in driving a car. However, the novelist is making a point—'Bama approaches everything he does as a craft he is determined to master. Most of the novel's undesirables possess delicately refined, noncerebral skills. Jones implies that while such abilities should be respected, they rarely are by conventionally respectable businessmen like Frank Hirsh or by consciously intellectual writers. Mastery of craft is, in his opinion, the special province of the proletariat. Further, art and writing constitute the intellectual equivalent of refined, practical skill. In an essay entitled "Living in a Trailer," Jones describes his admiration of the "crafts and skills" of the laboring class.[3]

Even so, 'Bama is an idealized character because he is meant to represent independence and honesty. He tells Dave that gambling and writing are the only professions left that still have room for "any individuality and freedom" (p. 580). This assertion calls to mind Mark Twain's veneration in *Life on the Mississippi* of riverboat pilots as the last free men in America. 'Bama even has an elaborate theory that writing and gambling are both controlled by a luck which is not external accident. Instead, luck is controlled by "some actual *physical* part of the brain" man has never learned to comprehend (p. 490). The writer and the gambler are seen as rare individualists who reject respectability and security. 'Bama's honesty is demonstrated in several ways: his blatant sexual promiscuity, his contempt for law-enforcement officers who are concerned only with their own protection, and his rejection of the hypocrisy of the American middle class. In addition, he can be brutally candid in analyzing the weaknesses of his fellow undesirables.

Jones goes to some effort to humanize the gambler. There is a hint that part of his initial motivation in seeking Dave Hirsh's friendship is a snobbish desire to befriend Frank Hirsh's brother, who happens to be a locally famous writer. Moreover, 'Bama becomes critically ill in the latter part of the novel; and while he makes a fiery speech of defiance to the doctor who orders him to take care of himself, he is no longer the same rebel. He turns gradually into "a flighty, irascible, often petulant man whose judgment was no longer dependable and whose grin, when he grinned at all, was bitter as gall and wormwood" (p. 953). The irony of Jones's attempt to humanize 'Bama is not that it fails; it is never really possible for the reader to idealize the character as the novelist intended.

The characterization of Ginnie Moorehouse fails for other, though somewhat parallel, reasons. Dave Hirsh, rather than Jones, comes to idealize her. Dave first knows her as an easy pick-up whom he cares about only as someone to sleep with, if no one else is available. During one night with her, he hears her life story. Coming from a desperately poor family, Ginnie has fantasized about sex ever since she can remember. Dave understands that such a preoccupation undoubtedly originated in a painful need for attention and affection. Ginnie's stepfather sexually abused her when she was twelve; her promiscuity began after that trauma. At the age of seventeen, she caught a venereal disease, which she then transmitted to a friend of her stepfather. Ginnie was sentenced to a year in a reformatory. The stepfather and the other adult males who victimized the girl went unpunished.

Dave is understandably touched by such a story and feels compassion for Ginnie. Sensing this, 'Bama becomes increasingly brutal and vicious in describing Ginnie, and Dave finds himself frequently defending her "as a human being" entitled "to a certain basic dignity and respect." At this point, one certainly sympathizes with Dave's viewpoint; however, 'Bama's apparently pointless vindictiveness toward Ginnie is part of a conscious plan, resulting from his understanding of Dave's capacity for self-destruction.

The gambler is aware that his friend is on the verge of a disastrous idealization of Ginnie. In fact, it takes only a short time for Dave to begin slipping into such a trap; he tells himself that Ginnie "was sort of a female symbol of the failure of all of us ..." (p. 903). Dave's devotion to Ginnie is finally brought to a climax after she becomes involved with a psychotic one-armed ex-marine. Ginnie meets the ex-serviceman in a bar and tells him an elaborately fictionalized story of her life: she was born the daughter of a wealthy local banker who lost his money and then died during the Depression; she disliked her mother and had learned no marketable skills because of her privileged upbringing and thus "had chosen to throw in her lot with the common people ..." (p. 1091). The ex-marine tells her a comparable story of unjust suffering. Coming from a family of rich Kansas wheat farmers, he had always quarreled with his father; he joined the marines when the war came, lost his arm at Iwo Jima, and "had a flock of medals"; returning from the war, he had again tried to work with his father, but couldn't stand it and left (pp. 1091–92). The two accept each other's fantasies and go to Kansas to get married.

Soon Dave begins receiving desperate letters from Ginnie. Her new husband's father, instead of being rich, is sunk in poverty as ugly as that she grew up in; the small farm on which they live is desolate and remote; and her husband has threatened to shoot her if she tries to run away. After three months, Ginnie escapes and returns to Parkman. She is now a terrified woman; her husband's threats had been frequent and arose "just on the mere suspicion that she might have been thinking about another man, or toying with the idea of leaving him" (p. 1163). It is at this point that Dave decides to marry her. His motives are complex. He has been rejected by the respectable Gwen French; his compassion for Ginnie has grown because of her experience in Kansas; and he has convinced himself that she would be an ideal writer's wife. Jones is never able to make plausible Dave's reasoning on the third point. The character's logic seems to be based on a patently ridiculous syllogism. He must find the source of his art among the "undesirables"; Ginnie is the epitome of such people; by marrying her he will wed himself to aesthetic inspiration. All of this ignores the fact that Ginnie is not a symbol, but a human being.

Ginnie's influence on Dave's art is disastrous. He has been

writing a revolutionary, brutal, completely unromanticized war novel for some time; suddenly he decides to add a subplot about a love affair "between a commonplace private and a low-class French peasant girl" in tribute to Ginnie, who is "... a symbol of the whole human race, and its own affirmation" (p. 1170). This destructive involvement with Ginnie soon comes to represent an even more basic threat because the psychotic ex-marine returns to Parkman determined to kill Dave for taking away his wife.

'Bama tries to dissuade Dave from marrying Ginnie by arguing that she will totally destroy him as an artist because all she wants is to become "respectable." This warning is one of the gambler's honest and accurate evaluations of a fellow undesirable. Dave refuses to listen; and after the marriage, Ginnie becomes antagonistic to his writing because it doesn't sell, pressures him to get a factory job, and starts refusing to sleep with him because sex is "unladylike" (p. 1209). Jones attempts two dramatic symbols to emphasize how much Ginnie is not what Dave idealized her to be. In one fight, she throws a saucepan that smashes Dave's typewriter. In another scene, Dave discovers that her childhood gonorrhea has left her sterile. Rather than being a source of artistic inspiration, the woman personifies opposition to creativity and the irrational, unfair blockage of it. Finally her ex-marine does murder the writer. Jones's formula is obvious and, in a romantic context, possible to accept: Ginnie's desire for respectability transforms her into an enemy of art, which must be based on freedom, rejection of security, and individuality. The essential aesthetic problem lies in the implausibility of Dave Hirsh's ever having seen her as a source of creative inspiration.

Jones is much more successful with his character of old Jane Staley. The grandmother of one of Frank Hirsh's mistresses, Jane is as promiscuous as the much younger 'Bama Dillert. The contrast between Jane's open flaunting of convention and her granddaughter's covert liaison with one of the town's respectable businessmen is clear. Jane, too, is meant to represent the honesty and independence of those people on society's fringes: "Whatever else she might be, Jane was a realist" (p. 81). There are two main reasons for Jones's greater success with the characterization of Jane than with 'Bama Dillert and Ginnie Moorehouse.

First, he is primarily content to let her be a character, rather than someone's personification of an abstract value. Further, he never allows her to take over and arbitrarily dominate any segment of the novel. She remains a minor character, but an important one. The one aspect of her characterization which has the potential of becoming implausible and obtrusive is controlled. Like 'Bama, Jane has something approximating psychic insight into the actions and motivations of the citizens of Parkman. Rather than expanding on this gift Jones instead quickly suggests a realistic origin of it:

It was amazing what she knew about the private lives and loves of the citizenry of Parkman extending generations back. In forty years or so of cleaning other people's houses it had apparently become a sort of a private hobby, an avocation, of hers. (pp. 689–90)

It is, of course, an old literary device to suggest that an individual's maid knows more about his private life than he realizes.

The most memorable aspect of Jane's characterization is the manner of her death. She dies of diverticulosis of the lower bowel without seeking any medical help because she mistakes the symptoms of her fatal illness for venereal disease and does not want to embarrass her granddaughter. She dies in extreme pain, but still defiant:

Powerfully, with those strong, man's arms, but quietly, she grasped the top of the headboard and pulled herself, almost all dead weight now, up to a sitting position. Sons of bitches! All of you! Think you can kill Old Jane Staley? Then she fell over sideways on her face, and everything faded out. (p. 1058)

An embattled undesirable all her life, Jane ultimately defies death itself. Still, there is artistically legitimate irony in her attempt to hide her disgrace from a granddaugher who is Frank's mistress.

The group of characters personified by 'Bama, Ginnie Moorehouse, and Old Jane Staley wins Dave Hirsh's allegiance. He perceives them as being more honest and more individualistic than the respectable townspeople, primarily represented by his brother. He ultimately looks to the undesirables for creative inspiration, and the story he is working on when he is killed is a tribute to them:

He did not know what to call it. He wanted to call it "The Plebeians"; or "The Plebes." But the connotations of both words, which had become a part of the English language over the intervening two thousand years, and in doing so had been almost completely divorced from the original Roman feelings and meanings—both words were too ambiguous, too double meaning. "Plebe" connoted West Point; "Plebeian" connoted hick or commonplace. And he wanted the old Roman usage, the meaning that had once existed in the Empire of Augustus amid the squalor, and the circus, and the put-on synthetic "Triumphs." Finally he decided to call it "The Peons." (pp. 907–08)

Jones's peons are anything but "commonplace," and Dave Hirsh sees them as society's last element of resistance to the kind of elitism and regimentation connoted by West Point.

IV   *The Attack on Middle-Class Hypocrisy*

Jones attacks middle-class hypocrisy almost exclusively through Frank Hirsh. There is nothing especially new or revolutionary in the satire of Dave's respectable brother. Frank is an inwardly desperate man shaken by a history of family scandal. His sexual maladjustment dates back to an Oedipal experience in which he tried to compensate for his inner weakness. His present compensation takes two directions: he seeks to attain control over women; and he works frantically to build a business empire and a family dynasty. The two drives are linked, and they allow Jones to investigate thoroughly his theme of the sexual maladjustment of the American male.

Frank's sexual problems originate in a childhood experience in which his mother caught him masturbating, chased him down and whipped him, and "... *momentarily, but only for a moment, he hated his own mother*" (p. 222). The pattern here is identical to that which Jones was to develop successfully in several short stories: a male child experiments with sex, is humiliated by his mother, subsequently hates and resents her, and feels overwhelming guilt for such emotions. While the formula is old, in short fiction Jones could make it convincing and important. In a long novel, with extensive analysis of adult reaction to such a childhood experience, he encounters difficulties.

Frank wants to control and dominate all women as surrogates for his mother. Like more than one of Jones's maladjusted males in later novels, Frank loves to fantasize about watching lesbian love-making. He clearly sees his wife, Agnes, as a substitute for his mother. At one point, he decides that their quarrels originate because he likes sex and she doesn't, and he asks himself if he must feel guilty all his life for enjoying it (p. 354). As a matter of fact, he doesn't enjoy sex; instead he needs the thrill that comes from secretly having mistresses and dominating them. Frank is compelled always to seek out women he can control and introduce to unconventional forms of sexuality.

His view of women is contemptuous: "Women, the poolroom sages maintained and Frank now believed, loved only one thing more than bed, and that was the fiction that they did not love it at all" (p. 72). Frank is devoted to the destruction of such a fiction in every woman over whom he can gain control. He needs the secrecy because it allows him to deceive Agnes:

Half the fun was in the secretiveness, he thought, really. . . . The doing of something wrong—and putting it over. (p. 208)

It is significant that Frank views his affair as "something wrong"; such a feeling allows him to continue the guilt he has felt since childhood.

Ultimately, merely having mistresses is not enough excitement; and Frank comes to need something more dangerous, more intoxicating to his guilt. Initially, he begins taking aimless walks at night seeking "adventure" and "danger." Then, one of his night walks almost turns into something truly dangerous: he finds himself looking through a window at one of his former mistresses undressing. After he has safely returned home, Frank reflects on what he has just experienced:

It was the most completely satisfying sexual experience he had ever had in his life that he could remember. He had more completely and fully *had*, and dominated, this woman tonight than he had ever *had* or dominated her in bed; and yet he had not even touched

84 JAMES JONES

her. He had merely seen her. He had *seen* her, naked, nude, while—
all unsuspecting—she had not even known anyone was looking. He
had *possessed* her. (p. 1139)

Frank continues his window-peeking because of this thrill of
possession:

Damn women. They didnt any of them ever care for you like you
cared for them. None of them, not any of them, ever really allowed
themselves to be possessed the way you wanted to possess them, the
way a *man* should possess them. (p. 1147)

The guilt and hatred Frank has always felt toward his mother
take a bizarre turn here. However, artistic problems arise, not
from the implausibility of Frank's behavior, but from the un-
necessarily long analysis Jones devotes to it.

Finally, Frank is left with no sexual outlet but his night walking. He needs business success as badly as he needs to possess
women (he especially enjoys secretive business deals), and he
longs for a dynasty to compensate for the disgrace his father
brought on the family name. After Dave chooses not to be his
surrogate son, Frank and Agnes adopt a son. This act of possession causes the businessman to relinquish power over his wife,
however. Agnes, finally tiring of her husband's adultery, leaves
with the boy and will not come back except under the conditions
that Frank abandon his mistresses and never try to sleep with
his wife. Because of the adopted son, Frank feels he has no
choice but to accept:

And, in the end, Agnes had defeated him. Finally and conclusively
defeated him, and driven his army from the field in rout, total rout.
All except, that is, for his going "walking." ... (p. 1193)

It is not difficult to see the contrast between 'Bama's open
promiscuity and Frank's night walking. Yet one must question
whether either form of behavior constitutes real sexual health,
the one being narratively idyllic and humanly arrogant, the other
passion-filled, but also invasive and callous. Jones wants one

other bit of ironic contrast and has Frank, after Dave's death, open a bar which he will not let "undesirable" persons enter.

Dave Hirsh suffers something of the same kind of sexual maladjustment as his brother, but is aware of his problem and its origins. This awareness, in conjunction with Dave's struggles to be a writer, allows Jones to introduce his theme of the alienated artist. Much is made of Dave's inordinate need "to be loved by the whole world" (p. 171). Writers, Jones editorializes, have too much love for the world and are, thus, inevitably bound to be hurt. The hurt will be worse because writers are, by definition, outsiders: "by its very nature, being a writer meant being an outsider, meant not living. . . . To live meant to act, and the very act of writing was itself an un-act—a putting of it down on paper instead of doing it" (p. 794). Accepting the role of artist entails, then, accepting an utter and complete aloneness, from which there is no escape (p. 1230). If such is the price, why would one accept the role? The novel gives two answers to this question, one idealistic and clear, the other apparently Freudian and quite incoherent.

The idealistic reason for becoming a writer is almost disguised by pessimistic diction that originates in Jones's vision of humanity's animalistic nature: "It might not be the highest work in the Universe; but it was the highest ever attained to by sniveling creeping man, scrambling along holding onto and clutching his goldbag and his scrotum like some hairy tarantula dragging along its precious egg bag" (p. 756). Artistic endeavor is worth the alienation it entails, because it constitutes man's most meaningful struggle. There are distinct echoes of "The Snows of Kilimanjaro" here—Jones and Hemingway both assert that the artist has no right to reject the pain and responsibility of his calling. The animalistic, and implicitly sexual, language of this passage leads inevitably to Jones's second concept of the nature of artistic inspiration.

V *Problems in Treating Artistic Inspiration*

Centering around the character of Gwen French, this concept represents Jones at his most confused and undisciplined. Much of the problem is implicit in the Gwen French characterization. Anticipating critical objection, Jones attempts a justification of her plausibility in a "Special Note":

There is a character in this novel which may cause surprise, or consternation, or even disbelief, among certain types of readers: that of the lady school teacher. In this connection, the author would like to point out that this character is . . . the result of the author's fascination with, and great admiration for, Miss Emily Dickinson. The author would like to, and chooses to, believe that such ladies could exist in 1950 as well as 1850.

There are basic problems with this justification: it is simply impossible to accept Gwen French as a plausible fictional representative of Emily Dickinson or even as a believable character, and it is even more difficult to admire her. Jones's failure lies in a failure to convince the reader that "such ladies" ever existed in any century.

Gwen French is an English teacher at Parkman College, absorbed in a critical study of the group of West Coast writers to which Dave Hirsh once belonged. She has an elaborate, though not original or profound, theory about the primal source of inspiration in all artists, and the ultimate source of failure in most. All art comes out of "agony," she says, and that agony is primarily manifested in unhappy love affairs:

". . . . My thesis was that its this unique and abnormally high potential for the falling in love process, the really abnormal need for it and the inability to escape it, that largely both makes and destroys the creative personality in any given individual." (p. 122)

She sees Dave's old group of writers as excellent illustrations of this thesis, as she explains to the returning prodigal at their first meeting:

". . . You see, in each case each of you arrived at a crisis with a woman in which you either got what you wanted—not only from her, but from life—or else didn't get it. But either way, it destroyed you as writers. By destroying in you the hunger *to* write." (p. 129)

Dave reacts to this by admitting its truth (he did have a painful love affair in Los Angeles) and by telling Gwen that she should be a creative writer herself, instead of a critic. However, she rejects such a goal as impossible: "... I dont have that drive, that abnormal hunger to be loved so badly ..." (p. 130).

Dave further decides that he is in love with Gwen and will seduce her. His attempted seduction of the lady schoolteacher becomes a driving obsession and dominates far too much of the novel. Moreover, Jones depicts their relationship in a way that distorts plausibility. Having carefully cultivated the image of an ultra-sophisticated woman who has become bored with sex, Gwen rejects Dave. Initially, the ex-writer decides that the rejection is actually the result of his being unattractive; then, in a wild leap of logic, he decides that the real truth is that Gwen is a nymphomaniac and is terrified of her inability to control her sexual passion. In truth, Gwen's image as a sophisticate is totally a lie. She is a virgin, terrified of anyone discovering that reality. Herself a victim of American sexual maladjustment, she has for years sought the courage to give herself sexually to a man.

The relationship between the ex-writer and the lady critic degenerates into something inadvertently approaching farce. In scene after scene, Dave belligerently attempts to sleep with her; Gwen refuses only after dropping broad hints that she has a dark secret and a gentler approach might be successful; Dave misses all the hints and leaves infuriated that a nymphomaniac will not go to bed with him. Then follows a cooling off period during which he brings his latest writing (usually inspired by 'Bama or the undesirables in general) to her for evaluation. This ritual gets to the absurd point of Hirsh digging up for the teacher one of his old poems entitled "Hunger" which has helped him seduce seven women who liked its "sincerity" (p. 259).

It is hardly surprising that Dave's approach is ineffective; and sexual tension between the two continues to build increasingly. In part, Jones is developing a theme in the characterization of Gwen that worked brilliantly in *From Here to Eternity*—the idea that individuals become so entrapped in the public roles they adopt that meaningful communication with others becomes impossible. (On a "Person to Person" telecast, Jones said that the novel illustrates every man's need for someone to love him more than he loves himself. Innate human selfishness makes such a desire impossible, both to realize and even to communicate, he added. The Dave Hirsh–Gwen French relationship is almost certainly meant to illustrate this universal tragedy.) However, Dave's convincing himself that Gwen, the virgin, is a nympho-maniac is so extreme an example of this problem that it verges on the comic. Gwen is finally so trapped by her own image, her own sexual fears, and Dave's crudely ineffectual attempts at seduction that she falls back on her father's pornography collec-tion for gratification.

The climax in this battle of nerves between Gwen and her would-be seducer occurs when Ginnie Moorehouse goes to the lady teacher and begs her to give up Dave. Despite all her humanistic training, Gwen is repulsed by Ginnie and, therefore, disgusted with Hirsh: "... He was actually sleeping with that—that—that—She could find no word sick enough. An animal. A female animal. No mind, no brains" (p. 917). After this meeting, Gwen gives up Dave entirely; and he ultimately marries Ginnie. After he is murdered by the ex-marine, Gwen faces all her inner turmoil and confusion. Receiving the manuscript of the war novel from Ginnie, she and her father edit out the love story and submit it for publication; she "confesses" her virginity and her repressed love for the dead writer to her father; she decides to become a creative writer rather than a critic; and she goes to a doctor to have her hymen surgically removed. Now that she has suffered a tragic love affair and is, at least technically, not a virgin, Jones implies that her dammed-up creativity will burst forth.

The elaboration of the formula that sexual frustration equals art, as shown in the Dave Hirsh–Gwen French relationship, would be aesthetically problematic in itself. But Jones does not stop there. He adds the character of Gwen's father, Bob French, a significant "minor poet" simply to intellectualize and editorialize the concept. In addition, Gwen's father ties the idea of sexual frustration producing art to a variation of the mysticism intro-duced by Jack Malloy in *From Here to Eternity*:

"... I have about come to the conclusion that the true artist, the great artist . . . is really only the last evolutionary stage the individual soul goes through, before it becomes that lowest of all the Initiates—as the "occult" books call them: the beginning Disciple, working consciously and specifically with some Great Master; and that all the anguish and suffering artists like you and I go through—all our great vanity... and our oversexualization... all these are both a sort of testing-ground for us.... (p. 820)

If Jones's analysis of the frustrated artist is the weakest aspect of *Some Came Running*, his depiction of post-World War II society as decadent and crumbling is the strongest. Sadly, the motif of doomed society is the least developed of any of the novel's significant themes. Still, there are passages which anticipate strongly the publication of *Whistle*, twenty-one years later. Jones fills his novel with references to men who have been physically crippled in the war: "It seemed that in the last few years the cripples had become a normal part of everyday life, a steady stream of them, rolling back from over both seas, hardly anyone even noticed them any more" (p. 11). But more important is Jones's vision of the returning GIs who simply cannot make the last step in the evolution of the soldier and adjust to peacetime life. One such character states his pain eloquently in the novel: the famous "Lost Generation" was lucky, he says, because they cultivated and loved their misery; while " 'we're not even a *lost* generation, my generation. We're an *unfound* generation. The 'Unfound Generation' of the 'Forties' " (p. 828).

Only during the war did such men have a sense of belonging, of being needed. Lacking any sense of direction since their discharge, they feel hopelessly lost in an America devoted to the ideal of rampant consumerism. The most memorable of "the Unfound Generation" characters in *Some Came Running* is Raymond Cole, who, after one humiliation too many, drives his car into an obscure, ice-covered river bottom, gets so drunk that he can't find his way out, and freezes to death. Dave Hirsh, surrounded by characters like Raymond Cole and witnessing the excessive spending of people like his brother, reflects:

What a nation we were turning into. It was like living in the last wild days of the Roman Empire. Everybody drinking and discussing and destruction sweeping down in hordes from the north. (p. 167)

He comes to think of the United States and the Soviet Union as "two crumbling skyscrapers which, tumbling, would knock each other down. In the unbearably melancholy twilight of the world" (p. 419).

Dave's inherent romanticism causes him to view men like Raymond Cole as latterday equivalents of the heroes of the Alamo, hopelessly out of place in a sterile, technological society (p. 826). Moreover, this society cynically exploits them whenever it needs more soldiers—they are "the modernday professional Roman legionary—though of course they were not aware of this" (p. 1095). The permanent condition of our time is warfare and the soldier is our prime symbol of the contemporary victim. To emphasize this point, Jones adds an epilogue to his novel in which a young man a great deal like Dave Hirsh dies a brutal death in Korea.

Despite the controlled power of this motif, *Some Came Running* is a flawed novel and there is no way to argue for its artistic success. Still, it cannot be ignored. Prefaced by some lines from Sir Walter Raleigh, the novel is Jones's attempt to set down his creed about many things:

> One Book among the rest is dear to me;
> As when a man . . .
>   .   .   .   .
> Sets down his Paternoster and his creed. . . .

While it generally fails, *Some Came Running* remains a sincere book containing much that will inform Jones's later fiction. After its publication in 1957, Jones's reputation was complex and confusing. He had published two extremely long novels, each attempting to say a great many things he felt strongly about. The first had been a spectacular critical and popular success, but the second became a notorious critical failure. Jones's career clearly had reached a crisis after 1957. In terms of critical reception at least, he largely canceled out the failure of his second novel with his next book, a brilliantly conceived novella called *The Pistol*.

CHAPTER 4

The Pistol *and* The Ice-Cream Headache :
Mastery of the Forms of Short Fiction

IN his "Introduction" to *The Ice-Cream Headache and Other Stories,* Jones reveals that *The Pistol* originated as a short story, but that somewhere "about five or ten pages into it" he realized that it would have to be "a short novel." He then defines his concept of his story turned novel: "I had something I had been looking for for a long time: namely, a subject around which to construct a deliberately, consciously *symbolic* novel; one in which the symbol is deliberately imposed upon the material from outside, beforehand, more in the European manner" (p. xv).[1] It is also of significance that Jones's references to his "army trilogy" always excluded *The Pistol.* Certain deductions can be drawn from Jones's description of *The Pistol.* For instance, the desire to write "a deliberately, consciously symbolic novel... more in the European manner" probably hints at a retreat from the naturalistic technique which dominated *From Here to Eternity* and *Some Came Running.* Apparently, he wished to achieve something in the mode of a fable or parable and felt that the accumulation of detail so functional in his first two books would not be appropriate here.

I The Pistol

The description of a symbol "deliberately imposed upon the material from outside, beforehand" implies the possibility of another kind of symbolism, which would emerge organically from an arrangement of plot, setting, and characterization. Prewitt's bugle in *From Here to Eternity* would be such an organic symbol. The bugle as symbol is so intricately bound up with Prewitt's personality and circumstances that it would carry little, if any, emotional impact without these associations. So definitely is the bugle Prewitt's that it could symbolically define no other character in the novel. In contrast, the pistol in Jones's novella can, and does, acquire a value which would fulfill the needs of many men. It soon takes on an ironically communal significance. It is so intensely fought over by individuals who see it as personal salvation that its ultimate function is to unify the shared fears and longings of enlisted men suddenly plunged into a war and their extreme vulnerability. Clearly a symbol imposed from outside, it does not depend upon the personality of a single character for meaning, but speaks to the needs of all the major characters in the novel. Thus, the pistol dominates Jones's novella in a way that Prewitt's bugle never could. *The Pistol* is, in truth, about the pistol, as *From Here to Eternity* focuses on Robert E. Lee Prewitt. The distinction is important; for it removes the criticism that the characterizaion of Pfc. Richard Mast does not carry the emotional power of Jones's depiction of Prewitt. Mast is conceived as secondary to a symbolic object.

The pistol fought over by Mast and five other major characters is Jones's most effectively rendered example of the talisman motif. *Webster's Eighth New Collegiate Dictionary* defines *talisman* as "an object bearing a sign or character engraved under astrological influence and thought to act as a charm to avert evil and bring good fortune." Omitting astrology, this definition captures the significance of the pistol to the men of Jones's "short novel." The weapon is seen by Mast and the others as possibly having the power to ward off, at least temporarily, the ultimate evil, which is death. Because of its supernatural associations, the pistol should not be discussed as a simple good luck charm.

Jones's first overt use of the talisman motif occurs in *Some Came Running*. Wally Dennis, the would-be novelist, acquires a set of knives early in the novel. The most precious of these is a Randall #1 which Wally still carries as a Korean War sergeant in the novel's "Epilogue." However, in the epilogue, the Randall #1 serves a function almost exactly analogous to Pfc. Mast's pistol. Wally's squad is trapped in a massive Chinese Communist attack, and he realizes the nearness of death. All that enables him to feel even a possibility of salvation is his Randall #1 knife:

And he loved it. It had saved his life on more than one occasion. . . . more than any other thing anywhere, his Randall #1 gave him a sense of comfort and luck. . . . If he could just keep his knife with him, and keep it clean and in good shape, he felt he might still yet get out—be one of those who wouldnt have to be hauled like cordwood in the trucks, dead. (p. 1262)

Like any object of religious devotion, the knife must be carefully cared for: to allow it to become dirty would be equivalent to an act of blasphemy against the only force that might offer salvation. When Wally is killed by a grenade, a Chinese soldier claims the knife as a trophy of war, tests its sharpness by slitting the throat of Wally's corpse, and then slashes the hand of one of his companions who attempts a theft. It is clear that the Chinese soldier will understand the Randall #1 to have the same talismanic value that Wally felt in it. Just as it was not the first, *The Pistol* is not the last time Jones uses the talisman motif. The focus at the beginning of *The Thin Red Line* is upon Private Doll's attempts to steal a pistol before landing on Guadalcanal. Given Jones's vision that Pearl Harbor resulted in an historical epoch in which warfare became the normal circumstance of humanity, it is not surprising that his symbols of salvation are weapons of destruction.

Despite this and other similarities, *The Pistol* is still a distinctly different kind of work from Jones's other novels. Here he consciously uses limited naturalistic technique in order to produce an experimental fable or parable. The exemplum of the parable is complex and debatable, but this ambiguity is not a sign of failure, but of success. In an extremely well argued essay, Allen Shepherd denies that military "authority" is really a major "enemy" in the novel and analyzes it as a study in the corruptibility of "human nature itself," the corruption resulting from the uncontrollable selfishness of the individual ego.[2] Given the book's emphasis on Mast's struggle to protect his charmed weapon from five other men, Shepherd's argument holds some clear truth. However, it is debatable that "authority" is not at least one of the enemies in *The Pistol*. In fact, Jones treats the military hierarchy in a manner consistent with the rest of his army fiction: "authority" is inconsistent, often bungling, but always threatening. It endangers the well-being of the individual soldier through blind oversight as often as through premeditated hostility. In fact, one of the main reasons that it is impossible to fight successfully against "authority" is that its power is so erratic and unpredictable. Shepherd approaches this point, but seems to back off from its obvious implications.

Probably a summary of the ways in which Pfc. Richard Mast acquires the pistol, struggles to keep it, and ultimately loses it is necessary before thematic points can be satisfactorily clarified. Mast is reminiscent of Stephen Crane's Henry Fleming in being isolated from the other soldiers because of superior intelligence and sensitivity. One of the novel's underlying themes is that such positive qualities can work to one's disadvantage in an organization like the army which rests upon a foundation of anonymity and impersonality. Mast acquires his symbol of salvation at the beginning of the novel when the Japanese attack on Pearl Harbor results in such bureaucratic confusion that a supply clerk allows him to keep a pistol issued on a temporary basis. One could certainly discuss the Freudian implications of the widespread envy inspired by Mast's possession of the weapon. In fact, analysis of the pistol as a symbolic phallic symbol would not be invalid. However, such an approach would limit one's understanding of Jones's masterful short novel. As Jones says in "Hawaiian Recall" there was an autobiographical inspiration for the account of Mast's acquisition of an illicit weapon. Revisiting the headquarters building at Schofield Barracks for the first time in over thirty years, he reminisces: "I had sat at the desk the morning of Pearl Harbor, carrying messages for distraught officers, wearing the pistol I was later able to get away with. The initial sequence of *The Pistol* had taken place right here on this floor."[3]

The body of the novel is simply an account of Mast's successful struggle to preserve his accidentally acquired totem of salvation from five men: Pfc. O'Brien, the first and most persistent rival; Corporal Winstock, a direct representative of "authority"; Sergeant Burton, who attempts to bribe Mast; Pfc. Grace, who commits the gravest sin in his obsessive need for the pistol; and

Sergeant Paoli, whose jealousy over Mast's prize stems from a fear ironically different from the other four. Shepherd correctly states that the primary risk Jones ran in writing such a novel was the boredom of repetition. His article effectively describes the techniques which prevented such a potentially damaging result. At the end of the novel Mast thinks he has won when Sergeant Pender notes that he may keep the pistol. But immediately Musso, the supply clerk who made the initial error, arrives to claim the weapon.

Shepherd correctly points out that the Pender-Musso incidents are introduced by Jones to emphasize "authority's" indifference to the individual soldier. Mast and all privates are simply insignificant to the bureaucratic army. However, indifference is anything but reassuring; it is not a basis for arguing against "authority" as a hostile force in the novel. In fact, to foreshadow this ending Jones goes out of his way to describe the various ways in which military bureaucracy has endangered the lives of virtually every soldier in Hawaii. Throughout the novel the American military establishment awaits a seemingly inevitable invasion of the island. Critical to any defense against invasion is the security of Makapuu Point. The Point extends out into the ocean, with "nothing between it and San Francisco" (p. 29).[4] Thus, Makapuu is perfectly situated for enemy attack. While the Japanese never come, the men assigned to defend this vulnerable spot endure another kind of attack: an awesome wind prevents any possibility of rest or comfort. In "Hawaiian Recall" Jones remembers the wind of Makapuu and writes, "In both the story *The Way It Is* and the novel *The Pistol*, he had used that never ceasing wind as a conscious symbol of pressure on the men."[5] Unable to find even temporary escape from the howling wind, Mast and his fellow soldiers soon feel complete isolation.

Mast's final chance for relief from the torment of Makapuu ironically comes as an indirect result of another series of bureaucratic mistakes. Before the Pearl Harbor attack, the army had ordered the digging of an enormous cave in a cliff overlooking the highway into Keneohe Valley. The plan, to fill the cave with explosives which could be detonated instantly if an enemy force invaded the island, failed when the army, fearing civilian protest and political repercussions, decided not to plant the explosives.

For a full month after Pearl Harbor, the vast cave is forgotten by military "authority"; then, when someone does remember it, the army wants the explosives loaded immediately. Again, a critical oversight results. The demolition cave is made ready to explode and block the Keneohe Valley highway, but no provision is made to protect the cave from an invading force. Reminded of this mistake, the high command orders a five-man volunteer road-guard to protect the cave at its most vulnerable point; no one doubts that such an assignment constitutes an obvious suicide mission. Thus, following a series of blunders, "authority" finds itself in the position of asking five men to place their lives in a situation which would be totally hopeless in the event of invasion. His account of the demolition cave allows Jones an opportunity for editorializing:

The story behind the creation of this roadguard was a complex one. But it can be explained easily with that phrase which has always done such excellent service in all the armies in the world: "Somebody" screwed up. "Somebody" forgot. And no one, of course, was able to figure out just who this "Somebody" might be. (p. 93)

Jones's characters are threatened by the invisible "somebody," just as Hemingway's Frederick Henry is vulnerable to destruction by an unidentified "they."

Despite its being a suicide mission, the roadguard receives more than an adequate number of volunteers. It becomes, in fact, an assignment coveted by almost all the men on Makapuu Point, including Mast. The roadguard offers escape from the unceasing torment of awesome wind and inadequate shelter. Men are willing to risk certain death in an anticipated invasion for the sake of basic animal comfort and contact with the surrounding world. Assignment to the roadguard is so desirable that Burton attempts to bribe Mast with guard duty and some money in exchange for the pistol. While most of *The Pistol* focuses on the threat to Mast's pistol from his fellow soldiers, the account of such a classic example of bureaucratic blunder clearly fore-shadows the ultimate defeat of the individual private by "au-thority."

Still Shepherd's evaluation is somewhat correct. "Authority" is not the only hostile force in Jones's parable. In fact, the central irony of the novel is Mast's expanding awareness that nearly every soldier in Hawaii shares a common nightmare, which in turn strengthens his belief that possession of the pistol is necessary for survival. O'Brien states the collective nightmare as memorably as any character in the novel:

"... What if I got captured? Did you ever see them Samurai sabers them Jap officers carry? You know what they do to prisoners? They cut them in two with them sabers. ..." (p. 44)

Two recurrent Jones themes seem relevant here: the idea that December 7, 1941, ushered in a new era in which warfare is the norm in human life, and the rapidity with which the old peace-time army had to be radically converted into an organization able to function in wartime. The characters in *The Pistol* are a great deal like those in *From Here to Eternity*—men who have come to the military as a refuge from the economic horrors of the Depression. Seemingly in the space of a moment, they find themselves in a war which promises unmistakably to be the bloodiest in human history.

The men cannot begin to anticipate many of the brutalities of World War II, but they can sense the coming horror. Thus, the image of the Japanese officer with the Samurai sword represents World War II, which is a present reality, and the inhumane world which was inevitably to follow it. It is ironic that the shared image of horror is primitive in nature, since the hideousness of both the war, and of the society which succeeded it, is predominantly technological. However, men like Mast, O'Brien, Grace, and the others could not begin to imagine the extent of technological destruction that December 7, 1941, introduced to the world. A further twist of irony is that the vision of the Japanese officer contains an element of reality. In *WWII*, Jones argues that the primary reason Japan could have been defeated by no other means than the atomic bomb lay in the fact that Japan was a curiously medieval society thrust abruptly into the age of technology, still clinging to its ancient warrior codes. In *The Thin Red Line*, captured American soldiers on Guadalcanal are mutilated in a manner even more horrible than O'Brien has envisioned. A famous photograph much circulated among American soldiers in the Pacific was that of a captured Australian being beheaded by a Samurai sword.

The characters' efforts to steal Mast's pistol and the resulting profound belief of each that the weapon *is* morally and factually his, indicate that one of Jones's main concerns in the novella is to depict the selfishness of the human ego, especially when faced with extinction. Nonetheless, the gradual revelation that each seeker of the pistol has a common fantasy of extinction and views the weapon as a talisman of salvation indicates a potential for communion. Mast, O'Brien, Grace, and all the soldiers on Pearl Harbor face a common threat, which can act to unite them as well as to pull them apart. Such communion is attained twice in the short novel. The first attainment is a false and unrealistic one; but the second, while startlingly brief, is notable. In the first incident, Mast is arbitrarily chosen as part of a patrol to guard another mountain pass and the Marconi Pass patrol becomes "the most pleasant experience Mast had during his whole time in Hawaii" (p. 107). The pleasure of this detail is twofold. First, Mast's image of the Japanese officer is not destroyed, but it is "abstracted . . . from an actual flesh-and-blood picture in Mast's mind to a mere idea." Equally a relief, "the constant, omnipresent, omnipotent authority of the army over every tiniest facet of their lives" is greatly reduced (p. 120). A false communion is suddenly possible because the greatest threats to individual safety have though only *for the moment* been pushed to the background. It is all the more unforgivable that it is in this atmosphere that the ironically named Grace attempts to steal the pistol. Grace's act shatters the truce of Marconi Pass and brings the imminence of extinction back to the minds of those men on the patrol.

The second instant of communion ends the novel and is quite real. When Musso, the supply sergeant, finally reclaims Mast's pistol, O'Brien shouts "upward": "You got no right. It ain't fair" (p. 158). The pronoun "you" takes on the intentional ambiguity characteristic of "they" in the fiction of Hemingway. *You* represents military authority and all the unknown, but sensed, terrors unleashed on the world of the common soldier (or all humanity) by the Japanese attack on Pearl Harbor. O'Brien, from the beginning the most determined of all to get the pistol away from Mast, is expressing a shared sense of helpless vulnerability when he shouts, not at the retreating Musso, but at the sky. O'Brien, Mast, and all the others are on the verge of beginning "the evolution of a soldier," the acceptance of one's anonymity and probable annihilation.

It is interesting that Musso is several times described as Satan: "If Mast's pistol was his savior, and his potential salvation, then Musso was Satan, the Devil, come to take it away" (p. 52). Musso is in reality a bungling supply room clerk; yet this external insignificance actually adds to his demonic stature. The evil that awaits men like Mast and O'Brien is as yet unknown, but it will be deadly, impersonal, and completely arbitrary. *The Pistol* is a parable of the vulnerability of all humanity in the new world created on December 7, 1941, and of its resulting need to find talismans of salvation from a nebulous, unavoidable enemy.

One should note a secondary reason for Mast's attachment to the pistol:

Wearing a pistol on his hip made him feel more like a real soldier, seemed to give him an unbroken lineal connection with the Army of the days of the West and Custer's Cavalry, made him feel that he was really in the Army, a feeling Mast did not often have in what to himself he termed this *crumby*, lazy outfit. (p. 13)

While there is clear similarity to Henry Fleming in this intensely romantic view of war, Jones's main reason for including it is to show how much it is necessary for Mast to mature before completing his evolution of a soldier. He is living in a new age of anonymous, technological warfare, but still dreaming of a time of heroic, individual conflict.

Allen Shepherd remarks on the tone of *The Pistol*, saying that Jones shifts between attitudes of "involved compassion" and "detached irony."[6] A better explanation of the curiously "cold" tone of the novella is that it is made inevitable by Jones's decision to subordinate characterization to a symbol "deliberately imposed ... from outside. ..." The experiment works well, but one price of its success is an extremely detached tone. The reader does not become involved in Mast's pain as in Prewitt's: rather, one's attention is on craft and technique.

The Pistol did much to restore Jones's reputation after the
failure of *Some Came Running*. He could hardly have written
a book better calculated to pacify critics. The charge that Jones
could not control his material, first directed at *From Here to
Eternity*, reached a peak after the second novel. Then he produced his short novel in which he successfully imposed tight
control on a difficult experimental form.

II   The Ice-Cream Headache and Other Stories

Jones's success with *The Pistol* indicates a considerable talent
for writing short fiction—an ability which might surprise readers
who know him only through *From Here to Eternity* and the other
long novels. His only collection of short stories, *The Ice-Cream
Headache and Other Stories*, is a major addition to his canon.
In fact, because of the volume's thematic variety and technical
versatility, it is aesthetically surpassed only by the army trilogy.
In the collection's "Introduction," written in 1965, Jones discusses
the fact that he has "written so few stories":

Then too there is the question of self-imposed censorship. One simply
can't write anything outspoken about sexuality and get it published
in any magazine printing today. This automatically rules out a whole
raft of subjects. If sexuality and an interest in it is one of your main
themes, as it is with me, this takes away from what you can write
a very large chunk of what you'd like to write. (p. xii)

Two main groups of stories in *The Ice-Cream Headache* are
army stories and tales of midwestern childhood, closely related
to his major novels. In addition, there are a few other pieces
which cannot be conveniently classified by subject matter and
which will not be examined in detail. Perhaps unexpectedly, the
midwestern childhood fiction constitutes the best work in the
volume. Jones, in fact, intended to do an entire volume of such
stories:

I had always meant to do a novel on childhood in the '20s and '30s
set in that beautiful, grim, frightening, land-and spirit-locked part of
the world. Ergo, why not do a book of childhood stories on it instead?

I thought it was a great idea. Novels on childhood, particularly middlewestern childhoods, were dime a dozen [*sic*]. It would be a fresh approach. (p. xiv)

While he never completed this project, *The Ice-Cream Headache* contains five such stories: the title story, "Just like the Girl," "The Tennis Game," "A Bottle of Cream," and "The Valentine." Certain motifs recur in all five: intensification of the inevitable pain and difficulty of adolescence by the sexual hypocrisy and repression of the midwest, intimidating and potentially castrating mother-figures or other personifications of this midwestern sexual repressiveness and sharp contrasts between weak father figures and frighteningly dominant grandfathers.

III   *The Midwestern Childhood Stories*

"The Ice-Cream Headache," not completed until after the rest of the volume including the "Introduction" was set, is the longest of the childhood stories. In his prefatory note Jones describes the story as having three subjects, the " 'near-but-not-quite-incest' thing, a much commoner experience in America than commonly admitted"; "the failed-family theme"; and "the curse of family alienation" (p. 213). Tom Dylan, the central character, is tormented by his sexuality, his family's decayed social position, and his hatred of his small midwestern town.

The story's opening sentence effectively sets the tone for what is to follow: "There was nothing so Faulknerian about the town, but there was sure something very Faulknerian about the family." Jones aims here at a mood which might be described as Midwestern Gothic; he is generally successful at achieving it. This and other references to Faulkner in the story make one feel that Jones is issuing a challenge: he seems to proclaim that Southern writers are not alone in having a heritage of families cursed by failure, long-smouldering hatreds, and nightmarish sexual fantasies to write about. "The Ice-Cream Headache" is, in fact, in a midwestern tradition probably the best exemplified by Sherwood Anderson.

During the lifetime of Tom's grandfather, the Dylan family were aristocracy in the small town. However, in an extremely

Faulknerian note, Jones emphasizes that the very qualities of the old man which allowed him to attain his ascendancy were what doomed his children to failure. Looking like photographs of Wyatt Earp, rumored to be "a quarter Indian," ruthless and physically brutal, the grandfather, while serving as sheriff, gloried in beating lawbreakers, and extended the practice of beatings to his own sons throughout their childhood. He was mystified that his "philosophy" of raising children, "practically universal" in this region, produced "four drunken weaklings." Then he attempted to guarantee the futures of his weak sons in two ways: by investing in "Instul stocks" and because of his conviction that the automobile was a passing fad, by training them to become veterinarians so that they could open livery stables. "The Crash" destroyed the stocks' security and "the rest of it was done by the cars" (p. 221).

Actually, only two of the four sons became veterinarians, "just the first son and the third son, Tom's father" (p. 222); but they all became weak, vindictive men who completely dissipated what little social prestige remained to the Dylans. Eventually Jones conveys the idea that the four sons' failed lives constitute an almost conscious revenge against the father they hated. Two authorial comments are essential to understand this point and the thrust of the entire story.

Tom has no doubt that responsibility for the "family curse" rests with the grandfather:

It was Tom's own personal theory that he, the grandfather, was almost certainly very highly oversexed, had frustrated and stifled that part of himself in him, and so instead had just taken it out on his four sons, in meanness. People did that. Only, how did you know with people like that from a generation like that that was all so stuffed up shut and ignorant. (p. 220)

The grandfather exemplifies the recurrent Jones characterization of the "oversexed" male turning to such perversions as sadism. A central irony here is that Tom, the grandson, can comprehend what his father and his uncles never could—that because of midwestern social taboos and restrictions, the old man was terrified of his own sexuality. All the whippings he administered to his

sons were simultaneously perverted sexual gratification to him
and attempts literally to beat such "evil needs" out of them.

Of course the sons grew up hating their father, secretly determined to thwart him. Afraid to state their defiance openly, they
resorted to the covert revenge of drunkenness and failure. The
other authorial comment helps clarify this point:

What the Dylan family had suffered from was, mainly, pride. Good
old *human* pride. . . . But which also caused more stubborn bitchery,
hard-headed meanness, hate, destruction, murder and organized mayhem than could be found anywhere else in the animal kingdom all
put together. Good old old-fashioned American, Middlewestern, kill-
me-but-I'll-never-budge pride. (p. 216)

Initially, Tom Dylan's ability to comprehend the complexity of
his family's suffering helps him very little. Tom is too wrapped
up in hatred—of his own father ("A drunk veterinary. It was
pretty obvious he hated his work. And what kind of life was
that. For a man.") (p. 224); of his mother for her bitterness and
puritanism; and of the town for ridiculing the Dylan family.
He is embarrassed by the family's vanished prestige (symbolized
by the old family home now lost) and terrified by his inability
to find an outlet for his own sexuality.

The purchase of some pornography during a stint in the
Civilian Military Training Corps in Indianapolis accidentally
leads to a potential release for Tom's sexual needs. Upon discovering that his sister Emma has stolen "three of his best pictures," Tom is stunned into a realization that ". . . girls might
have dirty thoughts, sexual thoughts, too, the way boys did"
(pp. 231–32). The degree to which Tom has already fallen victim
to midwestern sexual puritanism is clear. To him sexual desire
is "dirty" and a need generally linked to animalism. The discovery
of Emma's theft allows Tom to engage in some blackmail. He
demands that Emma and her best friend Joan meet him at the
deserted family mansion in order to engage in some orgiastic
activities. Tom's choice of the old Dylan mansion, so strongly
associated with his grandfather, symbolically reveals the inter-
relationship of his familial and self-hate. It is as if he intends to
consummate the family curse in the place of its origin.

Tom is ironically saved from an incestuous act only by an earlier good deed. While at the Civilian Military Training Corps camp, he had saved two small children from drowning during a sudden torrential cloudburst. Even though the children were the general's, Tom's courageous act did not win him a change of clothes or a dry place to spend the night. At this point in this story Jones quite arbitrarily introduces some satire of the military caste system. Since his return home soon after the rescue, Tom has suffered from pain which reminds him of the headaches he often had as a small child when his grandfather would allow him to eat too much ice cream. Partly because of associating it with his long ago "ice-cream headaches," Tom has not regarded his present physical conditions seriously.

However, on the way to the mansion for the proposed incestuous orgy, he becomes increasingly weak, short of breath, and hallucinatory. Initially, he assumes that this rapid deterioration is simply the result of sexual excitement. Again, Jones dramatically symbolizes Tom's sexual maladjustment in describing his association of desire with illness. Arriving at the mansion, he passes out. He wakes in his bed at home, hearing a doctor diagnose "double lumbar pneumonia." Before fainting, Tom has suffered a hallucinatory experience which symbolically unites all the story's main motifs. In the hallucination, he feels his illness to be a "punishment" and associates this retribution with his grandfather. Then he senses a "cardboard placard" advertising his grandfather's candidacy for sheriff. After looking like a photograph of Wyatt Earp, the placard then turns into surrealistic pornography:

The right eye and eyebrow [of the grandfather] turned slowly into one of the women's crotches from one of his pornographic pictures. Slowly it winked at him. . . . Breasts, crotches, delicious shaved armpits, delicious unshaved armpits, sixguns, mustaches, Western hats all revolved around each other now, turning, merging, separating, disappearing, reappearing, glaring, and then dimming as great lights flashed. (p. 237)

Intermingled with the surrealistic sexuality is an image of the grandfather beating Tom's father over the head with a pistol

"... while Tom, a very little boy, hid behind the bank building beside the filling station and watched." (p. 237)

The result of Tom's hallucination is an epiphany of forgiveness for his father, his entire family, and for himself. From his sickbed, he says to his uncomprehending mother and the doctor: "Nothing's that bad. Nothing is ever that bad. There's nothing in the world that's ever that bad. And they should never have let him do it to them. Guilty like that" (p. 238). The double lumbar pneumonia not only enables Tom to escape incest; it results in profound understanding and forgiveness of his father's weakness and his own adolescent terror. That guilt for oneself or others can be rejected, he realizes for the first time. The resolution of "The Ice-Cream Headache" seems arbitrary and forced, and much of the story is overwritten. Still it is important as Jones's most sustained example of Midwestern Gothicism and for its characterization of the dead grandfather as a personification of such terror.

"Just like the Girl" is Jones's best short story and one of the finest in contemporary American literature. The title, coming from the overtly Oedipal popular song, implies that destructive mother-son relationships such as the one in the story are so common in America as to be a treasured part of our popular culture. It is one of the five stories in the volume written in 1947, when Jones was only twenty-five. A painful prefatory note seems to make it clear that in the writing of this story Jones in part engaged in an act of vengeance against his own mother:

I once showed this story to a newspaper editor in my hometown of Robinson, Illinois, who had known and admired my mother. The strange, guilty, upset, almost disbelieving look on his face when he handed it back, which seemed to say: "Even if it's true, why *do* it?" was worth to me all the effort I put into writing it. (p. 13)

The mother in "Just like the Girl" is as frightening as the grandfather in "The Ice-Cream Headache." As the story opens, she is preparing her small son John, the central figure in the story, to spy on her husband after the man comes home. Her preparation involves a mixture of imposed guilt (" 'I've given my whole life to you children....' "); self-pity and propaganda

("'Everybody said I was the most beautiful woman in this
country and he was lucky to get me. Now he's cast me aside, for
any hotassed bitch that walks the streets.'"); unintentional revelation of her frigidity ("'Him with those great big arms and
strong as a bull. He hurts everything he touches, he'd kill any
woman....'"); and overt Oedipal appeal ("'When I go away
I'll take you with me and we'll go away forever.'") (pp. 16–17).
Against such an arsenal of psychological weapons, the father,
one of Jones's weak, alcoholic midwestern men, can only counter
by offering gifts and money for his children's affection.

   This inevitably destructive battle for the children's loyalty has
been going on for some time and has reached its climax in an
incident which occurred prior to the opening of the story. One
day, while frying chicken and suffering John's endless childhood
questions, the mother exploded with frustration; she hit the boy
with a kitchen fork. Immediately after John recovers from the
initial shock of his wound, the mother is able to shift guilt to
him through her mastery of psychological warfare: "... He had
felt very sorry for her and put his arms around her and told her
it was all right and it didn't hurt much and for her not to worry,
he did not really mind dying when he was still such a little boy,
but it only made her cry worse." When his father happens on
the scene, he gives John a half dollar; and John's reaction indicates the amount of emotional damage he has already undergone.
"If he had been cut over both eyes he bet his father would have
given him a whole dollar" (p. 19).

   The story begins on a night when John's assignment is to hide
in the back of his father's car, watch what he does with which
"hotassed bitch," and then report back to the mother. Undergoing
the confusion of puberty, John senses the possibility of considerable personal gratification in his task:

None of the kids had ever really seen anybody do it. They wouldn't
care if he was a drunkard's son or not, if he told how he had seen them
do it and just what they did. (p. 21)

   John, the child of a disastrous marriage, feels deeply the need
of some kind of personal and peer esteem. Like virtually all of
Jones's midwestern children, he views sex as a secret, ugly act

of considerable fascination. He has a fantasy that indicates his potential for sadomasochism:

> Some enemy soldiers were holding Priscilla Jenkins [a schoolmate] captive and going to torture her with red-hot irons. In his mind he saw Priscilla, a great lady now, standing tied to a tree, her clothes torn clear off of her and the enemy soldiers stepping up to put a red-hot iron against her thing–. . . (p. 20).

John's association of the penis with an object of torture is one of the story's most effective illustrations of the emotional damage his mother and father's marriage has done to John.

His spying mission turns out to be a disappointment. The only person his father picks up is Lab Wallers, an old American Legion buddy. The two sing, drive, drink, and talk. The dialogue between the father and Lab is among Jones's most effective dramatizations of the dominated midwestern male's virtually schizophrenic attitude toward women. Lab first enunciates some pious praise of the American woman: " 'Where would the world be, without the wives? Where would our kids be, if it wasn't for their mothers? Where would this nation be, if it wasn't for the women?' " (p. 22). Initially agreeing, the father applies this evaluation to his own specific situation but then unveils his anger and frustration: " 'I was lucky to get her. Everybody says so. If she just wouldn't devil me so. Goddam it, Lab, someday the men will be free' " (p. 22).

The painfully ironic ending of "Just like the Girl" cements its effectiveness. John falls asleep and awakens while being carried to bed by his father. The man has sensed the nature of the boy's mission but is not angry. Instead, the father praises his son— " 'You're a damned good man. You've got a lot of guts and I'm proud you are my son' "—and offers him "a quarter and *two* half dollars *both*" (p. 23).

The specter of his mother's disapproval enters John's mind, and he rejects his father and his money. The man then walks out in pain and some dignity. His son goes back to sleep thinking that his mother will be proud because he had not allowed his affections to be bought. The pain and inherent decency of the inarticulate father, the power of the mother who has bought her son's affections with psychological coin, and the future suffering of the Oedipally scarred boy are brilliantly condensed in this ending. The brevity of "Just like the Girl" forces a control on Jones that is somewhat lacking in "The Ice-Cream Headache."

Like the two preceding stories, "The Tennis Game" also centers on the explosive combination of an unresolved Oedipal relationship and a young boy's sexual awakening. Jones's introductory note reveals that it was published by *Esquire* in 1958 (after undergoing some ridiculous magazine censorship) and states its theme: "I think it's an interesting study of male masochism of which there appears to be a great deal in my generation, brought on of course by mothers like the mother in the story" (p. 195).

The mother in the story typifies Jones's personification of the puritanism and hypocrisy of midwestern women. She forces her son, Johnny Slade, to work constantly in the family vegetable garden and has numerous "good reasons" why he should do so—the Depression, his father doesn't make enough money and gets drunk, and Johnny must develop character. Johnny sees through all of this, however:

But the real truth was she couldn't stand to see him outdoors playing and having fun while she herself had to clean house and cook. She just couldn't stand it, he could tell by the look on her face, and so the whole thing was no more than one damned big lie. One of those grownup lies, that grownups told each other and pretended to believe, and that children because they were little had to accept and pretend to believe too, because they could not argue back. (pp. 200–201)

One of Jones's central thematic concerns was the power of those people in positions of authority to define "The Truth" and the helplessness of the subordinate individual to combat such definitions. This theme is central to *From Here to Eternity*—"truth" in the army tends to be what officers such as Dynamite Holmes decide it is. In the adult-child relationship, Jones found a perfect example of this theme—children are helpless in the face of adult definitions of truth.

Eleven-year-old Johnny Slade's means of combating his

mother's power are pitifully weak. There is a "big snowball bush" under which he hides to masturbate both for pleasure and for revenge against his mother (this is one "secret" he can have over her). In his introductory note Jones indicates that the mother's shrill dominance of her son is already pushing the boy toward masochism. As with John in "Just like the Girl" this boy's sexual fantasies are distinctly sadomasochistic.

In the climactic moment of the story Johnny remembers a visit "a month or so ago" from "Alice Pringle from the other side of town" (p. 205). The two had been playing outside when they suddenly begin childlike sexual exploration only to be interrupted by "his mother's voice, shrill, strident, demanding and insistent, like some all-seeing all-knowing powerful dark angel of God ..." (p. 206). Johnny instinctively admits what they are doing and is rewarded for his honesty by first having his mouth washed out with soap and then receiving "a whale of a whipping on his bare bottom" (p. 207). Remembering the Alice Pringle episode triggers Johnny's favorite and most elaborate fantasy, inspired by a *Collier's* story about a tennis match between Don Budge and Baron von Cramm. In the story Baron von Cramm loses and then commits suicide rather than return to Germany and persecution by Hitler.

Johnny loves to re-create this classic match in his mind, usually identifying most with von Cramm ("... in some strange way that he couldn't describe [he] was able to sense out and associate with the German's sad but strong feelings") and usually "losing" (pp. 208–209). At the end of the story Johnny indulges in this elaborate fantasy outside, while his mother entertains her Wisdom Club bridge ladies inside. Much of the pleasure of what he is doing comes from the knowledge that it is "secret" from his mother and her friends, even though it is happening only a few feet away from them. After going through the elaborate internal ritual of "losing" again as von Cramm, Johnny heads for the backyard "... to do what he always wanted to do when he felt like this. He wanted to play with himself" (p. 210). Jones puts some effective irony into the story's concluding dialogue. In response to his mother's question of what he is doing, Johnny answers: "'Playing,' he said grimly, his face a mask of German iron control, as became a Prussian" (p. 210). As Johnny walks away to hide and masturbate, his mother laughs and says to her Wisdom Club friends: " 'Playing! Oh, well, you know how children are. They're always playing some little game or other when they're by themselves' " (pp. 210–11).

Jones powerfully illustrates the degree of psychological damage the boy has received from his domineering mother: the association of masturbation (or sexual release) with death in the von Cramm fantasy would seem to indicate that this child could have little hope for any future healthy sexual adjustment. It is also of interest that in his acted-out game, which is the only thing over which he has real control, he elects to identify with the foreign "loser." Obviously, the degree of Johnny's estrangement from his environment is strong.

"A Bottle of Cream" and "The Valentine" are lighter fiction than the other three childhood stories, but the former contains elements of real interest. Jones called it "probably my favorite in the whole book. I like the mood and tone of it. . . . I like everything about it" (p. 169). Written in 1957, the story begins as its adult narrator reflects on going with a friend who has to pay a drunk driving fine. This situation allows the narrator some remarks relevant both to Jones's childhood stories and to all the long novels after *From Here to Eternity*:

But this is how serious the crime of drunken driving has become today. This, of course, is due to two things. One is that perforce we are a nation of drivers in the U.S., and the other is that we are a nation of drunkards. Really compulsive drunkards. . . . I myself attribute this peculiarly American type of drunkenness to the fact that as a nation we are so repressed in our social and sexual lives. (p. 172)

An aspect of the story peculiarly reminiscent of *Some Came Running* involves the characterization of Chet Poore, who provides the bridge between the "adult frame" and the central "childhood narrative." Poore is described as ". . . what you might call a criminal, sort of" (p. 171) and ". . . a house-breaker and a car-thief, as well as being an excellent pool- and poker-player" (p. 173). Chet Poore is a controlled example of Jones's fondness for the nonrespectable, if not actually criminal, element of society which reaches an extreme in the characterization of 'Bama Dillert in *Some Came Running*.

While the friend pays his fine, the narrator learns that Poore has been arrested in Detroit for stealing a car, making him a "three time loser." Poore's name triggers a series of childhood memories in which the reader learns that the narrator is Johnny Slade of "The Tennis Game," grown up and amazingly well adjusted when one recalls the foreshadowings of the earlier story. He operates a tavern and is married with "two small sons." He falls into a reverie about his childhood adventure with Chet Poore. Somewhere between the ages of six and eight, he was sent downtown by his mother for a bottle of whipping cream, interrupting another "replay" of the Budge–von Cramm tennis fantasy. Again the frustration of the family is effectively summarized:

I was angry at the cream and at my mother, who was angry at the cooking and at my father, who was angry at all the bills he had to pay and at God. Actually, of course, we were all angry at life but I did not know this then and apparently, though they were much older than me, neither did they. (p. 178)

On the way home, Johnny dropped and broke the bottle of cream and then lapsed into a "trauma" of helplessness:

Terrified, I knew I could not go back to my mother and tell her the truth. Not only would she whip me and yell at me loudly all the while as she did so, but also she would accuse me of wasting money we could not afford to waste, which would disturb me even more, even though I knew we were not anywhere near poor enough that we could not afford a second bottle. (p. 178)

Jones is focusing on the theme, central to "The Tennis Game," of the helplessness of the child in the face of the adult's ability to define "truth" and impose punishment for its violation. Again, the mother is a figure of threat and intimidation, lacking any true wisdom despite the name of her bridge club.

Johnny was rescued by Chet Poore, who was then twenty-four or twenty-five and a complete stranger to the boy. Poore kindly bought a second bottle of cream and sent the boy on his way. Johnny realized that, although "... it had meant nothing at all to him," the strange man had transformed his tragedy into simply a "horrible nightmare" (pp. 180–81), another example of the power of the adult to transform totally a child's reality.

Hearing that Poore is now threatened with life imprisonment (on a "habitual criminal" statute), the narrator begins to speculate about the forces that push some people across the border of legality. As a freshman in high school, he was himself arrested for stealing cigarettes from a store, ironically the one whose owner, though believing Johnny's account of the broken bottle, had forced Chet Poore to pay for its replacement. Johnny is caught in the cigarette scheme (the owner does, however, inflate the amount of theft to his own profit), but saved from any "record" by his father's influence. The contrast between this act of theft and Poore's decency to him over the bottle of cream leaves the narrator unable to anticipate anything meaningful about "Justice" or Chet Poore. The story ends with the information that Poore, now about fifty, is sentenced to life, with parole possible in twenty years.

Poore's name would indicate an implied naturalistic comment about "Justice." Jones's point seems to be that external forces (especially unthinking social approval or disapproval and pure chance) determine where, in relation to criminality, anyone in our "adolescent" society ultimately falls. Johnny Slade's childhood benefactor was one of those poor people who never got the right breaks and, as a result, developed the habit of criminality. The fact that America is a nation of drunken drivers, with rituals for dealing with acceptable and unacceptable cases of drunken driving, indicates that all its citizens can and may develop into criminals.

Despite his own partiality to the story, Jones really attempts too much in "A Bottle of Cream," and the story does not carry the power of "Just like the Girl" or "The Tennis Game." Still, its picture of the terrified helplessness of young Johnny when the bottle of cream breaks is memorable; and Chet Poore demonstrates that, despite the unsuccessful 'Bama Dillert, Jones could control his characterizations of the criminal, or near-criminal, personality.

Also written in 1957, "The Valentine" is mainly interesting for coming as close to triteness as possible without wholly falling into its trap. Another Johnny Slade story, it depicts the boy at twelve desperately "in love" with a girl who has never noticed him. The plot simply recounts his buying a box of candy for a Valentine surprise for Margaret; the presentation of the candy; and her amused reaction, which totally humiliates Johnny. What saves the story is some effective writing that emphasizes the helpless embarrassment of the boy in the face of adults like the condescending salesman at Woolworth's, where he buys the candy; of popular girls like Margaret who view him with amusement; and of his awakening sexuality. An effective ironic touch is Johnny's own scorn for the valentines of two girls "from Sacktown," who "were poor, and not very smart, and often not even very clean" (p. 167). This balancing irony is necessary to keep Johnny's characterization from total sentimentality. It also restates the Jones motif of the midwestern small-town caste system.

These five childhood stories are little known, but they are an important part of the Jones canon. They show an ability to handle the short story form with true sensitivity and are important as aids to an understanding of the sexual maladjustment theme that is central to the post-*Eternity* long novels. Since much about them is strong and, in form and delicacy, reminiscent of such classic American fiction as *Winesburg, Ohio*, one regrets that Jones did not complete his planned collection of "childhood stories."

IV   *The Army Stories*

The volume's four army stories—"The Way It Is," "Greater Love", "Two Legs for the Two of Us," and "The Temper of Steel"—vary in their effectiveness, but together represent an important complement to the military novels. They cover three major phases of a soldier's experience: prewar, combat, and postwar readjustment to civilian life. Jones's concept of the evolution of a soldier values each of these as a critical period with its own unique problems. "The Way It Is," published in the June 1949 *Harper's*, is described by Jones in *Viet Journal* as "one of my best short stories" (p. 244), and this evaluation holds true. The setting of "The Way It Is" is the Makapuu Head beach position so central to *The Pistol*, and Jones again utilizes the unrelenting wind as a symbol of intense pressure on men. Slade, the central character, has difficulty in even remembering his pre–Pearl Harbor Hawaiian experience: "... It was from another life, a life protected from the wind, a life where there were white clouds in the sun but no wind, just gently moving air" (p. 33). He occasionally likes to sit out on a culvert, facing and "defying the wind. But a man could only do it so long" (p. 40).

There are additional points of similarity to *The Pistol*. Like Mast, Slade is somewhat alienated from the other men by his greater intelligence and education. (One of course wonders if this Slade is the central character of the "childhood stories" now grown up and in the army.) Also, there is satire of the bureaucratic bungling which had necessitated the road-guard. "It was excellent strategy, for a makeshift, with the invasion expected truly every day" (p. 31). But perhaps of greater importance are the story echoes of *From Here to Eternity*. Slade, despite much pleading, has consistently refused to become an officer. His refusal has nothing to do with World War II, but with the army and how it works. It is, he says, a question of " 'belief' " and " 'who manufactures it' " (p. 39). Lieutenant Allison is the idealistic officer who debates with Slade the issues of his "cynicism" and his duty to the army. Slade says to Allison at one point: " 'I'm cynical about the Army. It's a helluva lot easier to be an idealist if you're an officer. The higher the officer, the higher the ideals' " (p. 38). Slade and Allison obviously resemble Warden and Ross, the officer who replaces Dynamite Holmes in *Eternity*.

The major plot twist of "The Way It Is" indicates that, like Jones's first novel, it is an example of proletarian protest. When asked for verification of his enlistment Slade responds, " 'Yes, sir.... But it was because I couldn't get a job' " (p. 37). Here again is Jones's emphasis upon the "old army" as a place of refuge for the economically desperate male during the depression years. At the beginning of the story, Sergeant Mazzioli, a by-the-book soldier, has stopped and prepared to search a car at the road-guard. Mazzioli is simply following his orders; but shortly after Slade arrives it is discovered that the car contains a Mr. Knight, one of "The Big Five," who control the island economy. Allison attempts to smooth over the incident by pointing out to the corporate giant that " 'a soldier's duty is to follow out his orders' " and promises him that " 'such a thing won't happen again...'" (p. 36). Mr. Knight leaves without speaking; but Allison still has faith that "'in the long run, it will all turn out all right because we did what was right. The Army will take that into account'" (p. 37). Allison's faith is betrayed when pressure from Knight causes the road-guard to be disbanded. Slade ends the story with the true but cynical comment, "'That's the way it is'" (p. 41).

Jones effectively presents in this story some of the major thematic concerns underlying *From Here to Eternity*. Because Mr. Knight has been inconvenienced, he takes action that potentially endangers the security of the island and thus of the entire Allied war effort. The point is not that he does what he does, but that he has the power to do it. Mr. Knight is big money, and big money can stretch its tentacles so far as to entangle the strategy of the United States Army during wartime. It is, therefore, not surprising that the army Slade, Milt Warden, and Robert E. Lee Prewitt know is dominated by a rigid caste system. The army will almost inevitably reflect the society it is designed to protect. One remembers "Mad" Welsh's refrain throughout *The Thin Red Line* that the war is being fought in the name of "property." Allison's idealism, if not shattered by colliding so painfully with "the way it is," may protect him from the fates of those Jones characters who perceive economic and social realities clearly—death for Prewitt and a cynicism bordering on madness for Slade, Warden, and Welsh.

"Greater Love," published originally by *Collier's* in 1951, was described by Jones as "my first real attempt at writing seriously about combat" (p. xiii). The story is set on Guadalcanal and is almost identical in tone to *The Thin Red Line*. The most intriguing character is the combat outfit's first sergeant, known only as "The First." A comment about him in Jones's prefatory note is of interest: "Almost anybody can recognize Sgts Warden and Welsh in 'The First'" (p. 123). Since the publication of *Whistle,* one can add the name of Winch to this recurrent character type.

The story constitutes a chapter in Jones's study of the evolution of a soldier; and its thematic development emerges from a contrast of "The First's" sardonic, battlewise philosophy with the naively idealistic views of Corporal Quentin Thatcher. Quentin is reminiscent of Fife in *The Thin Red Line* except that he is initially more preoccupied with the safety of his brother, Pfc. Shelby Thatcher, than with his own. Still, he undergoes a similar metamorphosis from idealist to a man intent only on killing the enemy. Jones's title is an ironic reference to the biblical passage (John 15:13) "Greater love has no man than this, that a man lay down his life for his friends."[7] The bitter wisdom of "The First" (as well as Warden and Welsh) is that combat leaves no room for such sacrificial concern with "friends" or brothers. All personalities, including one's own, must be forged into a necessary anonymity that allows for efficient annihilation of the enemy. The best way to insure such a grim impartiality is to have no friends; in *From Here to Eternity* much of Warden's apparent cruelty toward Prewitt results from the Sergeant's desperate attempt to keep himself above emotion.

However, one sometimes cannot help loving a brother, and Quentin Thatcher at the first of the story is far from possessing combat wisdom. When another soldier named Gorman says, " 'In a war, *every* man's got to take care of himself. That's my philosophy,' " Thatcher only laughs hysterically (p. 128). Gorman comes close to enunciating the "greater love" of combat— try to stay alive in order to kill the enemy. It is necessary that someone other than "The First" express this "philosophy," because "The First" does not teach by words, but by attitude and deed. Thatcher's first major step in his metamorphosis comes when he is sent on a graveyard detail. The macabre detail of this passage, in which the men dig up the bodies of dead Americans and then load them on a truck, is reminiscent of the scene in *The Thin Red Line* in which the men of C company expose the mass grave of dead Japanese.

During the digging a soldier named Al Zwermann discovers the body of his brother Victor and withdraws into a state of near insanity. Witnessing Zwermann's experience seems to affect Quentin very little; but when he does rush into combat, he still attempts to watch out for Shelby. Soon, however, the frenzied anonymity which is combat takes over his mind, and he completes the first major stage of his evolution into a soldier. In different ways, the style in the story's conclusion echoes both Fife's final change in *The Thin Red Line* and Henry Fleming's moment of battlefield maturity in Stephen Crane's *The Red*

Badge of Courage. Quentin sees Shelby fall to the ground, but does not perceive that his brother is dead. Instead he becomes enraged in the belief Shelby has fainted from cowardice. "Embarrassment for his brother made him suddenly hate him for failing in the clutch" (p. 138). Moments later, when Quentin shoots a Japanese soldier at close range, he experiences the same animal pleasure that Fife does. As with Fife, Jones spares no brutality of detail in describing his response.

The recoil slammed his shoulder and he kept both eyes open like he had been taught and saw the face open redly like a thrown tomato. A piece of bridgework popped out of the mouth.
"I got him!" Quentin yelled. "I got him!" (p. 139)

Almost from the moment of Shelby's death, Quentin has been accompanied in his charge by a man he cannot clearly see. This companion is called "the big man" in a manner reminiscent of Stephen Crane's referring to Fleming's companions as "the tall soldier," "the loud soldier," and so on. Jones, like Crane, substitutes a descriptive phrase for a name in order to stress both the main character's limited perception and the necessary anonymity of war. The fact that "the big man" turns out to be the First is important because of its inherent symbolic statement. After the battle, Quentin is still raging at Shelby's "cowardice"; and the First, who knows the truth, does not correct him. The story ends with this exchange:

"He [Shelby] ought to be shot," Quentin said.
"Watch the trees," the First said. "You're doing fine." (p. 140)

The First knows that Quentin has entered the realm of necessary combat wisdom and that he can do nothing but continue his evolution. Besides its value as a powerful story, "Greater Love" is important as Jones's first fictional study of combat and as a source of information from Jones on the characterizations of Warden and Welsh.

In the prefatory note to "Two Legs for the Two of Us" Jones writes that "*Esquire* published this one in September 1951, when *Eternity* was famous, after having turned it down at least twice

before that" (p. 43). (More than once in the Introduction to
Ice-Cream Headache Jones comments with bitter amusement on
the ease of publishing stories after he became a famous novelist.)
The prefatory note also states that this story constituted a scene
in "the early novel I wrote and re-wrote for [Maxwell] Perkins
and which was never published" (p. 43). The story is not
properly war-fiction: it is rather a postwar story which aims at
a theme recurrent in *Some Came Running*.

In both story and novel, Jones attempts to show the spiritual
devastation which the war bequeathed to the world. To symbolize
this spiritual maiming, he frequently creates characters who have
suffered either amputation of limbs or other severe and permanent wounds. "Two Legs for the Two of Us" is the story of an
unannounced visit which two amputees, George and Tom, pay
on George's ex-wife, Sandy. George and Tom are accompanied
by two prostitutes; and the dialogue is uniformly brutal and
bitter whether it focuses on recriminations between George and
Sandy, ridicule of the prostitutes, or the two men's "teasing" each
other about their shared deformity. Jones's greatest concern,
losses other than the physical, is indicated in the two men's
inability since the war to maintain any meaningful, sustained
relationship. Even though thinking about their wounds "turns
[their] stommick," both men constantly kid each other about
being "cripples." Feeling like freaks, George and Tom are special
kinds of war casualties—where once they may have possessed
self-respect and the capacity for affection, they now are controlled and defined by self-hate.

Sandy has contributed in the most cruel of ways to George's
loss of self-esteem by mailing him her wedding and engagement
rings while he was in the army hospital ward in Utah. On receiving them, George threw them out into the snowy Utah night.
Tom's marital history is that he has " 'been married four times
in five years' " (p. 48). The pain of all this is heightened by the
fact that George and Sandy still obviously care for each other.
Sandy says, " 'War is hard on the women, too' " (p. 48). It is.
Jones's point is a naturalistic one: it is all, finally, nobody's fault.

When George makes a sexual advance toward Sandy and is
rejected, he turns to one of the prostitutes. Finally, the divorced
couple exchange some deeply felt words:

"I just do what I have to," Sandy said.

"Sandy," George said. "You don't know what it was like, Sandy."

"No," she said. "I guess I don't."

"You goddam right you don't. And you never will. You'll never be. . . ."

George's last line is an echo of Hemingway's title "A Way You'll Never Be." Both writers convey the same idea—the impossibility of the survivors of combat conveying any real idea of its horrors to those who have never "been there."

The story's ending is moving as Sandy stands in the doorway watching the two men and the prostitutes leave, "moisture overflowing her eyes unnoticed, looking backward into a past the world had not seen fit to let alone" (p. 54). A war leaves many types of casualties; and one special kind is a woman like Sandy on whom "war is hard." The ending also emphasizes a peculiarly evocative symbol, introduced in the story—a red wine stain on a tablecloth which occurs when Tom spills a drink. As a symbol, its effectiveness stems in large part from its ambiguity; but somehow it conveys an idea of that despoiled past which George and Sandy can never bring back. "Two Legs for the Two of Us" needs more development of character and incident to be a totally successful story; but it is an interesting presentation of the world after 1945 as a wasteland.

The final war story, "The Temper of Steel," published as an "*Atlantic Monthly* First" in 1948, reveals the extent to which the young Jones was under the Hemingway influence. It attempts the Joyceian-Hemingway device of concealing the meaning of a story as carefully as possible without losing it entirely. The Jones of 1968 is afraid, however, that he did lose it; in addition to acknowledging Hemingway's influence in a preface, he explains the story's theme in a closing note.

The setting is a cocktail party attended by a young man named Johnny. Also in attendance is the central character, a rather mysterious figure named Lon who has "lived an adventurous life" (p. 4). Some rare knives are being exhibited at the party; and they inspire Lon to launch a discussion of the lore of knives and knife fighting. This discussion begins to bother Johnny because it brings to his mind a memory he habitually attempts to suppress.

As the focus switches to Johnny's consciousness, the feared

memory gradually emerges. First, he remembers having read a book by Archie Binns called *The Laurels Are Cut Down*, which forecasts the true nature of modern warfare and announces that "Chivalry Was Dead" (p. 6). Then flashes of digging trenches while serving on Guadalcanal impinge on his mind. Finally, the total memory emerges—Johnny's knifing of a Japanese soldier during that brutal campaign. Jones's mastery of naturalistic detail in this scene is as impressive as usual and foreshadows the evolution of a soldier theme. Describing the feeling of oneness between man and weapon that necessarily emerges in combat, he writes: "Quite silently it [his hand] unfastened the snap and freed the knife from the sheath strapped to his leg. Then it relaxed full length along his side, cunning as animals are cunning. Perhaps in the end that was all it was" (p. 8). Jones's ideas about the animal nature of mankind are also implicit in this passage. The scene climaxes brutally in understatement: "The Jap hardly made a sound, only a sharp 'unh' as the knife went into him. Such a silent war this one was" (p. 9).

The point of the story is not yet complete, and Jones needs one more bit of dialogue to complete it. Johnny and Lon discuss the scene in Erich Maria Remarque's *All Quiet on the Western Front* in which " 'Paul kills the Frenchman in the hole and then begs his forgiveness,' " agreeing that Remarque's book is " 'highly sentimental stuff' " and that " 'you couldn't write it that way now, could you?' " (p. 10). Jones's explanatory footnote reads:

The point is in the reference to Archie Binns and the quote about chivalry being dead, and in the boy's comparison of his own cold-blooded killing of the Japanese to the comparable scene in *All Quiet*. This is what modern warfare has come to be, with all of our blessings, and God help us for it. (p. 11)

In other words, Jones was here describing, as he was to do later much more effectively, the inhuman brutality of "modern warfare." The story *is* "young," as he also said later. The cocktail party setting seems artificial in itself; and the references to Binns and Remarque are introduced arbitrarily. The story's most vital moment is the description of Johnny's killing of the Japanese soldier. "The Temper of Steel" is nonetheless of interest because it contains so many of Jones's later themes and shows his early attempts to write in an overtly "Hemingway style" with mixed results. In addition, it is one of the two instances in which Jones put his own experience of killing the Japanese soldier on Guadalcanal into fiction.

The four war stories, ranging in subject from the period immediately after Pearl Harbor to the postwar wasteland, echo important themes of *From Here to Eternity*, *The Pistol*, and *The Thin Red Line*. Moreover, "The Way It Is" and "Greater Love" are highly successful short fiction.

Of the other stories in the book, "None Sing So Wildly" foreshadows the structural problems that Jones will have with *Some Came Running*, while "The King," on the other hand, is a highly successful example of what Jones calls a "double plot" story, in which two stories, "almost unrelated but spiritually connected, are taking place" (p. 141). "Sunday Allergy" also shows a talent for light comedy that Jones rarely exploited; but none supplement the theories behind his important novels like the Midwestern childhood and war stories.

The Ice-Cream Headache came as a major addition to the Jones canon. The best short stories—"Just like the Girl," "The Way It Is," "Greater Love," "A Bottle of Cream," and "The Tennis Game"—illustrate a sophisticated awareness of the control and discipline essential to the form. In *The Pistol* Jones had extended this mastery to the novella form with equal success. At his best, Jones is so accomplished with shorter forms of fiction that one longs for more of this kind of his writing.

CHAPTER 5

The Evolution of a Soldier, Part 2:
The Thin Red Line

IN *Cannibals and Christians* Norman Mailer writes a two-page commentary about *The Thin Red Line* which provides a revealing insight into both James Jones's fourth novel and Norman Mailer's flawed critical objectivity toward his rival war novelist. Mailer praises *The Thin Red Line* as ". . . so broad and true a picture of combat that it could be used as a textbook at the Infantry School. . . ." He further states that Jones's intent ". . . is not to create character but the feel of combat, the psychology of men. He is close to a master at this." Mailer insists correctly that, of all war novels, Jones's work is most reminiscent of Stephen Crane's *The Red Badge of Courage.* He finds Crane's novel superior, though he gropes for an explanation of its superiority. Admitting that in many ways Jones accomplishes more than Crane, Mailer can find no more specific flaw in *The Thin Red Line* than an assertion that it is "too technical," "too workmanlike." Mailer misses the old Jones (apparently of *From Here to Eternity*) who artistically risked wedding the realistic with the "mystical" in a prose that often evidenced a loss of authorial control.[1]

The Thin Red Line is anything but a "textbook"; it is a powerful novel which may require more than one reading to appreciate its author's success. Still, Mailer's insights that *The Thin Red Line* is about the "psychology of men" in "combat," rather than individual characters and that it evokes comparison to Crane's masterpiece are extremely perceptive. In this novel, Jones has reached the critical point in his concept of the evolution of the soldier—the time when face-to-face confrontation with a foreign military enemy demands the suppression of the self. The romantic individualism of a Prewitt, admirable though it may be, has no place in a situation where group cooperation is essential to minimizing casualties. Such combat is the situation for which Warden was attempting to prepare himself throughout *From Here to Eternity*; and, with one exception, the characters in *The Thin Red Line* have largely succeeded in sacrificing their egos to the welfare of C-for-Charlie Company. Such sacrifice is almost never the result of abstract loyalty or idealism; rather it is an instinctive realization that whatever safety is possible in combat lies in the smooth functioning of the company.

Peter G. Jones writes that "of all Jones's characters only Witt, at the bottom of the social scale, evinces signs of loyalty as a motivation."[2] After adding the name of "Mad" Welsh, whose loyalty is manifested in extremely subtle ways, one can accept this evaluation. Moreover, the loyalty of Witt and Welsh is only to Charlie Company, and not to any larger abstract entity such as the United States or even the army. As Peter G. Jones emphasizes, it is certainly not to the company's officers, whose ineffectuality merits no such respect.

The kind of brutal hand-to-hand combat about which Jones is writing in this novel necessarily involves the senseless, anonymous death which is central to Jones's concept of the soldier's evolution. This factor is the basis for the novel's lack of emphasis upon characters, as well as its similarities to *The Red Badge of Courage*. A conditional anonymity has been accepted by virtually all of the men of Charlie Company in a desperate, and by no means certain, attempt to avoid the irrevocable anonymity of death. As such critics as Maxwell Geismar, Edmond L. Volpe, and Lewis Gannett point out, the main "character" of *The Thin Red Line* is really Charlie Company—some of its enlisted men die and its officers are constantly changing, but the company continues to exist. Stephen Crane, depicting a parallel kind of anonymity, hit upon the device of referring to his characters as "the youth," "the tall soldier," and "the loud soldier" much more frequently than citing their names. There are, of course, different ways to approach the subject of death in combat. Joseph Heller, in *Catch-22*, treats it with a grim, black humor. Heller's logic is clear—a man in combat is potentially the victim of everyone and everything, although there is no "personal" animosity involved. Since this is patently absurd, Heller writes a novel whose structure is dominated by patterns of absurdity. Jones, in *The Thin Red Line,* chose naturalistic detail as his mode. This does not mean, however, that he is writing a "textbook."

A remarkable achievement of Jones's novel, which Mailer notes, is that, despite its focus upon the group entity of Charlie Company, the individual characters do not merge into an indistinguishable blur. Peter G. Jones comes close to explaining how the novelist achieves such a difficult effect: "[*The Thin Red Line*] . . . depicts the psychological states of men who fight, but is more concerned with a minute examination of their reactions and motivations, in the traditional sense of the psychological novel."[3] He further argues that "guilt," especially sexual guilt, is a major aspect of the novel's "psychological" concern. James Jones is intent upon a detailed examination of how various members of Charlie Company make the necessary sacrifice to anonymity. Thus, one sees various stages in which key members of the company suppress their human egos. Ironically, sexual guilt aids in such suppression—irrational shame induced in childhood helps one to minimize self-importance. Jones is utilizing the concept of the sexually immature American male. Because here it is a subordinate aspect of a bigger theme, the concept is controlled as it is not in *Some Came Running* and the later novels, *Go to the Widow-Maker* and *The Merry Month of May.* A central irony of *The Thin Red Line* is the implication that one reason for the American fighting man's success is his sexual immaturity. In the interview with Nelson W. Aldrich, Jr., Jones specifically ties the idea of male immaturity to false acceptance of such "animal" beliefs as "bravery." He expresses the hope that *The Thin Red Line* will reveal war for what it is and free a younger generation from preoccupation with doubts of its own physical courage.[4]

I   *The Campaign*

The novel follows Charlie Company from its initial landing on the Japanese-held island, Guadalcanal, to the termination of that bloody campaign. In a "Special Note," Jones writes that he chose not to create a fictional island for the novel's setting because "to have used a completely made up island would have been to lose all of these special qualities which the name Guadalcanal evoked for my generation." He does, however, fictionalize the campaign and create "smack in the middle of it a whole slab of nonexistent territory."[5] In *WWII*, Jones discusses the unique aspects of the Guadalcanal campaign. After pointing out that "Guadalcanal was the first American offensive anywhere," he writes:

> Fought at an earlier period of the war, when the numbers and matériel engaged were smaller, less trained and less organized, there was an air of adventure and sense of individual exploit about it . . . where small units of platoon and company strength still maintained importance, more than in the later battles of massed armadas, masses of newer equipment, and massed units of men in division and corps strength. It was still pretty primitive, Guadalcanal. (p. 49)

The brutal objectivity of tone in *The Thin Red Line* is an important ingredient in Jones's successful depiction of the "primitive" aspect of the historically significant Guadalcanal invasion. The men of Charlie Company have been taught to expect confrontation with a subhuman enemy; and the hideous nature of the hand-to-hand combat into which they are almost immediately thrust serves as a confirmation of their expectation. Thus, they become something less than human themselves in order to survive.

Guadalcanal was the campaign in which Jones himself received an ankle wound which sent him back to the States:

> I think I screamed, myself, when I was hit. I thought I could vaguely remember somebody yelling. I blacked out for several seconds, and had a dim impression of someone stumbling to his feet with his hands to his face. It wasn't me. Then I came to myself several yards down the slope, bleeding like a stuck pig and blood running all over my face. It must have been a dramatic scene. (*WWII*, p. 53)

In relation to *The Thin Red Line*, the most interesting aspect of this passage is its tone of detachment. Jones had obviously made considerable, if not total, progress in his own "evolution of a soldier" when he was hit. Perhaps not less important than the island's historic significance, a second reason for Jones's desire to retain the actual name of Guadalcanal in his novel was its personal meaning to him. It was there that he confronted death and became a casualty to be shipped home for the final stages of his "evolution."

He further notes, in *WWII*, that the complex of hills on Guadalcanal were called " 'The Galloping Horse' by some bright young staff officer because that was what it looked like in an aerial photo . . ." (p. 58). Charlie Company of *The Thin Red Line* is involved primarily in struggles for two "slab[s] of nonexistent territory," "The Dancing Elephant" and "The Giant Boiled Shrimp," so named because of their appearance in aerial photos. Jones has chosen to incorporate much of his personal experience in this work, but its tonal objectivity prevents it from reading like an autobiographical novel.

Saul Bellow has written about the thematic basis of this objectivity: "In apprehending what is real, Jones's combat soldiers learn a bitter and leveling truth and in their realism revenge themselves on the slothful and easy civilian conception of the Self."[6] That truth is best described by Jones himself: ". . . It is the individual soldier's final full acceptance of the fact that his name is already written down in the rolls of the already dead" (*WWII*, p. 54). If one is "already dead," then human ego and all the accompanying values of civilization become more than irrelevant—such a "normal" value system is an actual burden to the "professional" obligations of combat. This stage of evolution is the one which Jones said that he could never quite himself attain. As *From Here to Eternity* so eloquently shows, it would represent an almost impossible acceptance for an artist.

The characters in *The Thin Red Line* represent different methods and degrees of such acceptance. At one extreme is First Sergeant Edward "Mad" Welsh, and at the other is young Corporal Fife, the character most reminiscent of Crane's Henry Fleming. Because Welsh has virtually completed his acceptance of anonymity before the novel opens and Fife never fully accomplishes it, Jones needs additional characters to illustrate the evolution of a soldier. Most important are Private John Bell, whose intellectualism allows Jones to delineate the stages of evolution, and Pfc. Don Doll, who illustrates the process most completely.

In addition, Mess Sergeant Storm, Private Witt, PFCs Cash, Dale, and Bead, Corporal Queen, and Staff Sergeant Keck personify significant variations of the necessary struggle to suppress self. The novel opens with a description of the company's landing on Guadalcanal and their long march to quarters. Its bulk is devoted to the bloody fight for "The Dancing Elephant," with the taking of "The Giant Boiled Shrimp" as an anticlimax. Before the men are pushed into combat on "The Dancing Elephant," two scenes prepare them for the horror they are about to face. A group of men, most significantly Bell and Queen, discover a bloody, disintegrating American khaki shirt and then a mass grave of Japanese soldiers. The shirt and the grave serve as powerful symbols of the anonymity of combat death. In a perceptive essay, Paulette Michet-Michot argues that the novel is organized around the concept of crossing a line ". . . between the human and the animal, between reason and sensibility on the one side, and brutality and morbid cruelty on the other." She sees the bloody shirt and mass grave as Jones's announcement of Charlie Company's collective passing of the line and the direction in which the novel will develop."[7] Just before going into the struggle for "The Dancing Elephant," the company learns of the fate of two American soldiers who were captured by the Japanese. After torturing the two men to death, the Japanese mutilated their bodies in a hideously shocking way. Such news confirms the collective belief of Charlie Company that they will confront a subhuman enemy which can only be fought on a level of primitive barbarity. After these two scenes, the novel focuses upon the reactions of different members of the company to combat.

II   *Sgt. Warden/"Mad" Welsh*

Jones's introductory "Note" to *Whistle* confirms what one would have guessed—"Mad" Welsh is Milt Warden in combat. Peter Jones writes that "the consistently successful soldiers of *The Thin Red Line* have in common some interest that overrides the immediate fact of daily combat" and that "Welsh is fueled by gin and his endless contempt for everybody around him. . . ."[8] Gin is a major support for Welsh, but his "endless contempt" is primarily a means of masking, and attempting to repress, his concern for the men of Charlie Company. The mask is successful, and Welsh is a mystery to everyone around him, including Bugger Stein, his first commanding officer:

Welsh was mad. He was insane. Truly a real madman, and Stein never had understood him. He had no respect for anything or anybody. But it didn't really matter. Stein could afford to overlook his impertinences because he was so good at his job. (p. 11)

Like Milt Warden, "Mad" Welsh is "a good soldier." He is not yet truly "mad," however. Inwardly, Welsh does still care, and that concern is reflected in various covert ways and in one dramatically overt instance. Still he is fighting to deny the feeling, emotional side of his self; and such a struggle can only lead to madness (Sergeant Mart Winch, the Warden-Welsh figure in *Whistle*, does ultimately collapse into insanity).

Although Welsh has never been in combat, he has "pretty well lost his belief in, as well as his awe of, the mystique of human combat" (p. 22) before arriving on Guadalcanal. He is sardonically amused at himself because he had "outsmarted the nation" (p. 23) by enlisting in the army during the depression and is about to pay for his cleverness. He speaks contemptuously of such abstracts as "politics," "religion," "ideals and integrity," and "most of all, human virtue," and maintains that he believes only in "Property" (p. 23). Welsh does not attempt to acquire property himself; he simply recognizes that the human lust for territory is what controls governments and inspires wars. World War II is merely the most large-scale confrontation over "Property" thus far in human history. He has perfected the same intimidating grin which Warden uses to such great effect. Still, he is concerned about the young men of Charlie Company who are not prepared for the horrors they are about to face. To disguise that concern, he goes out of his way to humiliate them over petty matters; he is especially cruel in his treatment of Fife, his clerk and the most obviously unprepared soldier in the company.

In various ways, his concern does periodically become obvious to the reader, if not to the novel's other enlisted men. The company is about to go into combat on "The Dancing Elephant" as Welsh sees "... a whole stack of unopened handgrenade cases on the edge of the hill, and simultaneously realized somebody had fucked up somewhere along the line in not issuing grenades to C-for-Charlie" (p. 134). He immediately decides to issue the grenades himself by tossing them to the crowd of soldiers, parodying a forward passer in football, "Eggs! Eggs! Footballs! Footballs! Sammy Baugh! Sid Luckman! Rah rah rah! Who wants footballs! Bronco Nagurski!" (p. 135) By this act, Welsh has seen to it that the men do not go into battle lacking full equipment without dramatizing to them the incompetence of their own army bureaucracy. He takes this incompetence for granted; but understands that, in the present situation, such recognition is the last thing the men need. Of course, the soldiers of Charlie Company merely perceive this incident as one more example of Welsh's craziness. Ironically, it is appreciated only by a group of observing officers. Like Warden, Welsh does not care for the respect of officers.

After one particularly rough verbal assault on Fife, the sergeant is challenged by Mess Sergeant Storm, who asks why he can't occasionally be kind to the clerk. Welsh answers: " 'Because I don't mean to wind up playin nursemaid and havin to mother some kid, that's why . . .' " (p. 145). For Welsh, who inwardly does care so much, there is no possible middle ground between harrassing Fife and attempting to protect him. The novel's major irony is that he finally does "protect" Fife in the most significant of ways. When the young man is attempting to justify the possibility of accepting evacuation from combat at the end of the novel, Welsh makes him so angry that he immediately takes the chance to leave. Fife never comprehends what his sergeant has done for him.

The moment in which "Mad" Welsh's emotional, caring side cannot be controlled comes in one of the novel's most brutal scenes. Seemingly out of reach of any possible aid because of concentrated Japanese machine gun fire, a soldier named Tella lies hideously wounded. Hit in the stomach, he screams constantly, while attempting to hold in his intestines. Finally, a medic rushes out into the Japanese fire to give Tella morphine; but, just as he is about to insert the needle of the syrette into the wounded man's arm, he is killed and Tella is wounded again. Still, Tella does not die, and his screams increase and eat away at the nerves of the other soldiers. The situation seems truly hopeless, since the fate of the medic has just proved that no one can possibly reach Tella.

Suddenly Welsh leaps out from cover and rushes toward the wounded man. The sergeant's thoughts and actions during and after this spontaneous rescue mission reveal much about his character: "A curious ecstasy had gripped him. He was the target, the sole target. At last it was all out in the open. The truth had at last come out. He had always known it" (p. 241). Welsh is luxuriating in the paranoia which both makes him "a good soldier" and which must inevitably destroy him. Upon reaching Tella, the sergeant tells him to " 'stop that yelling' " because " 'it aint dignified' " (p. 243). Instinctively, his uncaring *persona* has asserted itself for a moment; but then he attempts to lift the wounded man and carry him to safety. The effort is hopeless, and Welsh can only give Tella all the morphine syrettes he can find on the medic's body. When he regains safety, Bugger Stein praises him and promises recommendation for the Silver Star. Welsh explodes:

"If you say one word to thank me, I will punch you square in the nose. . . . And if you ever so much as mention me in your fucking Orders, I will resign my rating two minutes after, and leave you to run this pore, busted-up outfit by yourself. . . ." (p. 245)

Welsh is frightened by what he has done—attempting to rescue Tella represented an open capitulation to his inner caring self, and such capitulation can only lead to defeat and chaos. He cannot possibly save everyone, in fact not anyone for certain.

Brooding on the incident later, he reaches an uneasy inner peace about it: ". . . Some penancemaking, selfdestructive thing in his nature . . . had made him go after Tella [and] would almost certainly make him liable to such acts in future, and [he] had accepted that" (p. 375). However, the acceptance is neither that easy nor that total. Welsh's most revealing moment comes during a lull in the battle for "The Giant Boiled Shrimp." In his foxhole on the side of a mountain, he stares at all he can see, including the head of "The Dancing Elephant" where so many deaths have just occurred, and is suddenly reminded of ". . . one of those sixteenth century bathtubs he had seen pictures of" (p. 409).

Imagining himself luxuriating in such a bath, he undergoes a series of realizations about himself. Admitting that a part of him actually likes all the ugliness and horror of combat, he immediately confronts his pity and concern for Fife. Finally, he faces the inevitable result of the uncaring exterior he has adopted:

There were times, moments, when Welsh realized that he was quite mad. Like: Three cherries on the same stem = George Washington. Two no, never. Three yes, always. Who would understand that if he told them? If he *dared* tell them. (p. 411)

Welsh knows that such "moments" will someday become a permanent state of being.

After the Guadalcanal campaign ends, Welsh, who has contracted malaria, becomes seriously ill, is hospitalized, and is offered evacuation himself. He refuses, and returns to his company where he "continued to recommend to everybody, smiling his sly, mad smile, that they try their damnedest to get themselves evacuated while there was still time" (p. 483). A number of factors make him feel that he cannot leave, even though it is obviously the sane thing to do. He is indispensable to the company where he "continued to recommend to everybody, smiling has long since cut himself off from his family; and, if he were sent home disabled, "his enemies the government" would commit him to a veterans' hospital run by "pipsqueak, hard-jawed Alexander-the-greats of doctors" (pp. 202–203). Welsh, like Warden, is so completely the soldier that no other identity is possible for him, least of all that of an invalid (the reality of precisely this fate is a key factor in the collapse of *Whistle's* Winch into insanity).

III *Corporal Fife*

Corporal Geoffrey Fife is never a total soldier, primarily because he is unable to adjust to the requisite sacrifice of self. Initially sensitive and idealistic in a manner quite similar to Crane's Henry Fleming, he does undergo some key stages in the evolution of a soldier. He even luxuriates in killing at the novel's end; still, he cannot rid himself of the crippling awareness of

self. During the landing on Guadalcanal, Fife, "who loved humanity," is shocked that such a bloody, brutal endeavor as war
is discharged "like a regular business" (p. 37). The impersonal
aspect of the "regulated business venture" in which men will
die seems "immoral" to him largely because it emphasizes his
own "unimportance" and "powerlessness" (p. 40). Throughout
the novel, Fife is incapable of separating abstract ethical judg-
ments from concern for his own safety.

To compensate for his fear of death and his constant humiliation by Welsh, Fife bullies his own subordinate, Bead. Once,
after berating Bead, Fife laments that " 'you just can't treat them
decent...'" (p. 58). Attempting to echo Welsh, the corporal is
constructing an external mask of toughness. Need for such a
mask intensifies after Fife agrees to homosexual acts with Bead.
Afterward his treatment of Bead is even more harsh for reasons
he can't comprehend: "... His reaction was an emotional response
he could neither understand nor control" (p. 123). Jones is not
making any comment about homosexuality *per se* in the Fife-Bead
relationship. Instead, he is underscoring the confusion in Fife's
mind, as well as the repressed sexuality inevitably present in
combat soldiers.

During the long march to battle on "The Elephant's Head,"
Fife explodes verbally at Stein, his commanding officer. Stein
is merely offering encouragement to the corporal and receives
an hysterical outburst in response. The officer is not totally surprised; because, after observing the young corporal for some
time, he has decided that Fife is "... a case of arrested adolescence" like "so many" in the American army (p. 113). One remembers, of course, Crane's trick of constantly referring to
Fleming as "the youth" to stress his immaturity. Stein had previously attempted to persuade Fife to apply for a commission in
the Administrative School "... because given Fife's personality
as Stein read it, Stein did not believe Fife would make a good
infantry officer" (p. 114). While the corporal's pride would not
permit him to accept such an offer, his superior's evaluation was
accurate.

After a brief period of pride in having confronted Stein, Fife
is immediately plunged into a dark depression arising from a
certainty that he will die soon in battle and everything, including

his old idealism, is therefore "pointless" (p. 117). While such a vision of the meaninglessness of all things parallels Welsh's philosophy, Fife is unable simply to accept it. The idea becomes an emotional rack on which he tortures himself for the rest of the novel.

Parallels between Fife and Henry Fleming intensify when the corporal enters combat. On the ground crawling toward "The Elephant's Head," Fife is astonished to discover all the other men running upright and well ahead of him. He then makes one of his several "heroic decisions." He stands up because "terrified as he was of standing up and being shot at by some invisible party, he was more terrified of being accused for his cowardice" (p. 140). Simply unable to maintain a mask of heroism, he soon adopts the role of the "honest coward," bragging endlessly about how frightened he has been. Locked in the prison of self, Fife cannot comprehend that everyone has been frightened—he is certain that fear has possessed only him. If he cannot be a hero, he will be a buffoon, since his ego allows no middle ground.

A crucial aspect of Fife's inner struggle comes when Bead, his target of harrassment and sexual partner, is killed. Fife attends the dying man. When Bead asks the corporal to take his hand, Fife hesitates for a moment out of fear of being revealed as a homosexual and is instantly overcome by guilt toward the man dying. After Bead's death, the corporal's pity switches to himself:

This was war? There was no superior test of strength here, no superb swordmanship, no bellowing Viking heroism, no expert marks-manship. This was only numbers. He was being killed for numbers. (p. 252)

Like Henry Fleming, Fife has imagined war as a gallant, heroic thing and is dismayed at the grim anonymity of modern mass combat. Edmond L. Volpe's insights into *The Thin Red Line* are as sound as his analysis of *From Here to Eternity*. Calling the combat novel "technically" Jones's best work, he argues that its main theme is the supreme power of "chance" which makes such abstractions as "heroism" and "cowardice" meaningless.

Chance also denies moral values and leads inexorably to brutal treatment of Japanese prisoners.[9]

Fife is then wounded himself by a mortar fragment and, after regaining sufficient consciousness, is delighted that he can walk away from the conflict without fear of being called a coward. On the way back to the hospital, he passes a dead boy in a stretcher who has been hit a second—fatal—time on the way to seeming safety: "Suddenly he wanted to shout at the whole world of men: 'Look what you *human beings* have done to this boy who might have been me! Yes, *me*, you *human beings!*'" (p. 346). He is dismayed to discover at the hospital that his wound is not serious enough to keep him out of action and then incurs the wrath of the officer-surgeon by pleading helplessness on the grounds of having lost his glasses.

After making a confession of cowardice to the unresponsive Mess Sergeant Storm, Fife returns to his company only to discover that his former clerk's job has been given by Welsh to someone else. Outraged, he challenges Welsh who answers that Fife should have been able to get himself evacuated. At this point, the corporal's mind is a chaos of conflicting emotions, and he chooses transfer to a rifle company merely to spite Welsh. Not only is he now back in combat, but he has lost the relative safety of a rear echelon clerical position. Fife has now evolved to a significant degree; he no longer views mankind with any idealism, and, out of necessity, he no longer crawls into battle. However, he is still tortured by fears, including a new one: "and the worst thing in his mind was that he might not be able to kill some Japanese or other who confronted him, and who, therefore, would kill him" (p. 438). The kind of hand-to-hand combat so basic to the Guadalcanal campaign seems to Fife a "primitive" thing beyond endurance or simple comprehension.

However, when the battle for the "Giant Boiled Shrimp" turns into an unexpected anticlimax and Charlie Company finds itself inside the final Japanese stronghold of Boola Boola village: "Corporal Fife scampered along . . . shooting every Japanese he could see, filled with both terror and elation to a point where he could not separate one from the other" (p. 449). Like Henry Fleming, Fife is never able to anticipate his reactions in any given encounter because he attempts to evaluate combat from the perspective of a rational self. In addition, Fife experiences for the first time in Boola Boola village what Jones calls "combat numbness," a temporary loss of ego which is essential for successful hand-to-hand combat. He does not know, like the others, that the "numbness" is only a temporary state and is convinced momentarily that he has evolved into a "real soldier." Drunk on this illusion, he later picks a fistfight with the clerk who replaced him as Welsh's subordinate and is generally belligerent.

When the "numbness" does go away, it is not long before Fife "rediscover[s] his cowardice" and engages in more fights desperately attempting to assert his manhood (pp. 485–86). At this point, "chance" steps in to help him. He reinjures an ankle initially hurt in high school football and, after some encouragement, reports it to the same officer-surgeon who earlier sent him back to his company. This time, he is offered evacuation—the doctor even promises him new eyeglasses. Fife considers staying; but, after Welsh insults him one last time, he accepts the doctor's offer. Fife does "evolve" to the point that he temporarily experiences combat "numbness" and even joins in the lust of killing the enemy. However, like Henry Fleming, he can repress belief in his own uniqueness only temporarily. Sometimes convinced that he is a coward and confident at other moments that he is "a real soldier," he never comprehends the role of "chance" in his reactions. In *Whistle*, Sergeant Marion Landers is a continuation of the Fife characterization; and he commits suicide out of despair at the loss of his idealism and irrational guilt over his behavior in combat.

IV   *Others of Company C*

It is through the character of Private John Bell that Jones most overtly explores two of the novel's major themes: the phenomenon of combat "numbness" and the effect of repressed sexuality on the man in combat. Bell is a mysterious figure to the rest of Charlie Company because it is generally known that he was once a commissioned officer. Fife discovers that Bell renounced his commission because of his wife. A First Lieutenant in the Corps of Engineers, he had been sent with his wife to the Philippines. Once there, Bell was ordered into the jungle to work on a dam. Tormented by the fact that his wife had to remain in Manila ("'You know what those pre-war officers' clubs were like . . .'") (p. 27), he resigned. Outraged, the army promised Bell that he would never get a commission again and that he would be drafted into the infantry. He feels surprisingly little bitterness about this treatment ("'It's their way of life, you know. And I was thumbing my nose at it...'") (p. 28); but he is tormented by sexual need for his wife, Marty, and fear that she is not being faithful to him. Increasingly, Bell becomes obsessed with Marty as he moves closer to combat; Peter G. Jones analyzes the significance of this obsession: "When men die around him in battle Bell thinks of his wife's marvelous body; this is the reaction of a healthy subconscious, feeding images of life to the threatened organism."[10]

Marty's role as Bell's source of subconscious health is clearly developed on the patrol which discovers the bloody American shirt and the mass Japanese grave. While staring at the shirt, Bell experiences a frightening hallucination:

He was both standing upright wearing that pierced, lifesoaked shirt and at the same time lying pierced and lifesoaked himself on the ground after having flung it away from him, while somewhere up behind him out of eye range he could nevertheless see a weird, transcendental image of his wife Marty's head and shoulders superimposed among the foliage gloom of the trees looking down at the two images sadly. (p. 65)

This surreal vision reinforces Bell's certainty of Marty's inevitable infidelity while, at the same time, sexually arousing him.

Later, during the battle for "The Dancing Elephant," he comforts himself with the superstition that ". . . if he and Marty both remained true to each other, he could make it back with his genitals intact" (p. 149). Bell continually surprises himself by volunteering for dangerous patrols and for a time cannot comprehend this "peculiar masochistic, self-destructive quality in himself." Then he remembers that, once as a child, he had been hiking in the woods when he discovered farmers at work in their fields just across a gravel road from where he stood. Then a car came, and a man and three women stopped to talk to some of the farmers. Retreating, he stripped naked and, leaving his clothes where he could not possibly retrieve them in time if discovered, returned to where he had first seen the farmers, hid behind a screen of leaves, and masturbated. The memory is a "revelation" to Bell: he comprehends that his volunteering is "... as sexual, and in much the same way, as his childhood incident of the gravelled road" (p. 276).

Later, Bell, suffering from malaria, is brooding about Marty's almost certain unfaithfulness when he falls asleep and has a nightmare—he is in a hospital watching his wife give birth and the baby is black; then he turns away in horror; and, when he looks back, the baby is not black, but Japanese wearing a "tiny, bent up Imperial Army forage cap, with a tiny, baby iron star" (p. 397). Awake, Bell attempts to analyze the dream and is most concerned about the fact that it sexually excited him. He concludes that his excitement comes from "the lascivious sensuality of knowing . . . he was cuckold," as contrasted to the unbearable pain of uncertainty (p. 399). To Bell's mind, the war will be to blame if he loses Marty; and the image of her giving birth to a baby looking like a tiny Japanese soldier symbolizes the worst that he fears.

Bell does ultimately receive a "Dear John" letter from Marty on the same day he is given a new commission as a First Lieutenant of Infantry. He has received that second commission which the army promised him he would never get. However, Marty is now lost to him; and he has nothing meaningful left. He gave up a relatively safe commission to protect their relationship and wound up in the infantry. Now, having lived through hideous experiences, he becomes an officer again when such a position can only reinforce the bitter irony of his loss.

Bell's intellectualism allows him to comprehend each step in his personal soldier's evolution. Early in the novel, he is enraged to think he might actually get hit by Japanese machine gun fire, ". . . slain not as an individual but by sheer statistical probability. . . . Mathematics! Mathematics! Algebra! Geometry!" (p. 189). Soon, however, one part of his mind accepts the inevitability of his death:

Some men would survive, but no *one* individual man *could* survive . . .

The whole thing was too vast, too complicated, too technological for any individual man to count in it. Only collections of men counted, only communities of men, only *numbers* of men. (p. 230)

That he still clings to the memory of Marty as a "talisman" does not represent an aesthetic contradiction on Jones's part, because much of the evolution of a soldier is inherently schizophrenic.

When the "combat numbness" hits him, he understands that ". . . instead of impairing his ability to function, it enhanced it, this sense of no longer feeling human." He whistles to himself ". . . a song called *I Am an Automaton* to the tune of *God Bless America*" (p. 267). He is concerned, however, about the possibility of becoming permanently "brutalized." Even between battles when the "numbness" seems to go away, Bell is certain that none of them "could really become the same again." He knows that only "long years after the war was done" could the men who fought it "avoid admitting they had once seen something animal within themselves that terrified them" (p. 339). After a time, he speculates, temporary lapses into animalism must inevitably become "a permanent state" (p. 452).

Not clearly so cerebral as Bell, Pfc. Don Doll undergoes the most total evolution of any of the novel's characters. In fact, Peter G. Jones argues: "The central figure of this novel is Don Doll. . . . His development follows exactly the plot's action and movement."[11] While it seems inaccurate to view anyone except the cumulative entity of Charlie Company as a "central figure," the critic's perception that Doll's characterization parallels the novel's structure is sound. Doll is first shown on the ship which will shortly put him on a landing craft at Guadalcanal. In an echo of Private Richard Mast, he is trying to steal a pistol as a protective "talisman." He has also made a recent discovery:

Nobody was really what he pretended to be. It was as if everybody made up a fiction story about himself, and then he just pretended to everybody that that was what he was. And everybody believed him, or at least accepted his fiction story. (p. 13)

The inspiration for this insight was a fistfight Doll had with one of the biggest and meanest men in the company. After they had battled on even terms, Doll suddenly realized that his opponent "was just as nervous about having the fight as he was, and did not really want to fight any more than he did . . ." (p. 14).

"Mad" Welsh intuitively understands Doll's need for the pistol and his sudden discovery about "fiction stories" and is almost as contemptuous of Doll as he is of Fife. However, Doll will move much further along the road to becoming a soldier than the idealistic corporal partially because he realizes everyone puts up a fake front. He never feels that only he is afraid, and he understands that by acting brave he will seem brave to others. Also, it isn't long before he comprehends the ineffectuality of his pistol in the face of modern warfare's technological sophistication.

During night air raids which completely terrify Fife, Doll forces himself to stand up in his foxhole when the bombs start exploding. Thus, he believes that he has proven himself "invulnerable" and finds that ". . . he could convince everybody he had not been afraid" (pp. 89–90). Combat shatters his sense of invulnerability; but, upon killing his first Japanese, he makes still another discovery:

Doll felt guilty. He couldn't help it. He had killed a human being, a man. He had done the most horrible thing a human could do, worse than rape even. . . . That was where the pleasure came. Nobody could do anything to him for it. He had gotten by with murder. (p. 198)

The comparison to rape makes it clear that Doll is experiencing another aspect of what Jones considered the essentially sexual response Bell had articulated to himself. Childhood sexual guilt, intensified by legalized "murder," helps transform Don Doll into an effective soldier.

Spurred on by this discovery, Doll begins to compete for dangerous assignments; and another motivation is introduced. Soon he and Pfc. Charlie Dale are engaged in a rivalry. Dale is inspired to volunteering by cold ambition; Doll is spurred on by a complexity of factors including the thrill of danger and resentment of the praise his rival receives from officers. On one mission, Doll, through a fortuitous combination of hysteria, instinct, and utilization of the "fiction story" concept, becomes a "hero." Part

of a volunteer platoon led by Captain John Gaff, he finds himself
pinned down by machine gun fire. He acts spontaneously and
irrationally:

Sweating, lying pressed flat in an ectasy of panic, terror, fear, and
cowardice, Doll simply could not stand it any longer. . . . Wailing over
and over in a high falsetto the one word "Mother! Mother!" . . . he
leaped to his feet and began to run straight at the Japanese emplacement. . . . (p. 272)

He empties his rifle, begins firing his pistol, and finally lobs a
grenade at the emplacement. When his pistol stops firing, he
realizes where he is and "luckily" runs in the direction of a protective ledge. As he runs, "a dark round fizzing object" falls in
front of him and he "automatically" kicks it away (pp. 272–73).
    Immediately afterward, Doll feels shame at having lost con-
trol; however, Gaff congratulates him on his courage and
"presence of mind" to run toward the ledge. The private then
utilizes an effective variation of his "fiction story" concept—he
modestly admits to having been frightened, but allows the im-
pression to remain that all his actions were rationally planned.
In the context of what he has just done, no one will believe his
confession of fear.
    By the end of the novel, the excitement of killing with im-
munity and constant praise from his superiors allows Doll to
develop a protective psychological armor impossible for Fife—
between battles, he simply never thinks about the possibility of
being killed. The new feeling isn't quite the same as his old one
of "invulnerability." He has been promoted to platoon guide and
senses the respect which officers and enlisted men alike have for
him. For different reasons, Doll, like Welsh, enjoys combat and
he is more than competent in it. He is almost forced into a painful
self-realization by an embarrassing incident after the capture of
"The Giant Boiled Shrimp" and Boola Boola village. During
combat, Doll has been sexually aroused by the feminine build
of Pfc. Carrie Arbre. In a drunken orgy celebrating the victory,
Doll makes a sexual advance to Arbre. He wishes the private to
accept buggery; but Arbre misunderstands and, unbuttoning his
pants, offers Doll oral gratification. The platoon guide is shocked

because, in his mind, what the private proposes is "queer" and what he intended is not (pp. 463–65). Doll has come close to comprehending the importance of repressed sexuality to his abilities as a soldier; however, the "protective" part of his mind blocks such an epiphany. In contrast to Bell, much of Doll's success in combat is due to his noncerebral nature. Since he changes from a boy attempting to steal a pistol as a protective "talisman" to an effective noncommissioned officer, Doll's "evolution" is the most completely developed in the novel.

Of the remaining characters, Mess Sergeant Storm and Private Witt are especially intriguing because Jones, in *Whistle*'s "Introductory Note," asserts that they correspond to Maylon Stark and Prewitt in *From Here to Eternity*. The Stark-Storm figure is the least convincing of the three "characters" Jones carries through each volume of his trilogy. It is not until the mess sergeant emerges as John Strange in *Whistle* that the main intentions behind the creation become clear. Essentially, Stark-Storm-Strange is intended as a direct contrast to Warden-Welsh-Winch. The top sergeant creates a facade of unconcern because he does care so much; the mess sergeant seems compassionate and devoted and is, thus, well-liked, but really does not feel strong emotion.

In *The Thin Red Line*, Storm's relationship with Welsh is described as an "armed truce":

Storm did his job and did it well, and Welsh left him alone. And Storm was aware that as long as he did his job well, Welsh would continue to leave him alone. That was enough for Storm. If Welsh wanted to be crazy, that was his own business. (p. 31)

It is also "enough" for Storm to protest periodically against Welsh's rough treatment of Fife knowing that nothing will change. Significantly, when Fife makes his desperate "confession of fear" to Storm in the hospital, the mess sergeant is uncomprehending and barely interested.

Still, Storm "does his job" more than "well"; he lets nothing prevent him from getting adequate food to Charlie Company: "Nobody'd ever say Storm didn't feed his people" (p. 53). After one slip, the mess sergeant refuses to do more than his job, however. Allowing himself to get swept into the heat of combat, he receives a hand wound and then is sent to the hospital for examination. On the way to safety, he helps escort some Japanese prisoners and participates in sadistic treatment of them. Everything about the combat experiences bothers Storm. He realizes the brutalization of the prisoners was a result of "that state of numbness," but still wonders if he is "so decent after all." Moreover, he is prepared to use his wound to get evacuated:

. . . he who had always believed in never letting a friend down, was here preparing to try and use his hand to get him out of the company, out of the Battalion, out of the whole fucking combat zone. And what was more, he knew it was the only sane thing to do. (p. 361)

One is meant to contrast this reaction with Welsh's refusal to leave, while telling everyone else to get evacuated. The hand injury does finally allow Storm to escape.

Before leaving, however, he returns to his company, if not to combat. Vowing to feed his men one good meal a day to relieve his guilt for avoiding combat, he becomes separated from his company. Initially he despairs that "modern war, after first wounding him, had finally caught up with [him] . . . in his work" (p. 427). Then he decides to cook all the hot food he can and distribute it to whatever troops pass, even if they are not from Charlie Company. There are effective symbolic overtones in this scene of Storm, the inwardly noncaring Christ figure, feeding "multitudes."

As the condensation of the name may have been intended to indicate, Witt is Prewitt reduced to an almost animal level. The idealism for all "underdogs" is gone, as well as the association with art. What is left is the stubborn "bolshevik" with a self-destructive loyalty to his company. The reader first meets Witt through Fife. The "bolshevik, . . . a small, thin, Breathitt County Kentucky boy, an old Regular, a former Regimental boxer" (p. 100), has been transferred out of Charlie Company by Stein and Welsh to Cannon Company, a new outfit made up of "the worst drunkards, the worst homosexuals, and worst troublemakers." Witt hates Welsh fanatically, but loves Charlie Company

("It's my compny") (p. 104) and periodically sneaks back to visit it. On one such visit, Fife pleads with him to request a retransfer from Stein. Witt angrily refuses (" '. . . I won't go to them and beg them. . . .' ") (p. 105) and, when Fife corrects his pronunciation of the word *travesty*, he becomes furious with his former friend. His "Kentucky code" will not allow him to hit Fife without warning, but he abruptly orders the corporal to return to his company.

For the rest of the novel, Witt switches back and forth from Charlie Company to Cannon Company. Whenever the fighting becomes especially deadly, he reappears in the midst of his old outfit and volunteers for the most dangerous patrols. Fife is incredulous at this behavior:

For a man to want to come back into a forward rifle company in the midst of attack was simply incomprehensible to him. In a way, though, it was very romantic. Like something out of Kipling. Or *Beau Geste*. (p. 208)

Whenever an officer makes a particularly stupid decision needlessly endangering the men, Witt returns to Cannon Company.

During the times in which he is fighting with Charlie Company, he is concerned with offering a kind of leadership which might save such men as "that punk kid Fife" (p. 264). Instinctively, he sees in John Bell a capacity of leadership equal to his own. After the successful struggle for "The Dancing Elephant," Witt is outraged to discover first that Bugger Stein had offered a plan of attack which would have saved the lives of countless men to his superior, Lt. Colonel Tall, only to have it rejected. For the first time, Witt feels a deep loyalty to Stein and does ask to come back permanently to Charlie Company, even revealing to Stein his "secret" desire to "*save* somebody" (p. 314). However, Tall soon relieves Stein of command; and Witt, in outrage, returns to Cannon Company.

Later, when he learns that his old unit is again deeply engaged in battle and that Tall himself has been promoted, he makes an incredible "odyssey" to rejoin them. On the way, he meets Storm, who asks why he is attempting such an ordeal. The Kentuckian can hardly understand the question: " 'It's the company, aint it?' "

(p. 429). He reaches Charlie Company just in time to volunteer for a roadblock patrol which turns out to be a suicide mission which only he and Bell survive. Before volunteering, he tells the new commander, Lieutenant "Brass" Band, what an insane idea the patrol is; afterward, he immediately goes up to Band and berates him: "... I hope yore happy! I love this compny bettr'n anything, but I wouldn't serve in no outfit commanded by a son of a bitch like you! If they ever kill you or get rid of you, I might come back" (p. 446). When Band is replaced, Witt returns again and, this time, does officially transfer back into the company.

Jones is consistent with his vision in the characterization of Witt. Robert E. Lee Prewitt's idealistic commitment to all underdogs (Witt dislikes blacks, for instance) and his artistic ego had no place in combat. Still, one feels that Jones had poured so much emotional intensity into the initial creation of Prewitt that he had little to add to the characterization in this novel and in *Whistle*. It is also possible that, as Jones grew older, he became more comfortable with the Warden-Welsh figure than with his "romantic bolshevik."

All of these men and many others who are characterized in ironic detail are part of the main character of *The Thin Red Line* —the enlisted men of C-for-Charlie Company. As Peter G. Jones points out, their officers are almost a liability to them. Bugger Stein is well intentioned but ineffectual; "Brass" Band becomes almost insane with personal ambition; and their third commanding officer, Captain Bosche, promises them total support and lets them down at the first crisis. Lieutenant Colonel Tall, reminiscent of Dynamite Holmes, is coldly and rationally self-serving. Discussion of the novel's satire of officers would not be complete without mention of the aptly named Captain John B. Gaff. Leading a group of volunteers on an especially dangerous mission, Gaff makes a bid for an unforgettable line as they are about to expose themselves to fire and says: " 'Well, fellows, this is where we separate the men from the boys ... the sheep from the goats ... ' " (p. 293). The respect the men have previously had for Gaff disappears instantly. Still, the line serves Gaff well—he receives the Medal of Honor and is sent home to sell war bonds. His unfortunate line becomes "a national slogan" and is the source of two hit songs (p. 493).

The novel brilliantly depicts the sacrifice of self that the effective combat soldier must make:

Their systems pumped full of adrenaline to constrict the peripheral blood vessels, elevate the blood pressure, make the heart beat more rapidly, and aid coagulation; they were about as near to automatons without courage or cowardice as flesh and blood can get. Numbly, they did the necessary. (p. 296)

The men of Charlie Company make that sacrifice, and the novel ends with those still alive preparing to invade another island, New Georgia. They are marching toward the waiting LCIs when they pass a man perching on a wrecked Japanese barge eating an apple. They pass on, and Mad Welsh chuckles that he doesn't need apples because he has his gin. All he hopes is that the numbness will "become a permanent and mercifully blissful state" (pp. 494–95). Welsh knows that, even if most of the men survive New Georgia, there will be another island and another and another. The boy eating the apple apparently does not have such knowledge; nor do the rest of Charlie Company, at least not to the degree Welsh does. But, if they live, they will learn it. In an excellent review, Maxwell Geismar summarizes the source of the novel's stunning effect:

... The whole impact of "The Thin Red Line" ... is just that Company C must go back into the battle line again. The whole unbearable and monstrous ordeal must be undergone once more.[12]

The symbolism in this last scene is subtly effective. What Welsh comprehends goes beyond good and evil and perhaps beyond the possibility of communication to others. The last line of the novel would seems to state the impossibility of communicating such bitter wisdom: "One day one of their number would write a book about all this, but none of them would believe it, because none of them would remember it that way" (p. 495).

The Thin Red Line is a brilliantly conceived and powerfully executed novel. It is often called "the best combat novel of World War II," and it did much in 1962 to restore Jones's reputation after *Some Came Running*. Already, he had the concept of the third volume of his army trilogy in mind. Sadly, *Whistle* was not to be published until after his death sixteen years later. In fact, the only truly important Jones books to appear between *The Thin Red Line* and the author's death were *The Ice-Cream Headache* (1968) and the 1975 analysis of military art, *WWII*. Two long novels, *Go to the Widow-Maker* and *The Merry Month of May*, exhibit many of the same weaknesses as *Some Came Running*.

CHAPTER 6

Two Studies of American Sexual Maladjustment: Go to the Widow-Maker and The Merry Month of May

IN *Go to the Widow-Maker* (1967) and *The Merry Month of May* (1971), Jones attempted long novels exploring his theme of the sexual maladjustment of the American male, a motif which had been dominant in *Some Came Running* as well as many of his short stories. Both of these late novels provide a foreground of intense action to which the sexual maladjustment theme more or less directly relates. The type of action differs greatly in the two works, however. Much of *Go to the Widow-Maker* focuses on a male-dominated world of skin diving in which proper observation of ritual is valued as a test of fitness. In *The Merry Month of May*, the Paris student rebellion of the late 1960s provides the foreground of action. Both novels are failures, although for slightly different reasons.

I A Skin-diving Epic

Jones was a serious skin diver; and *Go to the Widow-Maker* belongs to a school of American fiction represented most notably by Ernest Hemingway in which devotion to and proper observation of the rules of a physical activity make spiritual healing possible. Bullfighting is a sacred activity to Jake Barnes; and even Brett Ashley decides not "to be a bitch" and spoil the young bullfighter, Pedro Romero. Nick Adams begins to regain his self-confidence by rigidly observing the rules of fishing in the "Big

Two-Hearted River." Jones's contention for the advancement of
a book like *Go to the Widow-Maker* over the Hemingway "novel
of ritualistic action" was that it reflects a definite awareness that
this kind of world is a refuge for psychologically inadequate
males. The Hemingway glorification of escape to physical ritual
is "romantic" and seemingly unaware of its full implications;
Jones's book is an honest statement of perverted American sexual
mores.

Like *Some Came Running*, *Go to the Widow-Maker* is undoubtedly an honest book. However, Jones had difficulty in
learning that honesty alone does not equal art. In fact, Seymour
Krim has pointed out that *Go to the Widow-Maker* is a little more
than just honest—it is embarrassingly self-revelatory:

He [Jones] never spoke about Lowney Handy, the woman who
loved him and ran the Midwest writers' colony that sponsored him
while he hammered out *Eternity* and *Some Came Running*. Tom
Chamales, the war novelist who had killed men with his hands while
in the OSS, had a love/hate relationship with Jones, which led to
his sleeping with Mrs. Handy as revenge. Jones put it into *Go to the
Widow-Maker*.[1]

Accepting Krim's biographical reading, the fictional counterparts
of Jones, Mrs. Handy, and Chamales (Ron Grant, Carol Abernathy, and Doug Ismaileh) represent three of the most un-
pleasantly drawn characters in contemporary American fiction.

However, such a strictly autobiographical reading makes an
unnaturally limiting approach to Jones's novel. He is attempting
to interrelate two distinct themes and draw a final statement from
them. One group of characters in the novel—Doug Ismaileh; Al
Bonham, Ron Grant's skin diving teacher; assorted business entre-
preneurs; and Carol Abernathy—represent, in differing ways, the
perversion of ideal male-female relationships, and sexuality itself.
In contrast, Grant's ideal girl, Lucky Videndi, is struggling to
attain a healthy and liberating sexuality for herself and her lover.
Lucky has her own problems of adjustment: she suffers from
Oedipal attachment to her father, has been through a period of
almost legendary sexual promiscuity before meeting Grant, and
feels much guilt because of this past. However, one is meant to

feel that her essential sexual integrity is intact. At any rate, Ron is torn between the debasers of sexuality and Lucky for much of the novel.

Related to this theme is Jones's characterization of the world of skin diving as the last escape of individual man from the "bureaucratized, technological" postwar world. A fatalistic certainty that even the sea itself will inevitably be transformed into a bureaucratic wasteland is occasionally expressed in the novel. Thus Ron Grant, playwright and individualist, wishes to explore this "last frontier" as much as possible before it too is destroyed by modern technology. Symbolically, Jones attempts to create links between the freedom of skin diving and the beauty of sexual health on the one hand, and between debased sexuality and technological sterility on the other. Still, as his conversation with Styron in *Esquire* makes clear, escape into a world of romantic freedom necessarily results in the release of dangerous, chaotic "animalism."

The novel fails largely because it is difficult to like or even to believe in its sympathetic characters. Ron Grant appears so ego-centered throughout that one can hardly care about his spiritual redemption by Lucky Videndi and the sea. Carrying so much symbolic weight, Lucky hardly seems plausible as a character. Moreover, the charge of overwriting so often made against Jones is accurate for this novel, whose negative characters are almost totally depersonalized by Jones's anger and bitterness. Carol Abernathy is described so often as a witchlike figure that one has much difficulty adjusting when Jones attempts to give her more dimension as a desperate and frightened woman; and the macho overtones, primarily associated with Al Bonham, are stated so boldly that one has to stop and catch a breath when they are all discarded in Ron Grant's final epiphany.

Last, Jones has in the sea several quite obvious levels of symbolism, which he nonetheless fails to organize into an aesthetically coherent statement. The sea, as the origin of human life, has symbolic overtones of the womb (Carol Abernathy says, " 'The Sea is the Great Mother' ") (p. 186).[2] Thus, Jones relates this level of symbolism to the novel's strongly Oedipal overtones. In addition, throughout literature, the sea has represented female sexuality; and Jones attempts to create an analogy between its freedom and the sexual beauty of Lucky Videndi. Unfortunately, it often is impossible to determine which aspect of the sea-as-female he is stressing in any given scene.

In his "Dedication," Jones states that he meant to attempt in *Go to the Widow-Maker* a "great love story." The Ron Grant–Lucky Videndi affair is meant to be just that; and Jones develops two central analogies to describe both the idealized love his characters struggle to reach, and the enormous difficulties they encounter in that struggle. Grant has always wanted a Clark Gable–Carole Lombard love affair; and, as soon as he meets Lucky, he is sure that he has found it. One finds difficulty, of course, in accepting this reference to a relationship between two movie stars as a serious metaphor for an ideal of heterosexual love. In fact, the novel contains much celebrity name-dropping, which can be defended only by saying that the novel is, in part, about the lives of public people. At any rate, Ron and Lucky face enormous difficulties in becoming Gable and Lombard and are more often compared to Hansel and Gretel lost in the woods of modern bureaucracy and their own psychological problems. The Hansel and Gretel metaphor is also aesthetically problematic, although Jones undoubtedly intends a reference to both their powerlessness and their behavior, which is often childlike.

Grant, especially, has strong tendencies toward a childish self-destructiveness which he only confronts at the end of the novel. Like so many of Jones's male characters, the playwright is over-sexed and blames this problem partially on his real first name, Decameron. This name, given him by a father who "loathed the general frigidity of the local females like Grant's mother," has resulted in a "terrible and lifelong inferiority complex" (p. 79). One is apparently supposed to believe that Grant's abnormal sexual needs are a result of this sense of inferiority. In addition, Grant is burdened by an Oedipal complex blamed on an uncaring and generally absent mother. These traumas induced in the playwright by his parents produce several forms of desperation: he wants "everybody in the world to love him" (p. 217); he yearns to "possess" all beautiful women (pp. 220–21); he has a capacity for masochistic behavior and a terror of seeming cowardly. Complicating the parental misdirection is his adult relationship with Carol Abernathy. In addition to his literary sponsor, Carol has been his surrogate mother and his lover. She has, in effect, allowed him to act out his childhood Oedipal fantasies.

Despite, or partly because of, these psychological handicaps, Grant has succeeded in becoming "with the possible exception of Tennessee Williams . . . the most famous playwright of his generation . . . [which was] probably the best generation—because of himself and one other—since O'Neill's" (p. 1). As the novel opens, Grant is attempting to learn skin diving as a means of feeling *"manly"* (p. 23) and as an attempt to escape the dominance of Carol Abernathy. The diving is, to him, a Hemingway-like test which he must meet and conquer in order to subdue the fear constantly produced by a too active imagination: "the truth was, once he was in the water he was no longer afraid; it was just all the rest of the time" (p. 411).

After establishing the playwright's motivations in learning skin diving, Jones produces a long flashback of Grant's initial meeting with Lucky Videndi and begins to analyze her kind of psychological terror. Lucky is an extremely visible New York beauty and a kind of celebrity among celebrities. Not famous herself, she is widely known and admired by the public people of New York. She is a special favorite at social gatherings because of her total honesty which invariably produces a shock effect in an atmosphere dominated by polite hypocrisy. In fact, one of Lucky's characteristics which greatly unnerves Ron Grant at times during their relationship is an almost supernatural "deep intuitive knowledge" that is associated with her capacity for complete frankness. Much like Karen Holmes in *From Here to Eternity*, Lucky has a philosophical inclination which is manifested in a fondness for revising quotations from Spinoza: "She had also twisted for her own benefit Spinoza's 'Because I love God does not mean God must love me in return' to fit more the modern age: 'Because God hates me does not mean I must love God in return'" (pp. 32–33).

However, what first strikes Grant about her is not her honesty or her philosophical insight, but her incredible beauty. Jones's prose completely fails when he describes Lucky; in an attempt to make her seem the most beautiful woman imaginable, he merely succeeds in depersonalizing her. Each part of her body is analyzed in a prose of unrelieved superlatives, and the effect is rather like what would be produced if the speaker in Marvell's "To His Coy Mistress" were totally serious. Secretly, Lucky has always resented her great beauty because it has isolated her—men want only to seduce her, and women are often jealous. Her vaunted promiscuity is, in part, an ironic result of this isolation. Not surprisingly, Grant and Lucky make love soon after they meet; and Jones's description of their intercourse is even worse than his analysis of Lucky's beauty: "It always seemed to Grant afterwards that their two naked bodies had met in the center of the room with a smack like the clap of two huge and irate, omnipotent God-hands summoning a recalcitrant Universal Waiter" (p. 56).

After his initial meeting and affair with her in New York, the playwright decides that he must have this almost supernatural beauty, and Lucky has thought of such a union even before they meet. Their mutual determination, however, is frustrated for some time because of their psychological weaknesses. Grant fears a final break with Carol Abernathy and is still determined to have his skin-diving experience. Enraged at one point, Lucky blurts out at him, " 'You talk about your search for reality in diving. . . . Reality is me. . . .' " (p. 66) She does in fact represent a saving "reality" for the playwright; however, this "reality" is terribly confused by her own psychological weaknesses. Lucky is burdened by a severe Electra complex, which of course parallels Grant's Oedipal problems. Her father saved her from a "horrible convent childhood" and first taught her the necessity of intellectual honesty (p. 99); and she often feels that he was the "only really honorable man . . . she had ever met" (p. 252). In moments of extreme panic, she cries silently, "Oh, Daddy, Daddy! Why did you have to go and die so suddenly like that and leave your Little Girl?" (p. 253)

This dependence on her dead father becomes manifested in a conflicting need to see men as "authority" figures, and to humiliate them for any control they assume. Fearing her tendency to seek "authority" in lovers, she wishes to possess them. Thus, she is given to sadomasochistic fantasies in which the male figure becomes her "slave" who must "pay" for loving her. This side of her psyche corresponds to Grant's confused need to possess all beautiful women, while still being humiliated by them. Not surprisingly, their relationship undergoes some sick, destructive moments before peace is achieved. The characterization of Lucky becomes quite implausible as Jones attempts to establish the idea that, despite her Electra complex and associated guilt and hatred for men, she still embodies a healthy female sexuality which can save Grant. Her essential health is most embodied in her dislike of the "Super pro-male" (p. 263); she is always repulsed by the behavior of self-consciously "macho" men:

Brutality and insensitivity, was the upshot of it. Did men, when they got together in groups, have to become brutal and insensitive, to prove to each other they were manly? Did manliness and insensitivity have to go hand in hand? If so, it boded no good for the race or anybody. What kind of manliness was that? Not any kind she wanted. (p. 371)

Since it is precisely this kind of "manliness" that Grant is seeking in his skin-diving expedition, Lucky has her challenge clearly defined. Moreover, during much of the excursion, Carol Abernathy is present and determined to manipulate the playwright's Oedipal guilt. Thus, the battle lines are drawn: Lucky's essential sexual health is pitted against Grant's and her own psychological problems, as well as against the dual threats of the machismo world of skin diving and Carol Abernathy, with the soul of the playwright at stake.

Realistically, the battle is not easy; still Jones produces unnecessary tedium by dragging it out for almost seven hundred pages. One could accept the idea that Grant sees skin diving, in part, as a substitute for sexual involvement without Jones repeating it time and again. In addition, Jones needs to have Grant senselessly endanger his life while diving only once, instead of four or five times, to convey the concept that such behavior represents macho self-indulgence and escape from the female. He really does not need to repeat several times Grant's nightmare of being trapped underwater by a huge fish and his own "pride" to illustrate his main character's inner conflict. Finally, one episode in which Grant kills his prey in the sea and then comes up disappointed and frightened, rather than the several contained in the novel, would serve to illustrate the basic point that the playwright is seeking the wrong kind of masculinity for the wrong reasons.

Because their fights are always ultimately the same one, one also tires of Jones's compulsion to describe every ramification of every disagreement Grant and Lucky have. In a note strongly reminiscent of Catherine Barkley in Hemingway's *A Farewell to Arms,* Lucky begs Grant at one point not to let "them" destroy us since "'there's nothing the world hates more than a lover'" (p. 228). In fact, their relationship is most threatened by their own psychological inadequacies, rather than by any abstract external force.

Sadomasochistic aspects of their relationship dominate when Lucky begins to push strongly for marriage. The playwright vacilliates, uses diving as a means of avoiding the issue, and begins telling himself that anyone with Lucky's promiscuous past must be a "nymphomaniac" (p. 347); but finally he feels a sense of serious responsibility and capitulates. Angry at his period of reluctance, Lucky threatens him on their wedding night: "'Someday I'm going to cuckold you.'" After an initial shock, Grant reacts like a man who needs to be humiliated by a woman: "'Well, then if you ever do cuckold me, you'll have to let me watch it. . . .'" (pp. 352–53) This exchange creates an explosive atmosphere in which the playwright feels almost compelled to push his wife into adultery. His continuing resentment of her past love affairs, of course, adds to the stress of their relationship.

Grant's psychology at this point causes him to lash out at Lucky with the word *whore;* and her bitter reaction almost ends their marriage. In frustration, he begins to take more and more senseless chances in diving; and Lucky's terror and resentment of this attempt at escape becomes almost unbearable. The explosion comes when the playwright tells his wife the truth about his sexual past with Carol Abernathy whom he has described as only a sponsor and foster mother; to Lucky, this hypocrisy means that their entire love affair has been "a big lie" (p. 446) and she can, therefore, never trust him again. The reader wonders at this point why they do stay married; and Jones's best explanation is "the simple inertia of life" (p. 448). At any rate, they establish an agreement which allows Grant sexual intercourse whenever he wants, without emotional support or affection. Such an arrangement makes the playwright speculate even more on Lucky's hysteria at the word *whore*; and he decides that it originates in a " 'Fear-of-Whoredom Syndrome' " (p. 484), caused by guilt about her licentious life in New York.

Obviously, Jones has to bring this uneasy truce to an end soon, and he uses two incidents to bring about a saving epiphany in Grant. First, while her husband sleeps drunkenly in the next room, Lucky is propositioned by a skin-diving friend of Grant's named Jim Grointon. Grant awakes, finds evidence of Grointon's visit, and is certain that Lucky has carried out her threat of "cuckolding" him. Despite her denial when he accuses her, nothing can shake his certainty of her betrayal, and he begins to have visions of her nude in bed with a "faceless man" (p. 533). Paradoxically, Grant's jealousy produces an immediate overwhelming passion in Lucky for her husband; however, this passion only confirms what he already believes about her affair with Grointon. At this point, Jones introduces the second incident which contributes to the playwright's ultimate salvation. The playwright agrees to go on a treasure-hunting excursion with his skin diving teacher, Al Bonham, and several of Bonham's clients. Lucky hates Bonham; and the other members of the expedition are uniformly vicious, cruel individuals. The expedition for sunken treasure is obviously doomed to disaster from the start.

Besides disliking him, Lucky is terrified of Bonham's incompetence in anything beyond skin diving and begins to plead for Grant to protect her almost from the moment the ship leaves port. The point at which she can stand no more comes after the passengers on Bonham's ship encounter a group of hopelessly stereotyped Texans. Racism and decidedly ugly sexual perversion are but two of the characteristics of the Texans; and an orgy of drinking and petty violence ensues. Moreover, Grant's self-destructive tendencies almost result in his death when he foolishly attacks a giant shark while diving. Afterward, he begins to doubt his sanity; still Lucky leaves on a seaplane for civilization.

After her departure, the playwright's epiphany comes, in three stages. He first understands that his certainty of her adultery may be a result of his own inner guilt toward Carol Abernathy's husband. Then he starts to understand that the orgiastic involvement with the Texans is vicious and senselessly destructive. Before he completely repudiates this "manly" world, however, he gets into a drunken brawl with one of Bonham's more repulsive associates and suffers a broken nose. Returning to Lucky, he apologizes for his suspicions of her and elaborates his new understanding of the dangerous immaturity of the macho male:

"... It's like they're not men. Any of them. They're small boys, playing that they're men. And that's what makes it all so dangerous, because they *are* grown up, and what they do *counts*. *Nations* depend on it. The whole world depends on it. . . ." (p. 607)

Continuing his analysis, he asserts that the problem of all men who seek courage in the foolish way he has originates in a childhood penis envy of the father. This theory encompasses most adult males throughout the world who invent "games" like "politics, war, football, polo, explorers. Skin diving. Sharkdiving, . . ." in a futile attempt to "grow up to" their fathers' penises (p. 608). This speech is the key to *Go to the Widow-Maker* and is meant to negate the luxuriating in macho prose that has lasted for over 650 pages. Aesthetically, it is too simple and comes too late.

It satisfies Lucky, however; and she and her newly matured husband immediately go to bed in a scene which embarrassingly echoes Hemingway prose (p. 611).

The novel ends with the expressed hope that Grant and Lucky can someday regain the "strange wonderful Single Viewpoint they had once had" (pp. 617–18). Jones's attempt to write "a great love story" fails in part, however, because the internal and external conflicts of his characters are developed in such a tedious manner that one can scarcely care about, or even believe in, the lovers. This failure is somewhat analogous to the author's difficulties in handling the Dave Hirsh–Gwen French relationship in *Some Came Running*.

II *Problems with Flawed Characterization*

A different, though related, problem is involved in the flawed characterizations of Carol Abernathy and Doug Ismaileh. Both are primarily seen through Grant's eyes and emerge as such dark villains that any attempt to humanize them is doomed. The initial description of Carol, which becomes a refrain throughout the novel, casts her irrevocably as a witchlike figure: "... a sort of dark-dressed, spectral, mantilla-ed figure, with the gloom-sealed face almost hidden, standing on the church steps pointing" (p. 4). She is primarily a stock figure at which Jones can direct his rage at the Oedipal frustrations of American males. Her own artistic sterility and cultivation of occultism allow for even more ridicule: "... she deduced that she had been appointed a sort of occult Master of Midwestern Artists, doomed by some unknown Karma to the great sacrifice of aiding Creators while herself never being allowed the opportunity to create because of helping them" (p. 44). In fact, the one positive aspect of this character is its implicit repudiation of the superficial mysticism that mars *Some Came Running* and even *From Here to Eternity*. Like all mother-figures in Jones, she is an expert at manipulation through guilt and induced feelings of responsibility. Immediately after Ron announces his plan to go skin diving, she takes over the expedition and works to get the playwright hopelessly in debt to Al Bonham so that he will have to return to her.

Initially, Grant places most of the blame for his lost manhood on her and feels that he can escape her only while underwater. One scarcely subtle bit of symbolism in the novel is the fact that both Carol and Doug Ismaileh are completely incapable of diving. Besides guilt and responsibility, Grant also feels considerable fear of Carol; and she is constantly linked to imagery of blackness. Sensing his desire for a great love affair, she constantly tells the playwright that "*there is no such thing as love*" (p. 41). As soon as she becomes aware of Lucky, her attempted manipulation of him grows increasingly desperate. Besides his guilt, fear, and sense of responsibility to her, Carol even attacks the New York girl through Grant's duty to art: she has a theory that a wife and family will destroy any artist's "vital energy" (p. 272). However, the playwright hopes to defy her because he now has "charge of his craft" (p. 104). All this, of course, represents Jones's very simplistic approach to a concept of the Oedipal origins of art.

Jones does attempt to humanize his witch-mother figure by

discussing her deprived background and by giving her a few
legitimately pathetic scenes. The daughter of a Tennessee hill
family, she had met her husband while working as a waitress
in Bloomington, Indiana. He got her pregnant, paid for an
abortion which nearly killed her, and left. Later, he came back,
out of some "chivalric masochism of his own," married her, and
introduced her into Indianapolis society (pp. 42–43). Thus, she
is a woman who has always been a victim, and Jones is attempting to present the idea that a victim will always attempt to
victimize in return. Confronting the fact that she will not be able
to destroy Grant's love for Lucky, she begs him for an acknowledgment in his new play, then makes a fake suicide attempt,
and finally makes a rainy night visit to Lucky to accuse the playwright of homosexuality. This tragic past and these desperate
attempts to save her surrogate lover-son for herself are intended
to create compassion in the reader. However, she is depicted as
a black, threatening witch too often for Jones to succeed in his
attempt to balance the characterization.

In contrast, Jones makes no attempt to humanize Doug Ismaileh.
That he has the biblical name of an outcast is no accident; Ismaileh is a totally disgusting figure. His famous play is virtually
plagiarized from Grant's initial success, and he desires to make
a father figure out of the novel's main character in order to hate
him more completely and vindictively. Lucky immediately senses
that her husband's rival hates women; and, in fact, he is fond
of quoting his "Law" that " 'in any love affair he who quits first
wins...' " (p. 217). Ismaileh had been a pimp at one point and
learned that one could make women do anything if he was "cruel
enough" to them (p. 330). Self-consciously imitating Hemingway
as a heavy drinker, he even refers to himself as "Papa" (p. 503).
Angry and frustrated at Grant because of Lucky and because he
can't learn to skin-dive, he takes the strange revenge of seducing
Carol Abernathy. Their intercourse scene is a conscious parody
of the love scenes in *For Whom the Bell Tolls* (p. 334). He goes
to Grant, then, and proudly announces: " 'I've had your
broad...' " (p. 388). If Jones is making any aesthetic comment
with the Ismaileh characterization, it seems to be that he personifies the worst perversion of the Hemingway mystique: the

cult of masculinity devoid of sensitivity and fundamental decency.

Though he is in no way an artist, the skin diving teacher, Al Bonham, is apparently included in the novel for much the same reason, and this fact contributes to its confusion. Since Grant initially admires Bonham a great deal, the reader has difficulty for some time in discerning whether his values are meant to be repudiated or accepted. A physically huge man, Bonham functions brilliantly underwater but is "accident prone" in any aspect of human relations (p. 367). Lucky senses this flaw immediately, but, since the reader has difficulty in always being aware of her basic sexual health, the accuracy of her perception is clouded. Bonham is a central figure in most of the novel's excessively macho scenes. For instance, he personifies the concept that real men don't like their mistresses (p. 4), tells Grant that physical brutality is the way to handle Carol Abernathy and, in one scene, routs the crazed woman by stripping nude in her presence.

There are strong clues early in the novel of Bonham's essential sickness, but Grant's increasing hero worship makes it difficult to know how seriously to take them. A spectacular eater and drinker, Bonham confesses that alcohol is necessary for him to be able to stand himself and others (p. 171). His spear fishing is characterized by unnecessary violence. While secretly characterizing this tendency as that of "some primordial sub-human hunter" (p. 109), Grant also responds to its primitivism. It is clear from the first that Bonham is obsessed with succeeding professionally even to the point of capitalizing on Grant's role of a celebrity—he even has a theory that celebrities are "the Chosen Ones" created by "Mass Communications" and are peculiarly in need of excitement and the illusion of danger to feel that their lives are worthwhile. He is determined to capitalize on this need through the Tourist Trade, even though aware that he will be contributing to the destruction of the sea as a last frontier of individualism (pp. 364–65).

Grant senses a "moral irresponsibility" in Bonham's essential attitude (p. 151) but justifies it as the only option left to a real individualist in our age of conformity. Also, while it is Bonham who first introduces the insane idea of risking one's life with sharks as a substitute for sexual gratification, the playwright initially responds to this concept of adventure. Bonham even knows of a secret sharkhole where he often goes to engage in frenzied attacks on the dangerous fish; these attacks constitute an orgy of gratification through hatred. He believes that all life is "evil" and cannibalistic, with sharks merely representing the most extreme embodiment of the depravity of this planet (pp. 317–18).

Still, it is not until Bonham's sexual impotence with his Jamaican wife is discovered (by Lucky, of course) that Jones's intentions behind his characterization are made clear. Racism is first suggested as a cause for this impotence. The real reason is more complex and parallels Grant's and Lucky's psychological problems. Suffering from strong Oedipal feelings himself, Bonham believes that sex is "dirty" and, if his wife likes it, she must be morally impure (pp. 313–15). Feeling this way, he not surprisingly hates Lucky. When Bonham does have an affair with the wife of one of his clients, which indirectly destroys his entire business future, he likes it because the woman is "really *dirty*" and also not his wife (pp. 572–73).

One aspect of the Bonham characterization which especially seems a dig at Hemingway is his continual amazement at Grant's willingness to show his fear. Such lack of dignity is, of course, a violation of the Hemingway "code hero" concept. Paradoxically, Bonham seems to grow somewhat after he is totally destroyed in his business ambitions: he comes to Grant and Lucky, apologizes to her, and calls her a "hell of a *lady*" (p. 610). Besides being unmotivated, such a reversal is far too little to cancel out his primary role in the novel as a perennial "boy" playing "games" in a desperate attempt to feel "manly."

Besides flawed characterization, *Go to the Widow-Maker* is weakened by intensive philosophizing that is out of place in what is announced as "a great love story." When Jones, early in the novel, describes Ron Grant as a writer, one cannot help but feel he is writing about himself:

He didn't spend much time on delicate stylistic niceties but sort of bullassed right through. But his sensitivity about the physical world and his perceptions about people were so incredibly sensitized that they were almost feminine, and they made you stop sometimes with a feeling of 'Gee, I've felt that!' (p. 92)

For Jones at his best, this is an accurate assessment, but not for *Go to the Widow-Maker*. Too much anger and cynicism prevent the "sensitivity" that is so "delicate" in the army trilogy despite the three novels' "bullassed" style.

For the sake of his critical reputation, Jones needed a successful novel at this point in his career. Unfortunately, he did not achieve one with *The Merry Month of May*. Because of implicit parallels between the 1968 Paris student revolution and military conflict, one might reasonably have hoped that Jones would produce, in this 1971 work, something with the power of the army trilogy. Certainly the element of class distinction, which gives *From Here to Eternity* so much of its power, was somewhat relevant to the student revolutions. However, Jones was aware that the young Paris revolutionaries did not perfectly correspond with his army enlisted men—since many students were, of course, from middle- to upper-class families, a proletarian vision could not logically embrace them.

III   The Merry Month of May

In addition, the same tone of weary cynicism which is so distasteful in *Go to the Widow-Maker* mars *The Merry Month of May*. Jones simply could never obtain a comfortable philosophical position concerning the counterculture of the 1960s. This ambivalence is even reflected in a light detective "thriller," *A Touch of Danger*, which he published in 1973. Because of Jones's choice of narrator, a mood of cynicism and ambivalence toward the Paris student movement inevitably dominates *The Merry Month of May*. Jonathan James Hartley III, "failed poet, failed novelist," recently divorced, (p. 11)[3] is locked into a personal despair which clouds everything he sees. Attempting narrative complexity, Jones has Hartley state, more than once, a sense of uselessness in even bothering to recount his story: ". . . Why should I try? Even the desire isn't there any more" (p. 11).

Observing the separate stages of student insurrection does provide him excitement, if not purpose, for a while. His emotional detachment is shaken in three ways: when the workers join the students on the barricades, he momentarily allows himself to think real change may actually be imminent; he luxuriates in the thrill of isolated vulnerability when vital air traffic at Orly is suspended; and he observes with pain the destruction of historic Parisian landmarks. Despite Hartley's essential cynicism, his observations of these three aspects of the revolution give Jones's novel what power it has.

Hartley's cynicism is essentially a mask for a disillusioned, but not extinguished, liberalism. Arguing that all governments are basically corrupt and dishonest, he supports his thesis with a reference to the United States and Vietnam (p. 128). He especially has contempt for the French capitalistic class, the *Patronat*:

Everybody knew, at least every American did, just how antiquated the French *Patronat* was in comparison to our equally unloved American Establishment. It was about a hundred times worse, in just about every sense. (p. 153)

Thus, when worker support for the students reaches the point of nationwide strikes, Hartley has to struggle to keep down his own revolutionary fervor.

The Merry Month of May is not really about the student revolution, however; it is primarily another Jones study of American sexual maladjustment. John W. Aldridge complains that the novel's erotic obsession overwhelms all else and destroys any aesthetic plausibility.[4] The sexual maladjustment theme is developed around the conflicts of Harry Gallagher, an American film writer, with his wife and son and with one of the most unfortunate characterizations in all Jones's fiction, Samantha Everton. Intertwining the psychological conflicts of these characters with the student movement, Jones virtually succeeds in reducing the revolution to a cliché-ridden sexual battleground.

In addition to the implausibility of much of the plot and the offensiveness of the characterization of the bisexual Samantha Everton, *The Merry Month of May* is centrally flawed by Jones's symbolic reducing of the Paris student revolution to an outbreak of sexual immaturity. He misses no opportunity to emphasize this equation, and it renders the entire novel simplistic. In addition, the equation is strained because the Gallaghers are Americans and Jones introduces one French family, the DuPonts, solely to personify sexual health. To the degree that Jones is at all concerned with social revolution in this novel, one cannot help feeling that it is really the American unrest of the 1960s that concerns him. His very ambivalence to the 1960s American counterculture might have produced a good novel. Like Robert E. Lee Prewitt, Jones instinctively identified with all "underdogs." However, *The Merry Month of May* touches on some reservations about the Parisian revolt that would have been valid comments about much that happened in the United States in the 1960s—the students' ignorance of and contempt for irreplaceable artifacts of history, their naively cynical adoption of tactics of the government out of a certainty that they are "morally right," and their blind absolutism.

Such ideas are totally submerged by the Gallagher family's sexual conflicts, however. Jones's vision of the sexual immaturity of the American, while honest and containing some real insight, was ultimately not original or profound enough to support a long novel. It is unfortunate that *Go to the Widow-Maker* and *The Merry Month of May* were the last two serious novels published during Jones's lifetime. Their failures have much to do with the critical neglect of his best work at the time of his death. He was to publish one more artistically successful book before he died in 1977; however, *WWII* is a work of nonfiction, and fifteen years had passed since the appearance of his last important novel, *The Thin Red Line*.

CHAPTER 7

The Evolution of a Soldier, Part 3: Whistle

AS a concept, Jones's posthumously published novel, *Whistle*, goes back to the inception of his literary career. The novel's introductory "Note" reveals that, while Jones "first began actual work" on it in 1968, "it was conceived as far back as 1947, when I was still first writing to Maxwell Perkins about my characters Warden and Prewitt, and the book I wanted to write about World War II" (p. xix).[1] "The book" became three long novels which constitute the foundation of Jones's future reputation. In this introductory "Note," he adds:

I intended to write the third volume immediately after I finished *The Thin Red Line*. Other things, other novels, got in the way. Each time I put it aside it seemed to further refine itself. So that each time I took it up again I had to begin all over. (p. xx)

Among the "other things, other novels" which one wishes had not "got in the way" were *Go to the Widow-Maker* and *The Merry Month of May*. These two long novels were not the last works published by Jones during his lifetime, however. In 1973, the detective "thriller," *A Touch of Danger*, appeared; the next year Jones published an observation of the war in Vietnam, *Viet Journal*; and, in 1975, he wrote the commentary for *WWII*, the expensively produced study of "graphic art" inspired by the Second World War.

I   A Touch of Danger

Jones may well have intended the first of these as only light

164

entertainment. In an interview, he revealed that he had initially
conceived of the idea as a screenplay, that the novel was written
in six months, and that he had long been "a great fan of Hammett and Chandler."[2] At any rate, it lacks the power of Hammett
and Chandler's best work partially because it is obviously deriva-
tive. Jones does provide all the necessary ingredients for this
kind of novel—a private detective, Lobo Davis, whose cynicism
results from painful disillusionment; an upper-class woman whose
beauty masks inner corruption; and a convoluted plot involving
two gory murders. There is also an element of protest comparable
to the underlying tone of most of Hammett and Chandler—a
hopeless bitterness at the impossibility of stopping, or even
punishing, wealthy criminals.

The concern with the puritanical repressiveness of American
society that runs throughout Jones's fiction is also present here;
still, through Lobo Davis, Jones is expressing a mature awareness
of the destructive extremes of the 1960s "sexual revolution."
In the interview mentioned above, he endorses some of the main
causes of the counterculture, like the legalization of marijuana,
but asserts that the young need discipline and have been betrayed by their own leaders.

The novel also contains direct commentaries about the Vietnamese conflict, which probably indicate Jones's own views:

... I was against the Vietnamese war, just on military principles
alone, . . . and that we had no business there, and never had had, and
that we were maintaining a criminal government there, which was
also making a fortune selling heroin on the side, as well as ruining
our own economy on the operation. (pp. 225–26)[3]

II Viet Journal

It is important to remember that *Viet Journal* appeared only
one year after *A Touch of Danger*. The account of Jones's visit
to Vietnam in early 1973 has a curiously defensive tone; he
refuses to dismiss the American army, and especially the individual soldiers, involved in the Asiatic conflict as evil or corrupt,
and anticipates condemnation from the liberal establishment for
his refusal. The book is partially dedicated "TO THE UNITED

STATES ARMY TO WHICH MY FIRST NOVEL WAS ALSO DEDICATED"; and, as might be expected of an old soldier like Jones, once in Vietnam, he was not satisfied with information obtained indirectly. Instead, he constantly took risks by going into dangerous areas of combat. He was supported in this activity by high-ranking American officers; and this situation, while it could not have been otherwise if Jones was to see anything, gives the book a curious tone. The novelist seems himself to feel the strangeness of the spokesman of the enlisted man forced into a situation of almost exclusive association with officers. He writes convincingly of the dedication and courage of the officer class, but not with the emotional power of his tributes to the enlisted man of the "old army."

As its title indicates, *Viet Journal* is a random series of observations. These focus on two subjects: the American army and the Vietnamese political situation. Jones's comments about the U.S. Army are largely, but not entirely, favorable. He also views Vietnam as a tragic country destroyed by a history of external control and invasion and its own corrupt officials; but he refuses to idealize the Viet Cong and goes into detail about the atrocities he hears they have committed.

Inspired in part by the complexities of Vietnam, Jones decides to return to Hawaii for the first time since 1941. It is as if he wished to regain a period of relative innocence, when the U.S. Army was fighting villains as clear-cut as Hitler and Mussolini. The trip also becomes Jones's search for his own lost youth. "Hawaiian Recall" is included as an "Epilogue" to *Viet Journal* and, from its opening, conveys an evocative tone. He begins by quoting the military definition of "'*recall*: . . . a call on the trumpet, bugle, or drum, which calls soldiers back to the ranks, camps, etc.'" (p. 237). One is reminded of Prewitt and his bugle while sensing another connotation of the word—the attempt to call back the past.

Jones soon discovers, however, that the past is elusive. His Hawaii no longer exists; the tourist industry has obliterated it. When he goes to the Royal Hawaiian Hotel, he has difficulty locating the entrance and notices that "the corner where Maggio had had his fist fight with the two MPs had disappeared completely" (p. 240). After driving up to look at the house on Wilhelmina Rise which had served as the model for Alma's home, he returns to the Army-Navy Y on Hotel Street. The area which had been the "Mecca" for enlisted men before Pearl Harbor and which served as the setting of many of *From Here to Eternity*'s most important scenes is being decimated by urban renewal: "I looked at the corner bar, now closed, where Warden had come hunting for Prewitt when Prewitt was AWOL." Wu Fat's Chinese Restaurant is soon to be torn down (p. 243). Jones is suddenly overcome by the impermanence of human life:

Suddenly, without any preparation at all, tears were up behind my eyes. All that blood, all that sweat. How many men? Tears for thirty years, gone somewhere. Tears for a young idiotic boy in a "gook" shirt and linen slacks. (pp. 246–47)

Inevitably, Jones visits Schofield Barracks. Initially, it appears the same; and when he passes the Post Library, he remembers when he "... had first picked up Thomas Wolfe's *Look Homeward, Angel*, and heard some 'mystic' call telling me I was a writer" (p. 247).

Inside the barracks itself, however, he discovers that there have indeed been changes:

... the old caste system was gone. You couldn't *make* these youngsters do anything, you had to explain to them what you wanted them to do, and make them understand it, and then lead them. (p. 252)

As he had already discovered in Vietnam, it is no longer his army. Yet there is one constant: the enlisted men feel "lonely" (p. 253). "Hawaiian Recall" is an effective piece of nostalgic writing. Jones's account of his Vietnam experience, while sincere and at times provocative, is not likely to influence greatly anyone's views about that tragic moment in American history. It is significant that Jones left desiring to recapture a simpler, more comprehensible time.

III WWII

The following year, Jones was again distracted from completing *Whistle* when Art Weithas, "the head art director of *Yank*," contacted him about collaborating on a book about "World War II graphic art." Weithas was to coordinate the reproduction of World War II art in the book, and Jones was to write the commentary. Initially, the novelist hesitated—he was committed to finishing *Whistle* and felt, moreover, that he had nothing new to say about the Second World War. However, several factors influenced him to change his mind—he was deeply impressed by the originality and power of that art; and he became convinced that time had given the war ". . . a glow that it did not have" (p. 11).[4] Most importantly, perhaps, the project gave him the chance to correct what he believed to be inevitable historical inaccuracies. One segment of his narrative carries the subtitle, "Is History Written by the Upper Classes for the Upper Classes?" The opening line of the section quickly resolves the question: "It would seem that it is" (p. 70).

This phenomenon, he believes, applied to the Second World War: "As in most wars, in the United States in World War II . . . most of the commanding was done by the upper classes, and most of the fighting was done by the lower" (p. 70). The upper-class historian writes from the viewpoint of an idealism which his economic security allows him: "And this is not to say that the ideals are not eminently admirable. But they have almost no effect on your proletarian infantry soldier . . ." (p. 71). Thus the project offered Jones an opportunity to outline in nonfictional format the thematic basis of all his army fiction: the evolution of the (proletarian) soldier.

WWII is an important book, not only because it contains Jones's most detailed analysis of this concept, but also because Weithas's reproductions of the art work are vivid and unforgettable and Jones's discussion of the "graphics" is incisive. Moreover, the novelist makes significant and challenging observations concerning his personal war experiences and the historic background and implications of World War II. It is especially interesting to learn how much of his own experience is incorporated into *The Thin Red Line* and *Whistle*.

Jones describes the impatience of his company to be sent to the Pacific theater, despite what they knew would be brutal combat and despite the fact that their training "was woefully inadequate" (p. 41). He concisely summarizes the contributions of his Division, the Twenty-fifth Infantry Tropic Lightning Division, to the struggle for Guadalcanal:

> ... We had taken over from the First Marines, prosecuted the final offensive on the 'Canal, chased the Japanese to Tassafaronga in the whirlwind windup which gave us our name, and begun to move up to New Georgia for the next fight of the campaign. (p. 50)

This summary, of course, roughly parallels the action of *The Thin Red Line.* He recounts an experience of serving on "a Grave Registration detail on Guadalcanal," the details of which obviously inspired the story "Greater Love" and the mass Japanese grave scene in *The Thin Red Line* (p. 124). Again, in an echo of his combat novel, he recounts drinking the illicit concoction, "swipe," and watching "the tough little Southerner I eventually drew Witt from" crawl through the mud and bay at the moon (p. 130).

One curiously moving segment describes a brawl in Auckland, New Zealand, between the sick and wounded veterans of Guadalcanal and a new regiment of marines waiting to be sent into combat. No one clearly remembered what inspired the fight, but it soon assumed the proportions of a full-scale riot. Jones concludes his account of "The Battle of Auckland" by abruptly and effectively changing tone: "We must all have been half-crazy. When I started this little piece, I intended to do it humorously. Reading it over, I find that it's not, particularly. It seems more sad" (p. 61). The survivors of the horrors of Guadalcanal probably could not help but be "half-crazy" immediately afterward, and this is more than "sad." Writing about his days recovering at the Army hospital in Memphis, he remembers the

> ... cold silent unforgiving stare the overseas men at the hospital gave to everybody who was not one of them. It was not so much that they were specifically blaming anyone for anything, as that everybody remained unforgiven. I felt the same way myself. (p. 147)

The characters in *Whistle* also "feel the same way."

Jones's general discussion of World War II begins by analyzing a real, but largely unspoken, American fear after Pearl Harbor.

He discounts the argument that the Japanese sneak attack was a strategic blunder on their part because it united the nation. He remembers too well that, while many Americans did enlist immediately, others began calculating how to get rich on the war (p. 26). The unspoken fear was that a "peace-loving," "anti soldiering and soldiers" nation might not be able to produce the kind of fanatic warriors needed to defeat the Japanese and the Germans (p. 28). In an amusing echo of his recurrent theme of the sexually immature American, Jones speculates that many men enlisted to escape domineering mothers (p. 30). In contrast to the United States, he argues, Europe had been served by war as "tradition and heritage for a hundred generations" (p. 42), and the Japanese were devoted to a medieval code of blood and sacrifice. In the 1940s, the long-pampered army officer class was an unknown quantity in terms of effective leadership. However, the evolution process soon hardened the proletarian enlisted man; and the officer class matured under fire. Crucial to this hardening process was the grim presence of casualties: "Casualties are one of war's grimmer realities. In a way perhaps its most important element. An army that cannot take casualties cannot fight. And an army that takes too many will lose" (p. 89). Thus a code of behavior toward and among the wounded evolved spontaneously.

Most of Jones's remaining comments about the war can be divided into those concerning Europe and those focusing on the Pacific theater. To him, the North African campaign marked a turning point in military, and human, history: "the handling of Eisenhower's mass landings made it clear that the age of massed, managerial, industrial-production technological warfare had been born..." (p. 62). In this new method of military confrontation, the individual soldier became virtually insignificant. There would be no more temptation to write romantically about war. His account of the Normandy invasion is staggering, particularly in its emphasis upon the solitary role of Eisenhower. The general issued "a confident hortatory message" to every man in the armada prior to invasion and simultaneously wrote a "contingency" statement of "... withdrawal from the French shore due to invincible enemy resistance." Jones says accurately that "when one thinks of that, and the responsibility it entailed, it makes the hairs on the back of the neck move" (pp. 158–59).

He analyzes the Battle of the Bulge as a lost cause for the Germans from the beginning, but still praises the lonely, heroic American stands against the German onslaught: "They would also prove just how far the U.S. soldier had come in his professionalism since the early days in North Africa" (p. 205). The Ardennes were solely the triumph of the new "professional" American soldier (p. 208).

Two other events which unmistakably marked a new age in human history were the discovery of the Nazi extermination camps and the war crimes trials. Hitler, Jones writes, had resurrected "the barbarian concept of chattelized soul slavery" (p. 224). These atrocities represented "for the first time in two centuries" a reversal of "the struggle of Western man toward some measure of security and dignity and sanctity of the individual. . . ." For Jones, who had always believed in the animal nature of man, the implications of this regression were obvious— it produced ". . . an acute awareness of the shadows in us, the bestiality and vicious cruelty of which our race under its thin veneers of civilization was still capable" (p. 225). Concerning the war crimes trials, Jones writes that, while "the executed deserved to die," the Allies had established a frightening "precedent" for the treatment of future losers of wars (p. 228).

His overall view of the Pacific war was that it was necessarily a secondary effort by the Allies, a fact which the enlisted man could not help but know. In fact, modern "corporation" war first appeared relatively late in the Pacific; Jones marks the date as November 20, 1943, when the marines invaded the "Makin and Tarawa atolls in the Gilberts" (p. 104). For him, the invasions of Tarawa, Saipan, and Peleliu symbolized Pacific combat: "Probably nothing equaled them for prolonged intensity of fire and of fighting, and for the American casualties they exacted, which were staggering" (p. 105). The Pacific soon became a "head-on confrontation between . . . twentieth-century attack and seventeenth-century fanatical defense . . ." (p. 105).

While the outcome of such a conflict was inevitable, certain aspects of it were not. The kamikaze flights in no way altered the war, but they revealed the wartime fanaticism of the Japanese. Other events underscored the same. At Bayombong, the enemy executed their own wounded rather than allow them to be captured (p. 222). His analysis of this Japanese fanaticism leads Jones to a defense of Truman's use of the atomic bomb. He argues that the alternative was invasion of the main island itself, "but the way the Japanese were taking to their growing defeat with a sort of insane crazy self-destructive valor boded no good" for such a venture (p. 223). The enemy was devoted to a medieval code of suicide and cruelty, and the number of Allied casualties which would inevitably result from invasion was incalculable: "The loss of life on the U.S. side alone . . . would have more than tripled, quadrupled the combined losses of Hiroshima and Nagasaki" (p. 240).

While Jones believed the bomb had been necessary, he expressed doubt that man is ". . . evolved enough as an animal to be allowed to play with such destructive power." While the United States can be held accountable for inventing and first using the atomic bomb, ". . . no one can honestly claim the United States is responsible for developing the human race" (p. 249).

Some of Jones's commentary about the war cannot be labeled as specifically relevant to Europe or the Pacific. In two passages which anticipate *Whistle,* he condemns American war films for failing to portray modern combat with any realism or honesty and discusses the irreversible change in American middle-class mores and morality produced by the wartime economic boom. About the Teheran conference, he writes:

To what strange state had our hectic race risen in its long millennia of evolutionary process, that three such men, heroes or no, could sit together at a dining table, controlling the lives and deaths of so many of their fellow humans. (p. 145)

Most importantly, he asserts that World War II meant the end of free enterprise and the triumph of technology and the conglomerate: ". . . They would make of Americans wage slaves in a stricter tighter way than they had ever been during the nineteenth century Industrial Revolution."

From this vision, which is at the core of everything Jones wrote, one turns for relief to his discussion of World War II "graphic art." Jones believed deeply in art as perhaps the last sanctuary of the individual in a "conglomerate" world. The rule which he and Weithas devised for selecting material was simple: "... We would use no art work that was not done at the time by the original combat artists ..." (p. 25). A large percentage of the wartime graphics were necessarily propagandistic, but occasionally someone transcended that limit to produce great art "... which in the end can probably be defined simplistically as telling the whole truth beautifully, to create catharsis" (p. 16). This definition can probably be applied to what Jones always attempted to do in his fiction. Certainly he always wished to tell "the whole truth."

He focuses largely upon American graphic art of two kinds: humorous and satiric, and realistic. Humor was essential to maintaining sanity in face of "the dark side of humanity" which the enlisted man was being forced to confront everywhere, including in himself (p. 31). *Yank* magazine had "a curiously sophomoric quality," but some of its cartoonists, especially George Baker with "The Sad Sack," "reached the unsung souls of the hundreds of thousands of draftee GIs who never won a medal or earned a stripe" (p. 57). However, it was Bill Mauldin who truly caught the spirit of the enlisted man: "... Since he drew and wrote mainly about mud and infantry and the misuse of privilege by officers and noncoms and rear echelon types, we felt he was also drawing and writing about us ..." (p. 130). Jones even includes a section on "Nose Art," an analysis of the designs painted on the noses of American airplanes. He sees these designs as something akin to folk art.

Several individual realistic artists receive special praise from Jones. Among them, Howard Brodie of *Yank* is cited for his drawings of the Guadalcanal struggle: "Brodie somehow had permanently captured on paper the filth and misery and fatigue we had lived through. ... Somebody *had* understood. We *did* exist, after all" (p. 58). In discussing the work of Brodie, Jones is paying tribute to the power of art to make human experience real and permanent.

Life magazine commissioned some of the most important

World War II art, including the paintings of Tom Lea. Jones
writes that, until he witnessed the horror of Peleliu, most of
Lea's work was "high-grade propaganda." Peleliu produced a
change in the artist, and to explain that change, Jones concen-
trates on three paintings, *Two-Thousand-Yard Stare*, *Going In*,
and *The Price*. Jones believes that, in the first of these, Lea captured the essence of "combat numbness." *Going In* shows an
American soldier confronting another invasion: "He is no replacement, he's been there before, back down the line: Guadalcanal, Cape Gloucester, somewhere" (p. 116). Lea's *The Price*
is an almost unbearable painting of a wounded "marine (or
soldier)." Blood extends from just above his left eye, covers his
left shoulder and arm, and drips onto the ground. Jones accurately defines its effect as a combination of extreme realism and
"abstraction": "Unreal or not, it is a monument to the blood and
death that all of us, even those who have been there, prefer not
to see or think about when we are away from it" (pp. 116–18).
Kerr Eby, assigned by the Abbott Laboratories, ". . . sketched a
long series of charcoals on paper which perhaps more than any
other captured what it was like to fight in the Pacific jungles
and atolls" (p. 113). More than any other World War II artist,
Eby drew the grim "anonymity" of combat, which Jones conveys
through prose in *The Thin Red Line*.

Even though it meant that he was unable to complete *Whistle*,
one is glad that Jones agreed to do *WWII*. The volume stands
not only as an appendix to his army trilogy, but as an awesome
and powerful work. Jones's prose has rarely been more controlled;
and, combined with Weithas's reproductions, it overwhelms the
reader with the anger and pain of his vision. *WWII* so far transcends its genre as to make the label *coffee table book* in-
applicable.

IV Whistle

When Jones died in May 1977, there had been little discussion of his work, except for reviews of *WWII*, for some time. He
had not published a successful novel for fifteen years. His death
produced an outpouring of reminiscences and evaluations by
other writers. Great anticipation preceded the appearance of

Whistle. At his death, the narrative of *Whistle* was close to completion; the novel was to contain thirty-four chapters and Jones was well into Chapter 31. Jones had arranged that his close friend and fellow writer Willie Morris would, if necessary, complete the book, using notes and tapes Jones had made.

Thus an unusual atmosphere of expectant hope greeted the appearance of the novel less than a year after the death of its author. It was known that the novel would complete the army trilogy begun with *From Here to Eternity* in 1951. A general wish for *Whistle* to be a successful and important novel prevailed. However, *Whistle* met with mixed reviews. Writing in the *Chicago Tribue*, Philip Caputo praised the novel extensively: "... If the universal figure of this age is the soldier, Jones ought to be taken very seriously because no one has written about the soldier and his world more accurately and eloquently."[5] *Time* magazine, in contrast, dismissed the novel as incomplete and insignificant.

Other reviewers took a middle ground. After discussing Jones's frustrating inconsistency as a writer, Peter S. Prescott of *Newsweek* proclaimed: "*Whistle* is Jones' best novel in sixteen years; ... it recovers much of the passionate intensity that animates his better work; and ... it returns to thwack again at the only scene he ever handled with authority, the effect on men of war and the military life." Prescott does complain that, once again, Jones is unable to write convincingly about women or sex (February 28, 1978, pp. 80–82). Thomas R. Edwards called *Whistle* "a very badly written book" and Jones "a minor novelist," but added that "... he knew what he knew wonderfully well, and in *From Here to Eternity* and *The Thin Red Line*, and intermittently in *Whistle*, he told us much about how the military life shapes and marks those who follow it."[6] John W. Aldridge published the most perceptive analysis of the novel in the *New York Times Book Review*. Aldridge wrote that *Whistle* made clear "the developing theme of the trilogy as a whole": the end of "the almighty code of the old peacetime army under the pressures of a kind of warfare requiring for survival a radically altered mode of existence." Aldridge understands that there were reasons other than Prewitt's death in *From Here to Eternity* for Jones to change the names of the three characters who appear in each volume of the trilogy:

increasingly brutal experiences have "transformed [them] into altogether different people." In summarizing Jones's career, Aldridge writes:

Jones may not be recognized as a literary artist of the first rank. But he was a powerful naturalistic chronicler of certain essential responses of men at war, and he had a gift for being absolutely honest about what he felt and thought.[7]

Whistle does not attain the narrative power of *From Here to Eternity* and *The Thin Red Line*. It is structurally uneven and awkwardly written; but, seen in the context of the army trilogy, the novel is a significant achievement. Its focus is upon "The De-Evolution of a Soldier," described by Jones in *WWII* as a nearly impossible stage of the military evolutionary process. He explains that men who have been trained to kill and accept the inevitability of their own deaths and who have seen humanity at its most brutalized and most brutal simply cannot come home with the innocence they once possessed. However, the people back home cannot comprehend this fact, and a barrier grows up between the returning soldiers and civilians. The civilians can't comprehend that ". . . they have a lot of dead men around them, dead men who are walking around and breathing" (*WWII*, p. 54). Thus an *"esprit"* grows up among the veterans partly because of their alienation from civilian life; ultimately, this *"esprit"* becomes a shield against a now foreign homeland.

Whistle focuses on four "casualties" of the same infantry company which had fought on Guadalcanal and New Georgia. The four have been shipped home in 1943; the degree of their injuries varies greatly. Three of the four represent characterizations begun in *From Here to Eternity* and continued in *The Thin Red Line*:

So in *The Thin Red Line* 1st/Sgt Warden becomes 1st/Sgt Welsh, Pvt Prewitt becomes Pvt Witt, Mess/Sgt Stark becomes Mess/Sgt Storm. While remaining the same people as before. In *Whistle* Welsh becomes Mart Winch, Witt becomes Bobby Prell, Storm becomes John Strange. (p. xx)

As John W. Aldridge points out, there is a sense in which they are not "the same people as before"; still, Jones means that they represent a continuing characterization. The fourth character, Marion Landers, seems a refinement of Geoffrey Fife in *The Thin Red Line*. Mart Winch, besides dengue fever and malaria, is suffering from congestive heart failure; he has been warned to take extremely good care of himself or he might die at any moment. Bobby Prell has been wounded across both thighs by machine gun fire, and amputation of both his legs is considered a strong possibility. Strange, the least injured, has a hand wound from a mortar fragment; and Lander's right ankle was "smashed by a heavy-mortar fragment" (p. 5). The novel covers the fate of these four characters from their arrival in San Francisco to their ultimate destruction—Landers and Strange commit suicide, Prell gets himself killed in a brawl, and Winch goes insane. Most of the novel takes place in the fictional city of Luxor, Tennessee, which Jones says is based on both Memphis and Nashville.[8] (During his own period of recuperation beginning in Memphis in 1943, Jones came to know both cities.)

While the remainder of *Whistle* is written in the third person, its opening chapter is a first-person account of the reaction of other company veterans in the Luxor hospital to the news that "about the four most important men the company had had" were coming home (p. 3). This chapter functions much like a prologue in that it establishes the dominant mood and themes of the novel. The unnamed narrator says:

It was strange how closely we returnees clung together. We were like a family of orphaned children, split by an epidemic and sent to different care centers. . . . The people treated us nicely, and cared for us tenderly, and then hurried to wash their hands after touching us.

In describing "The Home Front" in *WWII*, Jones uses a very slight variation of this last sentence. The anonymous speaker in *Whistle*'s opening chapter continues to say that the old company ". . . seemed to us now the only family we had ever had," and that the "retreads" felt "arrogance" at being "infected" and "unclean" and "an insane loyalty" "for our own kind." While they wore Combat Infantryman badges, they considered all other medals "contemptible display" (in *WWII*, Jones writes that the real

soldiers in Memphis in 1943 felt the same way). The news of
the return of "the four" creates a "superstitious fear" among the
old company men in the Luxor hospital; it seems that "Our
God," which "could be likened to a Great Roulette Wheel," is
destroying the old company, "about the last thing we had left"
(pp. 4–7).

In their own ways Landers, Strange, Prell, and Winch come
to feel the same alienation and dissolution. As they approach
home, they view it with "anxiety and deep unexorcised fear, of
despair even" (p. 21); and their fear and despair are soon
realized. Two aspects of the new America which particularly
bother them are the economic affluence produced by the war and
the accompanying drastic change in morality. Discussing his plans
for *Whistle* in an interview, Jones emphasizes the "despair float-
ing around" in the economic boom years of 1943 and 1944.[9]
Jones is successful in conveying their outrage at wartime prof-
iteering, but his attempt to depict their dismay at changing
sexual mores is forced and unconvincing. He works very hard
to demonstrate that the repressive Puritanism in which they grew
up is largely to blame. Still, the women of *Whistle* never remotely
approach the stature of a Karen Holmes; they are simply the
enemy. Despite what most critics believe, this problem of characterization results more from execution than philosophy; however, it undeniably mars the novel. Except for Karen Holmes
and, to a degree, Alma Schmidt, Jones did indeed have difficulty
in creating believable female characters.

In addition, he makes the act of cunnilingus virtually the sole
symbol of the new American morality. In fact, John Strange's
discovery of this form of sexual gratification is part of what
destroys him. Jones is sincerely attempting to say something
about the disastrous effects on the male of a Puritanical upbringing in all this; but he overworks the subject to the point where
it almost becomes absurd.

Twenty-one-year-old Marion Landers, Winch's clerk in the
Pacific, is not an old army man, but he shares many similar perceptions. A college man, he is central to the novel because his
intelligence allows Jones to state key ideas; in this way, he
functions much like John Bell in *The Thin Red Line*. As mentioned, in other ways he is modeled on Fife. As the ship nears

San Francisco, he is hit by the impossibility of "caring" for such a big country; "and all his life Landers has been taught that to care was important . . ." (p. 25). He senses that he is on an "empty ship" approaching "an empty continent" and, in a metaphor that foreshadows his mental breakdown and suicide, feels that "another man called Marion Landers" is standing outside himself (p. 32).

Landers's mental torment began on a hillside on Guadalcanal when he looked down at the fighting and felt irrevocably estranged from a human race which could engage in such barbarity. He cannot overcome a certainty that he will be sent back to combat and senselessly killed. He is also tormented by an irrational guilt—after being wounded, he drank freely and "luxuriously" from a canteen while nearly starved men looked at him with "no envy." Despite their lack of resentment, Landers cannot escape the feeling that he sinned by drinking the water in front of them. When he attempts to discuss his feelings with Strange, the mess sergeant is uncomprehending and wishes "Winch were here with his wisdom" (p. 93). (There is a parallel scene between Fife and Storm in *The Thin Red Line*.)

Landers has always had trouble establishing meaningful human relationships; and when he reaches the hospital, he senses that the other men have lost the combat "numbness" and accompanying "disclaiming innocence of new experience." Since he has not lost the "numbness," he feels even more isolated (pp. 111–12). Marion Landers simply cannot accept the physical and spiritual violation of his combat wound and subsequent loss of idealism. The resulting sense of vulnerability causes him to rush toward self-destruction. He turns to women for comfort and falls in love with a Red Cross girl at the Luxor hospital named Carol Firebaugh. However, his own innocence and impatience prevent the relationship from growing. Increasingly frustrated and alone, Landers feels a "red rage" growing inside himself that he can barely control. The rage is "against everything, against life itself" (p. 130), and it frightens Landers. He seeks something to value and, in an effective scene, goes to the humane surgeon, Colonel Curran, to plead against the amputation of Bobby Prell's legs. There, he refutes Donne's quotation about a bond with humanity and says that he cares only about men of the old company: ". . . That's all the capital we have" (p. 131).

This sense of caring only for the company is heightened after a disastrous return to his Indiana hometown, where his family are socially prominent. He feuds with his father, who desires to show Landers off as a war hero. He begins to drink heavily and shocks the town by making a speech at the Elks Club to the local draftees about the "soldier's responsibilities": "'I can't in honesty tell you that you will be fighting for freedom, and God, and your country. . . . In combat you don't think about any of that. But I can assure you that you will be fighting for your life. . . . I think that's a good thing to fight for'" (p. 164). These words come from the Marion Landers who left his home-town as an extremely idealistic young man. He has no success with the girls in town, many of whom he frightens. When he passes out drunk one night, his father orders that he remain in jail overnight. The next morning, Landers cuts all ties with his family and leaves. A 1953 *Newsweek* feature on Jones indi-cates that he drew heavily from his own unhappy return to Robinson, Illinois, after being wounded on Guadalcanal for Landers's experience. For instance, he and "another veteran" shocked the Robinson Elks Club and "were thrown out."[10]

Increasingly, the men of the old company are all Landers has left; but since he is not "old army" and is a college man, that bond also begins to weaken. The "red rage" grows stronger and Landers becomes compulsively involved in senseless fist fights (at the end of *The Thin Red Line*, Fife is slipping into a similar pattern of behavior). After each fight, Landers is puzzled and shaken—he hasn't really wanted to hurt anybody. He analyzes his emotions and finds them dominated by "Anguish. Love. And hate. And happiness":

The anguish was for himself. And every poor slob like him, who had ever suffered fear, and terror, and injury at the hands of another man. . . . [The love is] for all the sad members of this flawed, mis-begotten, miscreated race of valuable creatures, which was trying and failing with such ruptured effort to haul itself up out of the mud and dross and drouth of its crippled heritage. And the hate . . . was for himself and every other who had ever, in the name of whatever good, maimed or injured or killed another man. (p. 245)

The "happiness" comes from the fighting, which provides him momentary emotional release.

Ultimately, Landers has a fight with a wounded officer at the hospital, has a verbal confrontation with the administrative chief, and goes AWOL for five days. Upon his return, he refuses to apologize, especially for the argument with the hospital's chief administrator: " 'He's never been shot at, he's never been in danger, he's never seen men blown up beside him. I'll probably be killed in this war . . .' " (p. 305). It requires all of Winch's ingenuity to save Landers from a court-martial and the stockade; but the young man is not grateful. Having developed a martyr complex, Landers wants the army to punish him and thereby reveal its corruption.

When the hospital's humane surgeon, Colonel Curran, attempts to counsel him, he reveals the full depth of his despair. Landers states that he is " 'futureless' " and can't see beyond " 'a curtain of fog' " (p. 309). Moreover, the human race is doomed to extinction because " '. . . we've overspecialized ourselves in war. A war will do us.' " " 'Human causes' " do not matter " '. . . as long as we continue to kill each other over them' " (p. 311). Winch again attempts to help his former clerk by offering him a position in his new stateside command. Landers refuses the offer as " 'indecent and immoral' " (p. 317). Winch still does the best he can and assigns Landers to the newly formed 3516th QM Gasoline Supply Company, instead of an infantry company.

To this point, Jones's characterization of Landers is an effective and powerful one. The young company clerk has been so shaken by combat's violation of his body and soul that he is groping desperately for a new set of beliefs. His speeches about feeling "anguish," "love," and "hate" for the "doomed human race" "overspecialized in war" can be read as Jones's personal vision. However, the characterization from the point of Landers's assignment to the 3516th becomes confused. He has a moment of "insight" which the novel simply does not support, blaming women for the breakup of the company and deterioration of all values: "[Women] had split the common male interest" (p. 312). Moreover, Jones allows Landers one last rebirth of his idealism originating in admiration for the commanding officer of his new company.

As Winch has foreseen, the officer, First Lieutenant Harry L. Prevor, "a Jew from Indiana," is soon destroyed by the army's anti-Semitism. The implausibility does not reside in Jones's vision of the army's corruption, but in the idea that any one man could resurrect Landers's idealism at this late stage. The new commander, Mayhew, is reminiscent of Dynamite Holmes; and Landers goes "over the hill" again. Now, Winch can only save his old clerk from the stockade by having him sent to the hospital psychiatric ward. There is an effective moment of ironic foreshadowing when Winch advises Landers to " 'just act crazy' "; " 'there's not much to doing it' " (p. 373).

In the hospital, Lander's despair grows deeper:

> What Landers hated were the war and humanity. And people. . . .
> The ones who wanted power. Who cared about having power, more than they cared about how they got it, or what they did with it when they got it. Like Mayhew. . . .
> And Winch? Winch did not count. Winch was an anomaly. (p. 382)

Jones says in his introductory "Note" that *Whistle* will complete the vision that evolves throughout the army trilogy. Landers's despair in the hospital is a crucial moment in the statement of that vision—we live, Jones felt, in an inhuman age of brutality and corruption in which individualistic men of integrity like Winch (and Warden and Welsh and Prewitt and Prell) are virtually extinct.

Landers appears before an Army Review Board ("this kindly, middle-class, bourgeois enemy") (p. 386) and is discharged from the army. Leaving the base, he purposely steps in front of a car driven by an officer's wife and is killed.

Jones places much emphasis on the sex of the car's driver, which ties in with Landers's earlier vision of women as a destructive force. Landers has been destroyed by a sense of irreparable violation of self in combat and the resulting loss of all ideals. The ground of faith has shifted from under him; and in the last analysis, women have little to do with his tragedy. Despite this lapse, the characterization of Landers is generally effective and is certainly central to the novel. As a "college man," he voices many of Jones's key ideas.

As is true with Maylon Stark and Storm, Jones has difficulty with the characterization of former Mess Sergeant John Strange. The novelist's concept of the Stark-Storm-Strange character is potentially intriguing. In all three novels, the mess sergeant, functioning as a contrast to Warden-Welsh-Winch, is an old army soldier who seems sincerely sympathetic to everyone, but inwardly does not care. He does have two things in common with Warden-Welsh-Winch: he does his job well, and he dislikes officers. Consistently in the trilogy, he fails to provide real understanding to the men who come to him to talk about internal torment. As an old army man, he intuitively understands elements of group dynamics which baffle a character like Landers; but, in comparison to the top sergeant figure, his commitment even to the old company is shallow. Ironically, Jones's problem with Strange in *Whistle* is inextricable from his overall concept of the characterization. Since Strange really does not care deeply about anything, his creator is hard pressed to formulate a basis for his ultimate destruction. He attempts to make Strange the prime victim of the revolution in American sexual mores and falls back upon the formula that women represent the "enemy." Ultimately Jones seems to be saying that Strange is most victimized by his own puritanically repressive upbringing; but, as is always the case in his long novels, his presentation of this idea is clumsy.

Because he sees through the shallowness of the mess sergeant's loyalties, Winch admires Strange:

The thing Winch admired about Strange was that he really did not give a damn about anything. The others, like Winch, pretended that they did not but, really, they cared. Strange really didn't. About anything. The Army, the outfit . . . success or humanity. Strange pretended to care but really didn't. (p. 19)

It seems valid to add that the mess sergeant believes that he does care about a lot of things, but is constantly surprised at how easily he recovers from bitter disillusionments.

Strange's problems with the American morality begin when

he visits his wife. Living in a house full of relatives, she seems to care only about the money she is making working in a defense plant. When he attempts intercourse with her, he becomes impotent; after she is asleep, he goes into the bathroom, "fantasizes" being back in Guadalcanal, and masturbates. Strange returns to Luxor, picks up a woman named Francis Highsmith, who shocks him by asking that he perform cunnilingus. He refuses. But the incident torments Strange; and the next time he goes home he learns that his wife has a lover, who is a lieutenant colonel in the air force, "a Princeton graduate . . . from somewhere on Long Island called Southampton" (p. 209). The lover sexually gratifies Strange's wife as he never has because he performs acts she refuses to describe. Embittered, Strange takes the money he and his wife have been saving since before the war for opening a restaurant and spends it on a Luxor hotel room. The room is to be a place for men from the old company to drink and make love.

The hotel room is a desperate gamble by Strange to hold off a chaos he feels growing all around him. He has always dreamed that after the war the old company would get together again: "Shared deaths, shared woundings, shared terrors had given it a family closeness it wouldn't be easy to find again" (p. 204). However, a horribly wounded company man named Billy Spencer returns from the Pacific with fresh news of how the company, because of casualties, has already evolved into a virtually new unit.

Having lost his wife, facing the reality of the end of the old company, terrified by a new sexual sophistication in America, he begins to feel a rage comparable to Landers's. In one particularly effective scene, he is enraged at the unreality of a war movie he attends. Jones's essay "Phony War Films" reveals autobiographical basis for this scene; in 1943, he shocked a theater audience by responding "with maniacal laughter" to the unreality of the film *Bataan*.[11] At about this point in Strange's characterization, Jones begins to focus upon the theme of sexual maladjustment. The former mess sergeant becomes obsessed with finding Frances Highsmith and performing whatever sexual acts she desires. Awareness that he sees the woman as a substitute for his wife does not diminish the power of his obsession. Soon he and the woman are engaging in sexual activities Strange has never previously dreamed about, including some with overtones of sadomasochism, and Strange is convinced that he is a "pervert" (p. 278).

Of course, he ultimately loses Frances. Strange believes that he cannot stand all that has happened. He has seen all his old "loyalties" diminish, and he has become a man engaging in conduct that morally repulses and frightens him. The major indication that John Strange can stand a great deal more than he thinks comes after Landers's suicide. At first, he is greatly shaken by the former clerk's death; but then he experiences his first American spring in six years and decides that "people, like the seasons, all had to end sometime" (p. 425). When he expresses this idea to Winch, the former first sergeant decides that Strange has gone crazy.

While he did not live to complete the characterization of Strange, Jones left notes for what was to happen to him. His final fate, as outlined by Jones and transcribed by Willie Morris, simply does not make artistic sense. Like Landers, he refuses a sinecure in Winch's office. In contrast to Landers, rather than accept an honorable discharge, he asks to be transferred to a new infantry company about to be sent overseas to Europe. Jones's plan was to have Strange become deeply attached to his new company and intolerably tormented by his knowledge of what they were to endure. Finally, this bitter foreknowledge leads to suicide. Jones's dictation reads in part:

He faces finally the fact that he simply cannot go through the whole process again. He simply can't go into England and into Europe with this new outfit knowing what he knows from the Pacific, and sit back in his relatively safe position as a mess sergeant and watch the young men be killed and maimed and lost. He can't stand being a witness again to all the anguish and mayhem [one remembers that the corrupt officer who finally drove Landers to suicide was named Mayhew] and blood and suffering. (p. 451)

It is consistent for Strange to become deeply attached to his new company and feel that he cannot bear to see them suffer. It is, however, not consistent for him to commit suicide over their anticipated suffering. Strange, after all, is the man who "really did not give a damn" and who has just decided that people pass away like the seasons. There are clues earlier in the novel that more is involved in Strange's suicide which Jones, had he lived, might have developed.

When he is wounded on Guadalcanal, he is filled with "the sense of fear, and the momentary feeling of total helplessness" (p. 45). From the first, he had decided that he would not die in this war; but his wounding made him realize that, like everyone else, he was vulnerable to chance. During two operations on his wounded hand, Strange has a dream of being tried for some unnamed crime. The judge is a huge, faceless figure clothed in white. In the first dream, Strange realizes that he has been found guilty: "The judgment was fair. In the dream he had felt a great sense of guilt, and then relief" (p. 178). In the second dream, the faceless figure points and says, " 'No, my son. You may not stay' " (p. 259).

The dream may well represent Strange's subconsciously confronting the fact that what he does finally care about is himself. Not a cerebral man like Landers, the mess sergeant would be capable of transferring that self-concern to others with no realization of what he is doing. Perhaps what Strange truly cannot "stand" again is risking his own life. Rather than admit that his own evolution into a soldier is incomplete, he will commit suicide.

Bobby Prell, twenty-three or twenty-four years old, has much of the Prewitt quixotic idealism that, in the characterization of Witt, had hardened into almost animal stubbornness. The symbolic heart of the company, Prell annoys Winch with his tendency to take risks:

There had always been a streak of the heroics-lover about Prell. . . . He was dead responsible, and steady, cool, calculating. But he was vain to a fault. He took bigger risks than the motorcycle-jockey, wild-ass kind. (p. 40)

Strange perceives that ". . . Prell was one of the ones who would always get hurt the worst, and the most often, in his life" (p. 49).

He has been hurt very badly indeed this time and faces possible

amputation of both legs or, at best, paralysis and life in a wheel-
chair. In addition, Prell is struggling with intense guilt because
of the manner in which he was wounded. Leading his men on
a patrol in New Georgia, he stumbled on an enemy troop concentration and spotted the Japanese commander of the entire
New Georgia operation, General Sasaki. The description of Prell's
patrol is one of the best pieces of writing in *Whistle.* A $1000
bounty has been placed on Sasaki's head by the American army.
Prell sights his rifle at the Japanese commander: "It gave Prell
a sudden thrill to know that he held the life of an important
man in his hands, and had carte blanche to kill him. He knew
how political assassins must feel" (p. 58). As he prepares to pull
the trigger, something clanks; his men are spotted; the Japanese
open fire; and Prell is wounded and two of his men are killed.

Try as he might, he simply cannot feel good about the patrol.
He had not voulnteered his men for it, "Prell never volunteered
his men for anything" (p. 43). On the other hand, it was not
originally his patrol; and even though he knows he got them out
as well as anyone could have, two men died. Still, the men had
risked their lives to make a stretcher and carry him to safety
and they had come to see him in a group before he was shipped
home. Reviewing the seemingly interminable moment when he
held Sasaki's life in his hands, he is confident that he was considering the outcome of the New Georgia campaign. However,
there was "the splintered fast flash of thought of the personal
fame and that $1000 he might get..." (p. 59). He has been
recommended for the Congressional Medal of Honor for the
patrol, but Winch has made it clear that he considers the entire
incident to have been a foolish risk.

During the first part of the novel, the Prell characterization
evolves around three points: his stubborn refusal to admit pain
or to have his legs amputated; his seething hatred of Winch; and
his struggle to reconcile ethically the acceptance of the Medal
of Honor. The pain is intensified by every movement, but Prell is
determined that no one would "see him blubbering" (p. 52).
This self-control requires such intense concentration that Prell
mentally compares it to a "religious experience. . . . He might as
easily have said mystical, but *mystical* was not a word Prell
used..." (p. 54). One remembers, of course, Prewitt's turn to

mysticism in the stockade. The pain is so intense that Prell knows he has no future, but he is still determined that he will not suffer amputation.

When Colonel Stevens attempts to talk to him about the leg and the Medal of Honor, he says that his "dream" has been to be "a thirty-year man" and that he isn't sure he deserves the medal, but he does "deserve the leg" (pp. 125–26). His mixed emotions about the patrol make it impossible to consider clearly the implications of receiving the Medal of Honor. In addition, he is not sure that anyone still alive could possibly "deserve it." But he is so certain about the leg that he suggests to Strange that the men of the old company sign a petition protesting the contemplated amputation.

The petition incident is the novel's most effective exercise in sustained irony. Nearly everyone to whom it is mentioned reacts identically: " 'A petition? In the Army?' " Still Strange does get the signatures of most of the men of the old company. Winch is so outraged by the idea of a petition in the army that he can't bring himself to say the word, but he does revise the "paper" and use it to stop the proposed operation. The petition incident in *Whistle* has been criticized as implausible; nevertheless, it allows Jones to convey, in an amusing manner, insights into the central characters. It is appropriate that Prell the "bolshevik" would have the idea, and that Winch, the old army manipulator, would manage its success while thoroughly disapproving of the idea.

Winch also uses his influence to get Prell's Medal of Honor finally sent to the wounded soldier. He does all this without Prell's knowledge, and their external relationship remains an angry one. Deciding that Prell is not healing because he lacks sufficient motivation, the sergeant visits him and insults him into an almost uncontrollable rage (" 'At least, you won't be going around leading any squads into any death traps...' ") (p. 149). Winch has calculated this action ("He would be... [Prell's] enemy. Everybody needed one enemy.") (p. 149). The effect is what he had hoped for—Prell becomes so outraged at him that he miraculously begins to get better. The ceremony in which Prell finally receives his medal is one of the novel's best moments:

When Stevens [the hospital commanding officer] placed the light blue ribbon with its white stars around Prell's neck, there was a hint of tears in Prell's black Indian eyes. But when he looked at Winch, immediately beside him, the glitter came back in them. (p. 153)

In an effective echo of Winch's inability to say the word *petition,* Prell now refuses to say the name of his former first sergeant.

In the last half of the novel, Jones makes Prell an almost subordinate figure, and his characterization becomes more pathetic than tragic. As with *The Thin Red Line,* one has the feeling that Jones had put so much passion and emotion into the creation of *Eternity*'s Robert E. Lee Prewitt that he had comparably little left to say about Witt and Prell. Also, as he got older, Jones seems to have become more comfortable with his first sergeant character than with his romantic, self-destructive young private.

Given his doubts about accepting it, it is appropriate that the Medal of Honor contributes significantly to Prell's final destruction. Somewhat miraculously, considering his wounds, he gets a nurse, Della Mae Kinkaid, pregnant and has to marry her. Almost immediately after the wedding, Della Mae stops having sex with him; and he discovers that she and her mother had planned the marriage because Prell has become a celebrity by selling war bonds ("People loved his simplicity.") (p. 341). In addition to his marital problems, Prell is disgusted by his new role as a professional war hero—surrounded by "Hollywood 'types,'" he begins to learn a "'show-biz' vocabulary from them" (p. 394).

A further blow comes when he learns of Winch's reassignment to his sinecure as a warrant officer: "That Prell hated Winch did not mean Prell thought Winch was an incompetent. . . . No; Prell would miss Winch. Badly. Hate or no hate" (p. 231). In fact, Winch and Prell's relationship is comparable to that between Warden and Prewitt—they are the best of soldiers who can never openly express mutual admiration because of extreme differences in emotional makeup. Next, Prell learns of Landers's death and is initially not deeply moved—Landers was not, after all, old army."

Typically, he is soon guilty for not having been upset and, in a war bonds speech, pays simultaneous "tribute" to Landers and to himself:

... Landers' wound came out in his version as much worse, a leg amputation, and he told them that Landers had died as a result of an additional amputation operation.... Landers had received no medals for his sacrifice, nor had wanted or expected any. (pp. 407–408)

This speech is really Prell's last moment of triumph in the novel. It is also a coded statement of his own despair. Truly, he had never wanted fame or a medal nearly as much as the right to be a fully functioning "thirty-year-man."

Landers's death is a signal too of how much the old company is breaking up. Winch is gone, and Prell's marriage is a farce. Recurring nightmares about the dead men in his patrol, which had stopped momentarily, return and "Landers was with them, in them" (p. 404). Desperately, Prell attempts to make Colonel Stevens a substitute for Winch. As with Strange, the Prell characterization was incomplete at Jones's death; but his notes indicate how he wished it to develop. Prell was to become disillusioned in Stevens and, left with nothing but a reputation as "war hero" and celebrity bond salesman, picks fights in dingy bars with the intention of getting killed. Ultimately, he was to succeed.

Prell's destruction does not have the emotional impact of Robert E. Lee Prewitt's. After the first half of the novel, he is too much a pathetic victim instead of a quixotic tragic hero. The Della Mae Kinkaid involvement especially cheapens the characterization. In Mart Winch, however, Jones regains much of the power of his first novel, especially when one remembers that Winch should be seen as essentially the same character as Warden and Welsh. For three long novels, "the First" has been walking "the thin red line" of insanity by struggling to repress his deeply ingrained emotions and feelings. He has been the clever manipulator protecting his men from the Japanese on Guadalcanal and the corrupt bureaucracy of the Army at home and abroad.

Forty-two-year-old Mart Winch is critically ill from the opening of *Whistle*. In describing Winch's physical condition, Jones writes: "Congestive heart failure was a gradual failure of the heart ... It wasn't so much a disease as a condition. And in that sense, it was incurable" (p. 15). Taken metaphorically, this passage effectively summarizes Winch's suffering. He is growing too old and too tired to be the self-sacrificing center holding everything else together. His "condition" is truly hopeless—he feels too weak to be everyone else's source of strength, but he has never known any other role. Jones seems to be saying that a man can selflessly give of himself only so long until there comes a time when nothing is left. In addition, Winch has come to a bitter epiphany about his reputation as one of the "charisma people": "What Winch had learned from charisma people, from being one, was that charisma people were a race, a den, a nest of Superliars.

"When you learned that, it took away everything.... It made it all worthless" (p. 11). "The First" has become so locked into the persona which he chose in order to manipulate effectively that he can't reveal his inner self to anyone. In fact, he is not a superhuman being with no feelings; and he feels hypocritical because everyone believes him to be. Thus, it is not surprising that the self-destructive side of his character is growing stronger:

In his mind was his constant admonition not to drink. Or smoke. He listened to both, constantly. Each time he took a drink or lit a cigarette, he listened to them.... (p. 73)

Jones subtly makes it clear from the first of the novel that Winch's sanity cannot last much longer—he is tormented by a "persistent sense of another him." Upon arriving in San Francisco, Winch picks up a woman named Arlette and has an extended orgy of sex and drinking with her which almost kills him. It is the last attempt to fulfill his "reputation" as the supreme hedonist. Before collapsing, he makes a wonderful public speech in Washington Square on the theme: " '*Soldiers of the world, unite! You have nothing to lose but your guns!*' "

"... Everybody else has unions, why not us? Jap soldiers, German soldiers, English soldiers, US soldiers. Russians, French, Australians. All united.... I'm a first sergeant.... But I'm more like a Jap first sergeant or a German first sergeant than I am like these civilized sons of bitches. . . ." (p. 81)

While this is a drunken outburst which ends with a gleeful flight from the military police, it is also a crucial statement of two of the central themes of Jones's trilogy: the exploitation of the proletarian enlisted men by officers and civilians and combat's inevitable destruction of the veneer of civilization.

Winch winds up in the hospital near death after the Arlette episode. He will be sent to Luxor and, after a period of recuperation, accept the safe position in the Second Army Command Personnel GI office arranged for him by an old friend: "It was one of those refined, delicate, shrewdly juggled pieces of old-Army-type manipulation, as finely balanced and calculated as any Winch had ever put together" (p. 71). Mart Winch cannot totally discard his old self, however tired he is. If he can no longer be the superhuman lover and drinker, he is still able, for a while, to help the men of the old company through his manipulation. In the hospital, the ravages of his "condition" show and even Landers feels ". . . much less in awe of Winch than before." Still, Landers knows that he cannot talk to "the First" without being totally honest: "Something in Winch demanded it" (p. 139). There is never any question that he will help Prell, "not that . . . [he] deserved it" (p. 133). His need to help the people he can is made even more desperate with the arrival of the horribly wounded Billy Spencer. The sight of Spencer, and his news, stun Winch even though he has always expected it: "The upshot of it was, there wasn't any old company any more. Only about fifty of the original hundred and eighty remained, most of them pfcs and privates" (p. 188). Winch is tortured by thoughts that he is needed in the Pacific to bring some order out of such a holocaust and furious with himself for feeling this "responsibility" (p. 191).

He needs some release and finally decides to go home to his wife and family in St. Louis (one of the shocks of reading *Whistle* is to discover that "the First" is married; the fact is not consistent with his characterization, especially in *From Here to Eternity*). Winch cares nothing for his family; and, when he discovers that his wife is being unfaithful with more than one officer, he is relieved. Jones seems to have added the detail about Winch's marriage primarily for the irony of having his militant spokesman for the enlisted man cuckolded by officers. It is one more example of the exploitation of the lower classes. That Winch has hardly been a model of fidelity himself is irrelevant to Jones's philosophical stance.

He quickly initiates a relationship with Carol Ann Firebaugh, the Red Cross girl Landers failed with. To emphasize his contrast with Strange, Winch introduces the girl to sexual acts other than intercourse. He enjoys " 'giving pleasure' " and knows that most American men are afraid of sex: ". . . Sex is all scrambled up in with our religion. Evil, dirty, filthy. Guilt. It shouldn't be. . . . But it's all tied in with our puritanism" (p. 294). There is no doubt that here Winch is speaking for James Jones.

While he knows that their relationship is inevitably doomed, Carol becomes one of the two forces which keep Winch sane for a while. The other is his need to help the men of the old company, which he continues to do even after being released from the hospital and transferred to Second Army Command. There is no doubt which of these two loyalties is the greater: "Prell and Landers and Strange were what was left to him of his real life" (p. 285). Upon leaving the hospital, he downplays his goodbye, an effort which puzzles and disappoints most of the men. For once, John Strange understands: " 'It hurt him too much, to say goodbye. It hurt him so much he sluffed it off.' " When Landers protests that Winch did not even say goodbye to Prell, Strange answers, " 'Naturally' " (p. 261).

Winch is now a warrant officer junior grade, a position which encourages his genius at manipulating officers—all they require, he has discovered, is that you lie to them and pretend to "respect" them (p. 286). He also has the opportunity to profit from many kinds of shady financial activities, but, of course, refuses. Despite his sinecure, pressures are mounting rapidly which must destroy Winch. His sanity is becoming ever more fragile as is made evident by constant nightmares. In these nightmares, Winch is always on a Guadalcanal hill looking down on his men trapped by Japanese fire and yelling, " 'Get them out of there! Get them out of there!' " No one can hear him. Once at night, he wrecks his car when a vision of a casualty from the

194 JAMES JONES

company takes shape on the windshield glass (pp. 298–99). Two other nightmares begin. One involves confrontation with a Japanese "either an officer with a sword or a tough, mean, old-hand sergeant." (The origins of this metaphor go back to *The Pistol*.) The other is of a wounded man lying just out of range of help, repeatedly being wounded again but never killed. (This image is based upon the Welsh-Tella episode in *The Thin Red Line*.) Winch desperately attempts staying up all night rather than wake Carol with his screams.

Moreover, he is losing the ability to help his men. He goes to Prell's wedding, but is disgusted by the way the wounded man is exploited by his bride and by the army. He has to leave: "'I can't stand parties like this'" (p. 343). His biggest shock is his complete failure to help Landers. Reminiscent of Prell's anguish over the patrol, Winch can logically convince himself that he did all he could for his ex-clerk, but still feels deep guilt over Landers's death. Then John Strange refuses assignment to his company, and Winch's alienation grows almost unbearable. The two men drink together in Winch's PX once; and, when Strange leaves, Winch shouts, "'You got to come back. You got to come back, Johnny Stranger.... Any time. Any time. Tomorrow'" (p. 432). Strange does come back once to announce his epiphany about Landers and the seasons. Winch feels that he can no longer even understand his old mess sergeant: "Landers was not the springtime, or anything near like it. Landers was a human man, ... and as such he could have been saved. Winch had just not known the combination" (p. 434).

Jones did not finish the Winch characterization, but Morris's transcription of his notes make clear the fate of "the First." The relationship with Carol Firebaugh ends; Landers is dead; Strange has shipped to Europe in a new outfit; and Prell is a war bonds salesman. Ironically Winch is to feel that Prell was "... the only one of the four old-company men to have found 'peace' for himself in the wartime noncombat areas" (p. 442). It is a final moving irony that the relationship of these two figures, Jones's symbols of the best in the human race, was to end on a note of complete misunderstanding. At the last, their carefully constructed masks broke down all communication. Left with nothing, Winch is to go insane.

More than any of the novel's incomplete strands, one regrets that Jones could not write the account of Winch's breakup. The sergeant has hated the canned music played on the PX jukeboxes throughout the novel; it epitomizes to him the sterility of the new technological society. (One remembers the emphasis upon various forms of proletarian music in *From Here to Eternity*.) Finally, Winch is to steal two hand grenades; sleep with them "defused" under his pillow "for two or three nights"; then sneak up to the PX a subsequent night; break a window and toss the grenades at the jukeboxes. He will blow up the machines and "most of the PX as well" (p. 447). Captured instantly, he is to be led away to spend the rest of his life in a Veterans' Administration psychiatric unit.

In *Viet Journal* Jones has described the vision embodied in the trilogy as "quite tragic" (p. 99). As Warden, Welsh, and Winch, "the First" has understood the full import of that vision. The Allies had to win the war to stop a barbarous fascism; but, whether they won it or not, the postwar world would be dominated by an impersonal bureaucracy and technology. The day of the individualist was over. Winch's assault on the jukeboxes constitute the character's last futile protest against this new dictatorship, which must overwhelm the human spirit. "The First" is too strong to commit suicide, but he cannot keep his sanity in such a world.

Whistle is not a totally satisfying novel. Of the four principal characters, only Winch is handled with consistent success. It does complete, however, Jones's "quite tragic" vision. For that reason, as well as for its moments of real power, one is grateful for its appearance even in a less than complete form.

CHAPTER 8

Credo

O NE has the feeling sometimes that there were two James
Joneses. There is the Jones who collected knives and guns,
had difficulty in writing convincingly about women, was a
fervent skin diver, and wrote best about men existing in an
exclusively male world. There is also the Jones who, in Willie
Morris's words, ". . . was a profoundly cultured and sophisticated
man, a student of literature, history, art, and music."[1] Indeed,
one of Jones's most interesting essays is an impressionistic
treatment of the work of the sculptor Alexander Calder. Two of
Jones's appearances in the mass media, only a year apart, show
this duality. *Life,* in the 1957 profile, presents an exclusively
macho personality. In February 1958, James and Gloria Jones
were interviewed by Edward R. Murrow on "Person to Person."
On this program, Jones emerges as a confident, but not aggressive,
man, interested in and articulate about his work and the profession of writing. He expresses no bitterness about the harsh reviews
of *Some Came Running* which were at that time just appearing.
Rather, he expresses quite calmly a theory of the inherent contradiction between the role of the writer and that of the critic.
Jones's writing often exhibited poignant sexual naiveté; he has
been repeatedly described as the most gentle of men, and he
once said:

. . . I've come to consider bravery as just about the most pernicious
of virtues. Bravery is a horrible thing. The human race has it left
over from the animal world and we can't get rid of it.[2]

While it is the "he-man" Jones who is often superficially the more
visible, it is the second who is the more important.

Two themes run throughout all Jones's work—the sexual malad-justment of the American male and the animal nature of man. As mentioned, Jones was unable to utilize successfully the sexual maladjustment concept as a main theme in long fiction (he was highly successful in using it as the basis for short stories). The animal nature of man concept has caused the most confusion about Jones's fiction.

Edmond L. Volpe has written the single most perceptive and balanced critical essay about Jones. Volpe asserts that Jones and Norman Mailer respond to a vision derived from the war of the destruction of individuality in contemporary society; he further asserts that Jones's and Mailer's "... reactions to this threat to individuality have been different, mainly because Jones is essentially a realist, and Mailer is essentially a romantic."[3] Not all critics would agree with this evaluation. The characterization of Prewitt, the implicit moral sanction of the oppressed enlisted men in *From Here to Eternity*, and the treatment of skin diving as a "last frontier" of "freedom" in *Go to the Widow-Maker* seem highly "romantic" to many critics. Leslie Fiedler views *Eternity* as a treatment of the suffering proletarian artist in the tradition of Goethe's *The Sorrows of Young Werther*.[4] Richard P. Adams sees the novel as making the same point as William Faulkner's Nobel Prize speech, demonstrating "man's enduring and prevailing spirit" in spite of the mechanized corruption of modern society and argues that Jones is "a thoroughgoing and reasonably sophisticated romantic writer."[5] Ben W. Griffith, Jr., describes Prewitt as the enlisted man's mythic hero in the tradi-tion of "Paul Bunyan, Pecos Bill, John Henry, and Robin Hood": "Prewitt is the folk hero standing alone against the organized system, the individual vs. the advent of the Age of Regimenta-tion."[6] David L. Stevenson believes Jones to be one with Jack Kerouac in romanticizing "subcultures" of society which make us question the values of the dominant society.[7]

Jones himself has used the word "romantic" in a negative sense in describing his reasons for preferring such later works as *Some Came Running* and *The Thin Red Line* to his first novel: "[*Eternity*] ... is a very romantic book, simply because in the writing of it I made all the characters better in the book—gave them more integrity, more intelligence, more sensitivity than they, in fact, would have had in life."[8] This analysis implies two points often missed by critics. Although it is a critical commonplace to refer respectively to Prewitt and Warden in *From Here to Eternity* as being Jones's "romantic" and "realist," Warden is romanticized in a more subtle, but no less important, way than Prewitt. In fact, the cumulative characterization of "the First" (Warden in *Eternity,* Welsh in *The Thin Red Line,* and Winch in *Whistle*) represents the Jones ideal of a soldier. Moreover, both Prewitt and Warden are doomed; "the First" is more realistic only in that he is always aware of the causes and inevitability of his doom.

All of Jones's characters are, in fact, doomed by the same interrelated causes: the animal nature of man and the anonymous nature of modern technological society. In an interview, Jones once referred to "...the ridiculous misuse of human strength which can include many subjects, not only physical strength, but technology, and all of the things that we live by." In the same interview, he defines morality as refusing to give another pain "even though one suffers himself." However, he is not hopeful about the triumph of such a morality: "...in all of us, there is this animal portion...which is not at all adverse to inflicting cruelty on others. This can be quite enjoyable at times.... It's in myself .... it's in all of us."[9] Jones views modern man as caught in an external and an internal trap. Human strength, which arises out of our "animal" nature, has been translated into an awesome technology which threatens the extinction of all individuality. Seeking escape from such anonymity, his characters attempt retreat to "frontiers" of individualism, only to find the "frontiers" already threatened by technology and to discover that they cannot escape their own "animal" heritage. In the course of discovering a "last frontier" of individual freedom, man, the animal, inevitably perverts and destroys it. War, and combat, are socially sanctioned outlets for man's animalism. The idealized First Sergeant carries awareness of this trap through three Jones novels until it destroys his sanity. Charles I. Glicksberg charges that the second half of *From Here to Eternity* collapses because Jones begins overtly to share his characters' "cynicism."[10] It is not cynicism, however, so much as recognition of the inevitable trap in which man is caught.

In *Go to the Widow-Maker* and in several essays, Jones seems to glorify skin diving as a romantic escape. An essay entitled "Why They Invade the Sea" asserts that skin diving ". . . is the Last Frontier, for the likes of us" and stresses its inevitable appeal to ". . . all the latter-day Wyatt Earps, Billy the Kids and Bat Mastersons who lament the passing of the Age of Adventure. . . ."[11] In another essay, Jones satirizes his own involvement in the sport as representing an attempt to conquer his "cowardice."[12] But Jones's most coherent statement about diving and the intended theme of *Go to the Widow-Maker* is contained in a joint interview with William Styron. First, he tells Styron that the appeal of skin diving is in living ". . . a dangerous life, where the percentages are not on your side." He adds: "I'd rather do that than work in an office. I'd rather *write* than do that." Jones continues by describing the novel (*Go to the Widow-Maker*) on which he is presently working. It is to be about a playwright who ". . . feels that not only his work but everything else is being encroached upon by government . . . and in trying to escape this, he winds up in . . . a sort of very animalistic world, with these diving guys who are all great individualists and who are in a way like some of the buccaneers. . . ." The character is to discover that a corollary of the free animalistic life is a total absence of law and protection and, subsequently, to become "terrified": "My guy realizes that he has to give up his individual liberty to live in the way he wants to live."[13] *Go to the Widow-Maker* does, in fact, present a playwright first enjoying, and then becoming frightened of, the "animalism" in his fellow divers and in himself. The novel is incoherent because this central idea becomes subordinated to Jones's vision of the sexual maladjustment of the American male. Still his description of his character's need to surrender "individual liberty" to live the way he wants is a concise summary of Jones's vision of modern man's entrapment.

Throughout his fiction, Jones presents apparent escapes from the anonymity of modern society. The army is to Prewitt a beloved "profession"; the characters in *Some Came Running* seem more honest than others because they exist outside "respectable" society; the bottom of the ocean is still pure and uncorrupted by man's technological advances. However, all of these escapes are dead ends; all men still have their "animal natures" which they carry with them everywhere. Critics often miss this underlying pessimism in Jones because, in his writing and in his life, he seemed to share his characters' need for romantic escape; but he was always aware that escape could not be attained. More than once, he said that the ultimate escape from social limitations was the brutality of combat where man's "animalism" becomes his main ally.

Volpe is correct then to call Jones a realist, in viewpoint. He possessed a grim vision of modern man's external and internal entrapment. As early in his career as 1953, Jones was described as believing that ". . . life is tragic, and that those who call for a serious American literature which can also be affirmative are asking the impossible."[14] After *From Here to Eternity,* the denial in Jones's fiction became increasingly strong. His vision was of a bleak contemporary tragedy which denied catharsis or any form of redemption. In technique, Jones is clearly in the tradition of the turn-of-the-century naturalists; he believes in "documenting" his setting thoroughly. In fact, some of Jones's reputation as a bad stylist derives from his commitment to a Dreiser-like dependence upon close detail.

Volpe accurately identifies the source of Jones's bitter vision as being his World War II experiences. Out of the horror of Pearl Harbor and Guadalcanal emerged the theme of the evolution of a soldier, which clearly rests upon the novelist's concept of man's "animal nature." The evolution of a soldier theme is the unifying element in Jones's army trilogy, *From Here to Eternity, The Thin Red Line,* and *Whistle. WWII* is a full and convincing nonfictional elaboration of the theme. However, perhaps the most concise summary of its core is contained in a Jones essay, "Phony War Films":

Most deaths in infantry combat are due to arbitrary chance, a totally random selection by which an unknown enemy drops a mortar or artillery shell onto . . . a man he has never seen before—and perhaps does not see at all! Such a death is totally reasonless and pointless from the viewpoint of the individual, because it might just as well have been the man next to him. It only has meaning when it is viewed from a higher echelon by those who count the ciphers. . . . About the only good thing that can be said for such a death, really, is that the individual is generally so dehumanized already, and so dulled emotionally and mentally, that being killed doesn't really hurt him half as much as he may have once imagined.[15]

The army, then, systematically dehumanizes the enlisted man to prepare him for the necessary anonymity of combat. The final anonymity potentially faced by every soldier in wartime is death.

World War II represented the peak of man's utilization of technology for the purpose of destruction. In such a technological war, each soldier became even more an expendable, anonymous "cipher." *WWII* defines the manner in which the army, using its awareness of man's inherent "animalism," carried out its dehumanization process; and the army trilogy illustrates the effects of such a process on the enlisted man.

WWII describes the concern of many Americans after Pearl Harbor that the United States, a nation of peace and individualism, might not be able to produce a fighting man equal to the German and Japanese soldier. Thus every experience of the draftee was designed to destroy his sense of self. A combat soldier had not only to know, but to accept, that as an individual, he had ceased to exist at the time of his induction. Basic training began the process of dehumanization, but actual batle experience was necessary to complete it. Combat brought home the final anonymity of death; a central moment in the infantryman's evolution came when he accepted the fact that statistically he had no chance to survive. Some men would survive, of course; but the odds made it clear that the individual could not. Acceptance of such a bitter truth necessarily transformed the combat soldier into a new kind of man:

He was about the foulest-mouthed individual who ever existed on earth.... And internally, his soul was as foul and cynical as his mouth.... He had pared his dreams and ambitions down to no more than relief and a few days away from the line, and a bottle of booze, a woman and a bath. (p. 70)

Since death has been accepted as inevitable, the infantryman existed on varying levels of final anonymity. In actual combat, he necessarily had to function as a selfless part of the whole to have any chance for temporary survival. He constantly saw the men around him die brutally at the hands of the enemy and chance. Any lingering vestiges of a civilized morality were sacrificed when he killed in an equally brutal manner. Relief from combat meant temporary relief from death and escape into whatever hedonistic outlets were available (usually quite few and quite inadequate).

Volpe has described the shock of his own initial vision of the anonymity of modern warfare:

Perhaps for my generation this . . . was the great trauma. We had grown up on Hemingway and Dos Passos and Cummings and we had no illusions about heroism and glory, but we were not prepared to be swallowed up and lost in the massive organization of the Army.[16]

There is in Jones's army trilogy none of the lost generation sense of disillusionment resulting from betrayed ideals. The end of ideals is a foregone conclusion; however, acceptance of the reduction of the self to an animalistic cipher is indeed a trauma. For such sensitive or artistic characters as Prewitt, Fife in *The Thin Red Line,* and Landers in *Whistle,* it is a trauma which cannot be survived. In *WWII,* Jones comments that acceptance of total annihilation represented a stage he could never himself reach:

. . . I think it was just there that my EVOLUTION OF A SOLDIER stopped short of the full development. . . . I simply did not want to die and not be remembered for it. Or not be remembered at all. (pp. 122–24)

Such an evolutionary stage would be difficult for anyone to reach; but it is especially antithetical to everything the writer or artist believes in. Artists perennially gamble that their work will insure them immortality and thus personal triumph over death. The need of the self to be remembered is at the heart of art and literature. Jones frequently talked about the masochistic, "exhibitionist" nature of the writer; he believed that writers worked out of an intense need for self-revelation, which was potentially painful in that it might expose them to harsh criticism.

Not for Jones personally, but for many other men, another step was required in the evolutionary process. It became evident in the last stage of the war that the Allies had won. This produced in the combat infantryman a realization that either he might not die after all or he might now die fighting a war long since won:

Such thoughts awakened all the pain he had learned so laboriously over the months, in many cases years, to amputate at the root.

It was the last metamorphasis that would be asked of him. And if he could weather that one, he would be about as fully a soldier as a non-professional could be, a "professional" among the Professionals. (*WWII*, p. 196)

Necessarily, the United States had produced a new kind of man, one who accepted the inevitability of his own death and the suspension of the Western morality in which he had been raised. If he survived the war, he had to return home and begin "The De-Evolution of a Soldier." This process was, in some ways, more difficult than the first. The returning soldier could not be the man who left home to fight. He had evolved into one who had seen, and participated in, the extreme limits of man's "animalism." Now he had to evolve back into a man functioning normally in respectable society. Jones emphasizes that many men simply could not make such a change—some went to the "booby hatch" and some returned to "The Profession." Central to Jones's pessimistic vision is the idea that the United States had created a new breed of "professional" soldier which it suddenly had no need for: "How could you be a professional when there was no more profession?" (*WWII*, p. 256) People who had not experienced the war were more than a little afraid of this new kind of American. It is significant that, in the Jones novels not set in the army, his main characters are always former soldiers or sailors.

It is, of course, the army trilogy which centers on the evolution of a soldier. *From Here to Eternity* (prewar peacetime army), *The Thin Red Line* (Guadalcanal combat), and *Whistle* (the embittered returning soldier) explore virtually every phase of the concept Jones outlines in *WWII*. Jones's "Note" to *Whistle* explains that he wished the three novels to be seen as a special kind of trilogy:

It was always my intention with this trilogy that each novel should stand by itself as a work alone. In a way that, for example, John Dos Passos' three novels in his fine *USA* trilogy do not. *The 42nd Parallel, 1919,* and *The Big Money* will not stand alone as novels. *USA* is one large novel, not a trilogy. (pp. xix–xx)

Partly to insure this intent, Jones decided to carry three character types through all three novels, but to give them different names in each volume in order to symbolize the changes circumstance and environment had produced in them. Thus, the rebellious private is Prewitt in *From Here to Eternity*, Witt in *The Thin Red Line*, and Prell in *Whistle*; the strong, competent First Sergeant is Warden in the first novel, Welsh in the second, and Winch in the third; *Eternity*'s Mess Sergeant Stark merges into first Storm, then Strange. The device is effective because the three become different men under different conditions, while consistently representing a basic character type. Despite some flaws, the army trilogy stands as the capstone of Jones's career. Each of the novels possesses power and artistic integrity; as a trilogy, they constitute the most sustained and thorough examination of the twentieth-century soldier and of World War II yet produced by an American novelist.

James Jones has written the most concise summary of his life and career:

In a way, I was in a unique position in that I was born into the upper classes (such as they were, in my small town), and for personal and economic reasons of my own enlisted into the lumpen proletariat of the old Regular Army; and then, since then, have moved back in among the upper classes by reason of a certain success as a writer. (*WWII*, p. 71)

Jones saw the American enlisted man as a new and inevitably doomed proletarian. While he always distrusted Marxism, or any political or social attempt to uplift a group of people, his artistic concern remained with that "lumpen proletariat" even after he returned to "the upper classes."

Jones has always been more appreciated by other writers than by critics, especially academic critics. Because of their friendship with Jones, the objectivity of William Styron, or Irwin Shaw, or Willie Morris is sometimes questioned. However, Norman Mailer, whose criticism of his rival war novelist more than once degenerated into quite personal attack, consistently praised *From Here to Eternity* and *The Thin Red Line* and wrote of Jones's potential for creating a new kind of American fiction. Mailer was one of the main beneficiaries of the new frankness which *From Here to Eternity* introduced into the American novel.

Ultimately more significant than Mailer's grudging respect for Jones's art, if not for his life-style, is the praise from a younger American writer whose fiction embodies all the strengths which Jones's work is often alleged to lack. Joan Didion, who never met Jones, uses a most economical and concise style and is certainly a master at characterizing women. One of the finest of young American writers, Didion made what she called a "courtesy call" to Hawaii after Jones's death. "I was making this trip for the same reason I had walked the Oxford [Mississippi] graveyard, a courtesy call on the owner." Didion explains her concept of ownership:

Certain places seem to exist mainly because someone has written about them. Kilimanjaro belongs to Ernest Hemingway. Oxford, Mississippi, belongs to William Faulkner . . . and not only Schofield Barracks but a great deal of Honolulu itself has always belonged for me to James Jones.

She is not offended by Jones's fictional preoccupation with war and the army because she understands something often forgotten by critics: "James Jones had known a great simple truth: the Army was nothing more or less than life itself."[17]

That so many other important writers hold so much respect for Jones derives from two things: their understanding that an artist discovers in the intensity of his personal experience "great simple truths" and gives them universal meaning, and their appreciation for the struggle implicit in maintaining the uncompromising honesty found in all of James Jones's work. Despite his commercial success, Jones never settled for slick and fashionable writing. All his novels attempt presentations of complex historical and psychological themes. He was a writer's writer, as Didion recognizes.

Though it never mentions James Jones, John Gardner's recent book, *On Moral Fiction*, says much that is relevant to Jones's critical reputation. Gardner's primary thesis is that contemporary American literature and criticism are dominated by an "immoral" concern with technique, rather than content, and that this introverted concern diminishes the strength of fiction. Attacking the critical fashion of the Barth-Barthelme-Pynchon school, Gardner argues that the most influential contemporary critics look only at the technical surface of fiction. Thus, he says, "critical standards built on the premise that art is primarily technique" ignore "the effect of emotional honesty" and are inadequate for analyzing writers such as Dostoevski, Poe, Lawrence, Dreiser, and Faulkner, whose strength lies in emotional honesty, rather than consistent technical perfection and effect.[18] James Jones should be added to such a list. Though *The Pistol* is proof that he could write a structurally tight book, Jones generally preferred to attempt honest and thorough lengthy analysis of man's fate in a hostile technological universe.

Gardner also argues that fiction should depict "life-like characters" whom "we come to understand."[19] As Maxwell Perkins first realized, a character like Prewitt had never been made fully comprehensible before *From Here to Eternity*. Further, the cumulative characterization of "the First" in Jones's trilogy is a brilliant accomplishment—one sees Warden-Welsh-Winch sacrificing himself to protect others until he has nothing left with which to save himself. Jones's work is filled with other characters whom we come to understand and care deeply about—Maggio, Karen Holmes, Alma Schmidt, Johnny Slade, Mast, Fife, Bell.

Finally, Gardner asserts the superior insight of artists into art:

The artist's character—the whole complex of his ideas and emotions— is his final authority on what is, and what is not, art. Except insofar as they are really artists, critics have, finally, no authority at all.[20]

Like much in *On Moral Fiction*, this is an extreme position, quite open to challenge. However, it reflects something to us about the admiration of such writers as William Styron, Irwin Shaw, Norman Mailer, and Joan Didion for Jones's work. The creator of the army trilogy wrote with "the whole complex of his ideas and emotions."

Notes and References

Chapter One

1. Norman Mailer, *Advertisements for Myself* (New York, 1959), p. 414.
2. *Twentieth Century Authors: A Biographical Dictionary: First Supplement,* ed. Stanley J. Kunitz (New York, 1955), pp. 500–501.
3. Willie Morris, *James Jones: A Friendship* (Garden City, N.Y., 1978), pp. 31–32.
4. *Twentieth Century Authors,* p. 501.
5. Quoted by Lee A. Burress, Jr., in "James Jones on Folklore and Ballad," *College English,* 21 (December 1959), 164.
6. Quoted in *Saturday Review of Literature,* 34 (February 24, 1951), 11.
7. James Jones, "Hawaiian Recall," *Viet Journal* (New York, 1974), p. 249.
8. *Twentieth Century Authors,* p. 501.
9. Interview by Nelson W. Aldrich, Jr., *Writers at Work: The Paris Review Interviews, Third Series* (New York, 1967), pp. 245–46.
10. "James Jones: A Talk before the End," recorded and photographed by R. T. Kahn, *Book Views,* June 1978, p. 6.
11. James Jones, *WWII* (New York, 1975), p. 25.
12. *Viet Journal,* p. 2.
13. *WWII,* pp. 137–39.
14. *James Jones: A Friendship,* p. 46.
15. *Viet Journal,* pp. 48–49.
16. Ibid., p. 48.
17. Willie Morris, "A Friendship: Remembering James Jones," *Atlantic Monthly,* June 1978, p. 49.
18. A. B. C. Whipple, "James Jones and His Angel," *Life,* May 7, 1951, pp. 143–57.
19. Robert E. Cantwell, "James Jones: Another *Eternity?*" *Newsweek,* November 23, 1953, p. 106.
20. Whipple, pp. 143–44.
21. *James Jones: A Friendship,* p. 53.

22. A. Scott Berg, *Max Perkins: Editor of Genius* (New York, 1978), p. 435.

23. Maxwell Perkins, *Editor to Author: The Letters of Maxwell E. Perkins* (New York, 1950), pp. 273–74, 295–99.

24. Whipple, p. 150.

25. Bernard DeVoto, "Dull Novels Make Dull Reading," *Harper's*, June 1951, pp. 67–70.

26. Ernest Jones, "Minority Report," *Nation*, 172 (March 17, 1951), 254–55.

27. John Lardner, "Anatomy of the Regular Army," *New Yorker*, March 10, 1951, pp. 117–19.

28. David Dempsey, *New York Times Book Review*, February 25, 1951, p. 5.

29. C. J. Rolo, "This Man's Army," *Atlantic Monthly*, March 1951, pp. 83–84.

30. Ned Calmer, "The Real Enemy Is Hard to Find," *Saturday Review of Literature*, February 24, 1951, pp. 11–12.

31. Cantwell, p. 102.

32. Maurice Dolbien, "What NBA Means to Some Past Winners," *New York Herald Tribune Review*, March 1, 1959, p. 11.

33. Cantwell, p. 102.

34. David Ray, "Mrs. Handy's Writing Mill," *London Magazine*, 5 (1958), 35–39.

35. Robert La Guardia, *Monty: A Biography of Montgomery Clift* (New York, 1977), pp. 102–103.

36. La Guardia and also Patricia Bosworth's *Montgomery Clift: A Biography* (New York, 1978).

37. *James Jones: A Friendship*, pp. 83–92.

38. All quotations in these two paragraphs from interview by Aldrich, pp. 235–38.

39. Gloria Jones in conversation, August 1978.

40. "Briefly Noted," *New Yorker*, January 18, 1958, p. 102.

41. David Dempsey, "By Sex Obsessed," *New York Times Book Review*, January 12, 1958, p. 32.

42. Edmund Fuller, "In Praise of the Yahoo," *Saturday Review*, January 4, 1953, p. 13.

43. *Advertisements for Myself*, p. 415.

44. A. Scott Berg, "The Elusive Man Who Was America's Greatest Literary Editor," *Esquire*, July 18, 1978, pp. 55–68.

45. *James Jones: A Friendship*, pp. 114–22.

46. *Advertisements for Myself*, p. 414.

47. John W. Aldridge, "The War Novelists Ten Years Later," *Con-*

temporary American Novelists, ed. Harry T. Moore (Carbondale, Ill., 1964), pp. 33–34.

48. Maxwell Geismar, " 'Numbly They Did the Necessary' " *New York Times Book Review,* September 9, 1962, p. 1.

49. Lewis Gannett, "Guadalcanal: Mindlessly, They Prevailed," *New York Herald Tribune Book Review,* September 9, 1962, p. 1.

50. John W. Aldridge, "Twosomes and Threesomes in Gray Paree," *Saturday Review,* February 13, 1971, pp. 23–26.

51. James Jones, "Letter Home: Sons of Hemingway," *Esquire,* December 1963, pp. 28, 30, 34, 40, 44.

52. "Notes on People," *New York Times,* February 26, 1974, p. 74.

53. Gloria Jones in conversation, August 1978.

54. *Advertisements for Myself,* p. 414.

55. Willie Morris in conversation, August 1978; see also *James Jones: A Friendship,* pp. 252–53.

Chapter Two

1. Richard P. Adams, "A Second Look at *From Here to Eternity,*" *College English,* 17 (January 1956), 205–10.

2. James Jones, *From Here to Eternity* (New York, 1951). Page references will appear in the text.

3. Edward L. Volpe, "James Jones—Norman Mailer," *Contemporary American Novelists,* ed. Harry T. Moore (Carbondale, 1964), p. 109.

4. Peter G. Jones, *War and the Novelist* (Columbia, Mo., 1976), p. 34.

5. *Celebrity Register,* Earl Blackwell, Editor-in-Chief (New York, 1973), p. 258.

6. Adams, p. 208.

7. Leslie A. Fiedler, "James Jones' Dead-End Young Werther," *Commentary,* 12 (1951), 252–55.

8. *Writers at Work,* p. 244.

9. In an interesting article, Lee A. Burress, Jr., analyzes the "Re-Enlistment Blues" as an example of ". . . the communal theory of ballad authorship" and attempts to discover with little success how Jones knew of such a theory, "James Jones on Folklore and Ballad," *College English,* 21 (December 1959), 161–65.

10. Jerry H. Bryant, *The Open Decision* (New York, 1970), pp. 123–30.

Chapter Three

1. *Writers at Work*, p. 240.
2. James Jones, *Some Came Running* (New York, 1957). Page references will appear in the text.
3. James Jones, "Living in a Trailer," *Holiday*, July 1952, pp. 74–76, 78–79, 81, 83, 120.

Chapter Four

1. James Jones, "Introduction," *The Ice-Cream Headache and Other Stories* (New York, 1968). Page references will appear in the text.
2. Allen Shepherd, " 'A Deliberately Symbolic Little Novella': James Jones's *The Pistol*," *South Dakota Review*, 10, (1972), 111–29.
3. *Viet Journal*, p. 251.
4. James Jones, *The Pistol* (New York, 1959). Page references will appear in the text.
5. *Viet Journal*, p. 254.
6. Shepherd, p. 112.
7. One also remembers Wilfred Owen's World War I poem entitled "Greater Love," but the context of Jones's story makes it seem likely that he had the biblical quotation in mind.

Chapter Five

1. Norman Mailer, *Cannibals and Christians* (New York, 1966), pp. 112–13.
2. *War and the Novelist*, p. 175.
3. Ibid., p. 139.
4. *Writers at Work*, p. 247.
5. James Jones, "Special Note," *The Red Thin Line* (New York, 1962). Page references will appear in the text.
6. Saul Bellow, "Some Notes on Recent American Fiction," *The American Novel Since World War II*, ed. Marcus Klein (Greenwich, Conn., 1969), p. 162.
7. Paulette Michet-Michot, "Jones's *The Thin Red Line*: The End of Innocence," *Revue des Langues Vivantes*, 30 (1964), 15–26.
8. *War and the Novelist*, p. 175.
9. Volpe, pp. 106–19.
10. *War and the Novelist*, pp. 139–40.

11. Ibid., p. 173.

12. Geismar, p. 32.

Chapter Six

1. Seymour Krim, "Final Tribute," *New Times*, June 10, 1977, p. 76.

2. James Jones, *Go to the Widow-Maker* (New York, 1967). Page references will appear in the text.

3. James Jones, *The Merry Month of May* (New York, 1971), p. 11. Page references will appear in the text.

4. Aldridge, pp. 23–26.

Chapter Seven

1. James Jones, *Whistle* (New York, 1978). Page references will appear in the text.

2. Barbara A. Bannon, " 'A Touch of Danger,' " *Publishers Weekly*, May 7, 1973, pp. 38–39.

3. James Jones, *A Touch of Danger* (New York, 1973), p. 234.

4. *WWII*. Page references will appear in the text.

5. Philip Caputo, "An Eloquent Farewell to Arms," *Chicago Tribune Book World*, February 19, 1978, p. 1.

6. Thomas R. Edwards, "Something About a Soldier," *New York Review of Books*, May 4, 1978, pp. 30–31.

7. John W. Aldridge, "The Last James Jones," *New York Times Book Review*, March 5, 1978, pp. 1, 30–31.

8. Quoted by Willie Morris, in "Introductory Note by Willie Morris," *Whistle*, p. xvi.

9. Bannon, pp. 38–39.

10. Cantwell, pp. 102–107.

11. James Jones, "Phony War Films," *Saturday Evening Post*, March 30, 1963, p. 64.

Chapter Eight

1. *James Jones: A Friendship*, p. 26.

2. *Writers at Work*, pp. 246–47.

3. Volpe, p. 107.

4. Fiedler, pp. 252–55.

5. Adams, pp. 205–10.

6. Ben W. Griffith, Jr., "Rear Rank Robin Hood: James Jones Folk Hero," *Georgia Review*, 10 (1956), 41–46.

7. David L. Stevenson, "James Jones and Jack Kerouac: Novelists of Disjunction," *The Creative Present*, eds. Balakian and Simmons (Garden City, N.Y., 1963), pp. 193–212.

8. "The Writer Speaks: A Conversation between James Jones and Leslie Hanscom," in John R. Hopkins, *James Jones: A Checklist* (Detroit, 1974), p. 10.

9. Ibid., pp. 15, 12–13.

10. Charles I. Glicksberg, "Racial Attitudes in *From Here to Eternity*," *Phylon*, 14, (1955), 385.

11. James Jones, "Why They Invade the Sea," *New York Times Magazine*, March 14, 1965, p. 55.

12. James Jones, "Flippers! Gin! Weight Belt! Faceplate! Gin!" *Esquire*, June 1963, pp. 124ff.

13. James Jones and William Styron, "Two Writers Talk It Over," *Esquire*, July 1963, pp. 57–59.

14. Cantwell, p. 107.

15. *Saturday Evening Post*, March 30, 1963, p. 65.

16. Volpe, p. 105.

17. Joan Didion, "The Coast: Good-bye, gentleman-ranker," *Esquire*, October 1977, pp. 50, 60, 62, 64.

18. John Gardner, *On Moral Fiction* (New York, 1978), p. 145.

19. Ibid., p. 139.

20. Ibid., p. 147.

Selected Bibliography

PRIMARY SOURCES

1. Books

From Here to Eternity (novel). New York: Charles Scribner's Sons, 1951. Signet paperback edition published in 1953.

Go to the Widow-Maker (novel). New York: Delacorte Press, 1967. Dell paperback edition published in 1968.

The Ice-Cream Headache and Other Stories (short-story collection). New York: Delacorte Press, 1968. Dell paperback edition published in 1971.

The Merry Month of May (novel). New York: Delacorte Press, 1971. Dell paperback edition published in 1972.

The Pistol (novella). New York: Charles Scribner's Sons, 1959. Dell paperback edition published in 1969.

Some Came Running (novel). New York: Charles Scribner's Sons, 1957. Abridged Signet paperback edition published in 1958.

The Thin Red Line (novel). New York: Charles Scribner's Sons, 1962. Signet paperback edition published in 1964. Originally serialized in *Playboy*, August 1962, September 1962, and October 1962.

A Touch of Danger (novel). New York: Popular Library, 1973.

Viet Journal (nonfiction). New York: Delacorte Press, 1974.

Whistle (novel). New York: Delacorte Press, 1978.

WWII (nonfiction). New York: Grosset & Dunlap, 1975. Ballantine Press paperback edition published in 1976.

2. Short Fiction

John R. Hopkins's *Checklist* (see below) provides a complete bibliographical history of the individual stories in *The Ice-Cream Headache* and of the published excerpts from Jones's novels through 1974. "Million-Dollar Wound" (excerpt from *Whistle*), *Esquire*, November 1977, pp. 106–10, 198, 200, completes the list of Jones's published short fiction.

3. Essays and Interviews

"Buying Out of Vietnam: Three Women, Three Prices" [excerpt from *Viet Journal*], *Oui*, November 1973, pp. 39, 40, 116.

"'Flippers! Gin! Weight Belt! Faceplate! Gin!'" *Esquire*, June 1963,
    pp. 124–27, 129–30, 132, 134, 136–39.
"Hawaiian Recall," *Harper's*, February 1974, pp. 27–31. [Reprinted in
    Viet Journal.]
"In the Shadow of Peace" [excerpt from *Viet Journal*] *New York
    Times Magazine*, June 10, 1973, pp. 15, 17, 46, 48–50, 54,
    56, 59.
"James Jones: A Talk Before the End" (Interview by Willie Morris,
    recorded and photographed by R. T. Kahn), *Book Views*, June
    1978, pp. 6–7.
"Letter Home: Sons of Hemingway," *Esquire*, December 1963, pp. 28,
    30, 34, 40, 44.
"Letter Home," *Esquire*, December 1964, pp. 22, 24.
"Living in a Trailer," *Holiday*, July 1952, pp. 74–76, 78–79, 81,
    83, 120.
"Phony War Films," *Saturday Evening Post*, March 30, 1963, pp.
    64–67.
"Story Behind the Book: 'A Touch of Danger'" (Interview by Barbara
    A. Bannon), *Publishers Weekly*, May 7, 1953, pp. 38–39.
"Too Much Symbolism," *Nation*, May 2, 1953, pp. 38–39.
"Two Writers Talk It Over" (with William Styron), *Esquire*, July
    1963, pp. 57–59.
"Why They Invade the Sea," *New York Times Magazine*, March 14,
    1965, pp. 47ff.
Writers at Work: The Paris Review Interviews, Third Series (Inter-
    view by Nelson W. Aldrich, Jr.). New York: The Viking Press,
    1967, pp. 231–50. Originally published in *Paris Review*, 20
    (1959), 34–35.
"The Writer Speaks: A Conversation between James Jones and Leslie
    Hanscom," in John R. Hopkins, *James Jones: A Checklist*, Detroit:
    Gale Research Company, 1974, pp. 5–18.

SECONDARY SOURCES

1. Biographical

ANON. "The Good Life and Jim Jones," *Life*, February 11, 1957, pp.
    83ff. Photographic "Close-Up," prior to publication of *Some
    Came Running*.
BERG, A. SCOTT. "The Elusive Man Who Was America's Greatest
    Literary Editor," *Esquire*, July 18, 1978, pp. 55–68. Biographical
    study of Maxwell Perkins, contains account of Perkins's discovery
    of Jones.
————. *Max Perkins: Editor of Genius*. New York: E. P. Dutton &

Co., 1978. Contains a more extended account of Perkins's discovery of Jones.

CANTWELL, ROBERT E. "James Jones: Another *Eternity?*" *Newsweek*, November 23, 1953, pp. 102–107. Biographical essay focusing on Jones's success after *From Here to Eternity*.

GOODFRIEND, ARTHUR. "The Cognoscenti Abroad—II: James Jones's Paris," *Saturday Review*, February 1, 1969, pp. 36–38. Interview-essay focusing on Jones's success after *From Here to Eternity*.

KRIM, SEYMOUR. "Final Tribute," *New Times*, June 10, 1977, p. 76. Biographical essay upon Jones's death.

KUNITZ, STANLEY, ed. *Twentieth Century Authors: A Biographical Dictionary: First Supplement*. New York: The H. W. Wilson Co., 1955, pp. 500–501. Contains valuable information about Jones's family background and childhood.

MORRIS, WILLIE. "A Friendship: Remembering James Jones," *Atlantic Monthly*, June 1978, pp. 47ff. Biographical essay, especially important for details about Jones's military discharge and his last years on Long Island.

————. *James Jones: A Friendship*. Garden City, N.Y.: Doubleday & Co., Inc., 1978. The most complete account of Jones's life now available.

RAY, DAVID. "Mrs. Handy's Writing Mill," *London Magazine*, 5, (1958), 35–41. Debunking account of Lowney Handy's Marshall, Illinois, writers' colony.

SHAW, IRWIN. "James Jones, 1921–1977," *New York Times Book Review*, June 12, 1977, pp. 3, 34–35. Tribute upon Jones's death, contains Shaw's comparison of the importance of Jones's army fiction to Stephen Crane's *The Red Badge of Courage*.

STYRON, WILLIAM. "A Friend's Farewell to James Jones," *New York*, June 6, 1977, pp. 40–41. Tribute upon Jones's death, contains Styron's analysis of Jones's importance as a literary descendant of Sherwood Anderson, Theodore Dreiser, and Mark Twain.

WHIPPLE, A. B. C. "James Jones and His Angel," *Life*, May 7, 1951, pp. 143ff. Story of Jones's literary apprenticeship with Lowney Handy.

2. Criticism

ADAMS, RICHARD P. "A Second Look at *From Here to Eternity*," *College English*, 17 (January 1956), 205–10. Argues that the novel is a "romantic" assertion of man's capacity to "endure." Contains a convincing analysis of the novel's structure.

ALDRIDGE, JOHN W. "The Last James Jones," *New York Times Book*

Review, March 5, 1978, pp. 1, 30–36. Aldridge's final evaluation of Jones: "Jones may not be recognized as a literary artist of the first rank. But he was a powerful naturalistic chronicler of certain essential realities of warfare and of the responses of men at war, and he had a gift for being absolutely honest about what he felt and thought."

————. "Twosomes and Threesomes in Gray Paree," *Saturday Review*, February 13, 1971, pp. 23–26. Review of *The Merry Month of May* in which Aldridge dismisses Jones as a writer with "a thoroughly commonplace mind seemingly arrested forever at the level of its first adolescent ideas."

————. "The War Writers Ten Years Later," *Contemporary American Novelists*, ed. Harry T. Moore. Carbondale: Southern Illinois University Press, 1964, pp. 32–40. Dismisses Jones as a victim of "having lived too long abroad."

BELLOW, SAUL. "Some Notes on Recent American Fiction," *The American Novel since World War II*, ed. Marcus Klein. Greenwich, Conn.: Fawcett, 1969, pp. 159–74. Praises the objectivity of *The Thin Red Line*: "In apprehending what is real, Jones's combat soldiers learn a bitter and leveling truth and in their realism revenge themselves on the slothful and easy civilian conception of the Self."

BRYANT, JERRY H. *The Open Decision: The Contemporary American Novel and Its Intellectual Background*. New York: The Free Press, 1970. Compares *From Here to Eternity* to Norman Mailer's *The Naked and the Dead* as warnings that "the real danger to American democracy is not the armies of Germany and Japan, but the fascists within our own system."

BURRESS, LEE A., JR. "James Jones on Folklore and Ballad," *College English*, 21 (December 1959), 161–65. Analysis of "The Re-Enlistment Blues" as illustrating "the communal theory of ballad authorship." Contains letter from Jones which describes his transfer from the Air Corps to the Infantry.

CALMER, NED. "The Real Enemy Is Hard to Find," *Saturday Review of Literature*, February 24, 1951, pp. 11–12. Most perceptive initial review of *From Here to Eternity*, discusses novel's basis in social protest and its theme of the need for human communication.

DeVOTO, BERNARD. "The Easy Chair: Dull Novels Make Dull Reading," *Harper's*, June 1951, pp. 67–70. Attacks *From Here to Eternity* and Norman Mailer's *The Naked and the Dead* as examples of arrested "infantilism."

DIDION, JOAN. "Good-bye, gentleman-ranker," *Esquire*, October 1977, pp. 50, 60–61, 62, 64. Account of Didion's visit to Honolulu after Jones's death ("a courtesy call on the owner"). Jones had established literary "ownership" of "not only Schofield Barracks, but a great deal of Honolulu itself," just as Hemingway "owned" Kilimanjaro and Oxford, Mississippi, "belonged" to Faulkner.

FIEDLER, LESLIE A. "James Jones' Dead-End Young Werther," *Commentary*, 12 (1951), 252–55. Describes *From Here to Eternity* as being a "romantic" glorification of the suffering young artist in the tradition of Goethe's "archetypal" *The Sorrows of the Young Werther*.

GANNETT, LEWIS. "Guadalcanal: Mindlessly, They Prevailed," *New York Herald Tribune Book Review*, September 9, 1962, p. 1. Favorable review of *The Thin Red Line*, emphasizes Jones's skill in making C-for-Charlie Company the "hero of the novel."

GEISMAR, MAXWELL. "James Jones: And the American War Novel," *American Moderns: From Rebellion to Conformity*. New York: Hill and Wang, 1958, pp. 225–38. Calls *From Here to Eternity* "perhaps still the best single novel of its period." Analyzes Jones as a "country writer in an urban age of American literature."

————. " 'Numbly They Did the Necessary,' " *New York Times Book Review*, September 9, 1962, pp. 1, 32. Favorable review of *The Thin Red Line*, especially perceptive in evaluating the role of the novel's ending in creating its total impact.

GLICKSBERG, CHARLES I. "Racial Attitudes in *From Here to Eternity*," *Phylon*, 14 (1953), 384–89. Analysis of the implied attitudes toward ethnic minorities in the novel. Argues that "the second part of the novel collapses" because "the author inwardly sympathizes with and reflects the overall cynicism of his principal characters."

GRIFFITH, BEN W., JR. "Rear Rank Robin Hood: James Jones's Folk Hero," *Georgia Review*, 10 (1956), 41–46. Describes Prewitt as "the foot soldier's folk hero" and as being in the tradition of "Paul Bunyan, Pecos Bill, John Henry, and Robin Hood."

HASSAN, IHAB. *Radical Innocence: The Contemporary American Novel*. Princeton, N.J.: Princeton University Press, 1961. Describes Prewitt as "the perennial collector of injustices, the consecrated underdog" and argues that the novel's "focus . . . is the nature of power or authority as defined by the responses of men to them."

JONES, PETER G. *War and the Novelist: Appraising the American War Novel*. Columbia, Mo.: University of Missouri Press, 1976.

Emphasizes Prewitt's self-destructive guilt and praises *From Here to Eternity* as "the best American war novel, one of the finest novels of the twentieth century." Argues that, while *The Thin Red Line* is "unsurpassed . . . as a fictional account of combat," its main emphasis is on psychological motivation.

KAZIN, ALFRED. *Bright Book of Life.* Boston: Little, Brown & Co., 1973. Discusses *From Here to Eternity* as a naturalistic study of men trapped by a frustrating and self-limiting "maleness."

LARDNER, JOHN. "Anatomy of the Regular Army," *New Yorker,* March 10, 1951, pp. 117–19. Mixed review of *From Here to Eternity:* "If it is . . . the most realistic and forceful novel I've read about life in the Army . . . it's because the English language is capable of absorbing, and condoning, a good deal of abuse from a man who has something to say and wants very desperately to say it."

MAILER, NORMAN. *Cannibals and Christians.* New York: The Dial Press, 1966. Mixed review of *The Thin Red Line.* Praises Jones as a "master" at capturing "the feel of combat, the psychology of men" and compares the novel to Stephen Crane's *The Red Badge of Courage.* But calls Jones's novel "too technical" and "too workmanlike."

MICHET-MICHOT, PAULETTE. "Jones's *The Thin Red Line*: The End of Innocence," *Revue des Langues Vivantes,* 30 (1964), 15–26. Argues that *The Thin Red Line* achieves its "significance" as a study of men crossing a line "between reason and sensibility on the one side, and brutality and morbid cruelty on the other." This line "separates the human from the animal."

PRESCOTT, PETER S. "Warriors Out of Work," *Newsweek,* February 20, 1978, pp. 80, 82. Mixed review of *Whistle* and of Jones's career. Praises Jones's knowledge of "politics, at least the kind practiced within the Army," but criticizes his style and his characterizations of women.

SHEPHERD, ALLEN. " 'A Deliberately Symbolic Little Novella': James Jones's *The Pistol*," *South Dakota Review,* 10 (1972), 111–29. Effective analysis of *The Pistol* as an experimental work. Argues that the violence in the novella is "not solely the product of corrupting institutions, of the Army, or of Authority, from whatever source, but of human nature itself."

STEVENSON, DAVID L. "James Jones and Jack Kerouac: Novelists of Disjunction," *The Creative Present: Notes on Contemporary American Fiction,* ed. Nona Balakian and Charles Simmons. Garden City, N.Y.: Doubleday & Company, Inc., 1963, pp. 193–212. Argues that Jones and Kerouac glorify "subcultures" which exist outside the American mainstream and thus bring into question accepted cultural values.

VOLPE, EDMOND L. "James Jones—Norman Mailer," *Contemporary American Novelists*, ed. Harry T. Moore. Carbondale: Southern Illinois University Press, 1964, pp. 106–109. The most perceptive single essay on Jones. Argues that Jones is a "realist" responding in all his fiction to a vision of contemporary man.

3. Bibliography

HOPKINS, JOHN R. *James Jones: A Checklist*. Detroit: Gale Research Company, 1974. This is a thorough guide to Jones's published work.

Index

223